The God's  Honest Truth

Darin Hufford

Copyright Information

Master Press Publications

The God's Honest Truth
Copyright © 2005 by Darin Hufford

ISBN 0-9673250-2-1

www.darinhufford.com

Requests for information should be addressed to:

Master Press Publications, 13613 N. Cave Creek Rd.
Phoenix, Arizona 85022

---

*Cover design by Kodis Design, Copyright © 2005 Kodis Design
Interior design by Kodis Design*

http://www.kodisdesign.com

Printed in the United States of America

DEDICATION

This book is dedicated, first, to the very one who inspires everything I do in life. It is through my love for my wonderful wife, Angie, that I hear the whispers of God Himself. You are my world and my life. I love you.

Also, I dedicate this to my four precious daughters: Landin, Sidney, Emma and Eva. There are simply no words to describe the love that I have for you. You are the total sum of who I am.

Finally, I dedicate this to Jay and Suzie Dolan. Your hearts have spoken more revelations than a thousand sermons. Thank you for your encouragement and love.

CONTENTS

The God's Honest Truth

Introduction[0]

The sun had just set as the 6:00 p.m. train reached its speed from Union Station to Gatwick. My wife and I had just spent four wonderful days in London, England touring the rich historical buildings and visiting the many castles and dungeons. Our minds were now settling down to a comfortable numb. So many sights and memories had transpired over the last few days that our brains were on overload. Only the sound of the rolling train passing over the creases in the tracks filled the space between us. It was as if the train wanted to rock us to sleep with its hypnotic sounds and motions. If we had not been in such a foreign place, we would have been tempted to succumb to its charm. In fact, I should not say "we," because my wife was already sleeping soundly on my shoulder. It was only I who was awake, and the passing countryside that seemed to be running away from me as if it were in a hurry to leave. I was not offended, because I was ready to go. I had a child at home waiting for me to return and I missed her terribly.

Clank-clank, clank-clank, clank-clank, the aged buildings and warmly lit houses raced by my window too quickly for me to see inside. My eyes strained to peek deep within each dwelling in an effort to join them for dinner or a cup of tea. Each window stirred a new emotion within me. One would have the flickering glow of a fireplace and a picture on the wall. Another would parade the silhouettes of people living their lives. The next window showed me a man talking to his television while a woman sat near by. *Clank-clank, clank-clank, clank-clank,* each pane of glass told a different tale that made me want to know more: a stove with steaming pots, an empty bedroom, a candlelit dining room, a coat draped over an old chair. It was like someone else was changing channels on the television, looking for something worth watching, and every time something caught my attention, they would change it again. I wished the engineer would stop for just an hour, so I could introduce myself and learn the people's names. Perhaps, (if they would let me) I would walk from room to room and get acquainted with their houses and ways of living. I wanted to explore the rooms I couldn't see. I found myself longing to hear the sound of their voices around the dinner table. What were they eating? Where had they been all day? What were they talking about? I wondered who they were and what they were like.

Clank-clank, clank-clank, clank-clank, I felt almost criminal because of my desire to invade their privacy. Surely they must have expected that I would do this, I thought, since they lived so close to the tracks. It was an open invitation to anyone riding the train. It was an invitation that said, "Come on in, as far as you can." It was an invitation that left a thousand unanswered questions racing through my mind. I would have been satisfied to stand outside with my face against the glass of their living room windows, but the train would not hear of it.

Only a glimpse was allowed and nothing more. By the time our little train reached Gatwick, I was feeling a bit cheated. I must have walked fifty miles in London, studying the history and admiring the sights of that great city, but something was lost in the trip. What I truly wanted to experience required an invitation that I had not received.

It's funny how we spent all our money going from place to place trying to get a feel for London, but it was all missed. *The sights reserved for tourists only told of the history and not the heart.* One would have to meet a family who lived there and share a meal before they could truly say they visited London. With my tiny credit card loaded to the limit, I was now receiving the revelation that I had not really been in London. I had only seen it from a racing trolley on my way home. London was in my head but not in my heart. I had studied it for four long days but never once did I experience its innermost heart. It was at this moment that God began to flood my spirit with the truth of what He desires. It was a truth that concerned the entire body of Christ and me personally. Over the next few years, this truth began to grow until it ultimately overtook my entire ministry and redefined my calling. I now realized that my trip to London was not in vain. I had hoped to see the queen from a distance, but I left having met the King of kings in the most intimate and personal way.

Whether or not we realize it, we all have had this boxcar experience when it comes to the heart of God. From childhood on, we were handed fleeting glimpses that revealed bits and pieces of who He is and what He is like. Unfortunately, not all the windows tell a true story. In fact, most of them tell more about the history of the building rather than the truth about who is inside.

Many images that should have been swallowed were only tasted, and others that should have been tasted and spewed out were swallowed like poison. Like passing windows viewed from a racing boxcar, we have been given nothing more than a flutter of half-truths concerning His heart.

For many of us, it was our earthly father that stamped the image of God on our hearts. For others, it was a pastor or leader in our church. Perhaps one of the many traveling evangelists we encountered or a book we read gave us lasting imprints of God. There are so many that come and go so quickly, just like the windows I passed on my train that day. They were there for just a moment and then they were gone. In the end, we are left with tangled fragments that paint an incorrect and compromised image of God's heart. Modern day Christian doctrine is many times based on these pictures. It's the accumulation of every popular teaching and religious slogan. It's mixed with the unforgettable pain of our past experiences and just a touch of truth, all wrapped into a neat little contradicting explanation of God.

These passing windows reminded me of the day my father came to my second grade classroom for a visit. It was the great daddies' day show-and-tell event, where all the children's fathers came and presented themselves before the class. This is very much what we endure in modern day Christianity. Every pastor, teacher, leader and author is bringing his daddy for show and tell. Some daddies are mean, some are strict, and some are cold and heartless, while others are sweet and patient. After a lifetime of enduring the different daddies, we begin to connect the dots in an effort to draw an accurate picture of the heart of God.

God is NOT your daddy, He is your Father.

More often than not, we end with a picture that falls drastically short of truth. Why? Because each daddy contradicts the other, and God is NOT your daddy, He is your Father. Over time, our understanding of the heart of God has been so warped and contorted that we find ourselves terrified to stand in His presence.

It's no wonder why we have to force ourselves to read our Bibles and pray. It's not surprising to find us sleeping in on Sunday morning or holding back during praise and worship. This is not the age of rebellion that we so commonly hear about. We are not in the midst of a God-hating generation; we are in the midst of a God-unawareness generation. It's a generation that is reacting rationally and normally to what it has been given. It's a generation that is straining to look deep into the heart of God, but the train of life is moving too quickly to focus on any one thing.

> *We are not in the midst of a God-hating generation; we are in the midst of a God-unawareness generation.*

The Journey Begins

I would like to take you on a journey. It's one that will change your Christian walk forever and redefine your view of God in a way that will leave you feeling naked and speechless. It is only fair to warn you of a few things before we get started. Every religious teaching you have been brought up with is about to be shaken and stirred. Your preconceived ideas of who God is and what He wants from you will be dashed to the ground and shattered. Be prepared to receive the spiritual challenge of a lifetime. We are about to stop the train and have a cup of tea with the Father of Heaven and Earth. By the end of this journey, you will have swallowed what others have only tasted. In the end, I promise you will be stronger and closer to God than ever before.

There are a few rules before we get started. First of all, you must promise yourself that you will not hold to traditionalism for tradition's sake. I am not asking you to blindly believe anything you read, but I am at the very least asking you to let go of the very thing that holds most people back from true relationship.

Jesus Christ defied almost every tradition that the Pharisees believed in. Tradition is a recipe that the mind creates in an effort to re-erect a spiritual move that originated in the heart. Jesus Christ defied almost every tradition that the Pharisees believed in. Just because a man fell in love with his wife from across a crowded room, does not mean that every time the two of them are in a crowded room they will fall in love all over again.

> ✝
> *Tradition is a recipe that the mind creates in an effort to re-erect a spiritual move that originated in the heart.*

Tradition believes in the crowded room and overlooks the heart.

Secondly, you must approach the following chapters with a naked spirit. That is to say, it is imperative that you remove every religious and jargon-driven piece of clothing you are wearing regardless of how attractive you feel it is. This includes all the little catch phrases you incorporated into your belief system after listening to your favorite evangelist or pastor. Your faith in their surefire "truth" can stunt what God is about to do in your heart. These things can become like a tightly tangled ball of Christmas tree lights in your head. It is my desire to remove them all and replace them with one soft white light of truth. You will understand what I am talking about shortly.

Thirdly, you are NOT allowed to take your head on this journey. This is a journey of the heart. God is a heart person, and nothing from your head will ever comprehend what is about to be told to you. Your head will only weigh you down. It will cause you to over analyze and spit up what was meant for the heart.

Lastly, you must enter this journey with total and complete honesty. This is perhaps the most important thing of all. It is absolutely imperative that you are willing to do this. Without honesty, you cannot move another spiritual inch. You must be willing to open every secret part of your heart and lay it out truthfully and sincerely before God. No one else has to know but you and God. No true revelation can ever be received without this one thing happening first. This is precisely why there had to be a John the Baptist. His ministry was to prepare the way for the Messiah. That preparation was all about honesty with self. Once this is established, there is no limit to what God can show you.

There is one more thing. You must *not* cut out early because you got offended. You need to commit to reading this book entirely. Weigh everything carefully and prayerfully before making judgments. Much of what you are about to read will contradict many things you have been taught throughout your life. You might even find yourself feeling like you are doing something wrong throughout this process simply because much of this will be totally foreign to your theology. Nevertheless, you must keep reading until you are finished.

Without honesty, you cannot move another spiritual inch.

If you are ready, buckle your seatbelt and turn the page.

Losing My Religion[1]

The auditorium began to fill up with people who had traveled from all parts of the country to attend our annual "Married to the Master" conference. It was the opening evening, so there was a line at the registration table surrounded by small clusters of people wearing nametags and holding conference schedules in their hands. Some had come alone, while others were part of a group that had arrived on their church bus. There was the usual anticipation in the air that so commonly is felt at Christian events such as this. As the worship team exploded into song, the crowd doubled in size in just a few minutes, and soon we were on our way.

There is this little room behind the curtains on the stage, where I often retreat to just before I preach. It gives me time to collect my thoughts, look over my notes, and say a quick prayer before entering the main auditorium. I especially like this room, because it allows me to watch all the people without them knowing. In fact, I will sheepishly admit that many times I skip praise and worship altogether, because I enjoy watching them so much. Every time I do this, I find myself falling in love with them all over again. The voice of God is clearer than ever before when I am in this mode, so it has become a practice of mine to do this.

As I stood there watching, I began to notice that there was something different about the spirit of this crowd, something that stuck out to me like a sore thumb. Oddly enough, it was a mixture between anticipation and disappointment. If I were to give the exact breakdown and ratio, I believe it was about ten percent anticipation and *ninety percent disappointment.* I suppose I could have rationalized that they were all in sin and needed deliverance, but for some reason God would not let me retreat to that excuse. These people were basically disappointed with their religion. It was as if they had been sold something by a con artist and once they got it home, it didn't work.

Surely you have seen those late night infomercials where they advertise those "amazing" life changing products that you can't find in stores. For example, there's the closet organizer that is guaranteed to make all your problems go away. The recipe is pretty much the same, with whatever they are selling. They have the charismatic hyperactive spokesperson that swears that his closet organizer can save your marriage, heal the sick, and raise the dead. Then there is the skeptical simpleton sidekick who publicly finds the answers to life through the ninety-mile-an-hour demonstrations. And finally there is the mystified studio audience who simultaneously erupts in a series of *scripted* "oooos" and "ahhhhs" followed by uncontrollable and obviously insincere applause. Before you know it, they have you believing that this closet organizer can hang your shirts, file your suits, hold your shoes, walk your dog, and drive your kids to school.

So what do you do? You grab your credit card and race to the phone; after all, if you call in the next five minutes without thinking it through, they'll include the "twelve-compartment laundry hamper" at no extra charge. Five weeks later, your miracle working purchase arrives in the mail, and before you know it, you are sitting in a pile of tangled poles, hooks, and hangers that look nothing like what you saw on TV. In the end, where do these two thousand loose parts end up? Piled in your closet creating even more clutter than before.

The night of our conference, I stood in my cubbyhole peeking out at several hundred people who honestly felt like they had been deceived into buying a religion that didn't meet up to its charismatic claims. With cluttered emotional closets, they mindlessly attended conference after conference in a feeble effort to find out what went wrong. What part was missing? What did they miss in the direction manual? Where was that mystery clamp that was supposed to hold everything together? Why isn't it working like they said it would? Why doesn't it look like the picture on the box? Perhaps if they were lucky, they might find a screw here and a fastener at the next seminar, maybe even a pole at the next. But history has proven to them that it is very unlikely that this conference would be any different than the rest, and so there they stood with their laminated name tags, their schedules, and their hands in the air trying to be faithful, positive, and believing like good little Christians. In their hearts however, they were skeptically watching another Christian infomercial that would most likely fall short of its exaggerated claims.

The last thing these precious people needed was another sermon full of empty promises and quick fix formulas. By now, they had heard it all. They had tried every recipe, read every book and prayed every prayer. They've tried giving all their money, anointing all their windows, and binding all their demons.

They've pleaded the blood, put on the armor, and fasted themselves to skin and bones. They had declared it, claimed it, confessed it, chanted it and even commanded it until they were blue in their spiritual faces. These people had heard every power preacher on the planet, and for some reason when Monday morning rolled around, they were right back where they started.

As the final song was being played, I nervously approached the stage and posed a question to everyone in the room, a question that would change the entire course of my ministry. I asked how many of them had been basically miserable for the largest part of their Christian lives?

To my amazement, almost every hand
in the building went up.

Let me remind you that this was not a group of baby Christians who needed a little more guidance and encouragement in their walks. These people were an active part in their churches. Many were pastors and leaders who had come with their groups. These were people who had been saved for many years. I do not believe that this was an isolated incident. In fact, I am certain that this predicament is running through the veins of the majority of Christians in the Church today. In fact, a recent survey done by The Billy Graham Evangelistic Association and the Southern Baptist Association has now proven that Christianity is the fastest declining religion in America. Another study done by George Barna has produced staggering facts that the Church might be embarrassed to admit. In this study they found that almost fifty percent of regular Protestant church attendees are not born again. In other words, they do not believe that their salvation hinges on the life, death and resurrection of Jesus Christ. As a solution to this problem, Protestant denominations are launching a world-wide evangelistic crusade to save the souls of those who go to church every Sunday. Amazing!

I would like to make it abundantly clear that it is not my intention - nor has it ever been my intention - to "bash" the body of Christ. I do not believe that this is in God's heart. I have never felt that my calling was to nitpick and finger-point at everything I see wrong with the Church. I don't believe that anyone is called to do this. Truthfully, I am surprised to see how many people will claim such a calling. This body-bashing mentality is directly from the spirit of the enemy and in no way lines up with the heart of God. The purpose of this book is not to expose the faults of the Church, but to declare the truth and beauty of God. Having said that, allow me to continue.

For the next hour of our conference, we started down a path of total honesty. Once we had established a covenant of openness between ourselves (just as you and I have), we began to frankly ask a few questions that had been begging for answers for the majority of our Christian lives. I'm talking about those questions that would make you feel almost pagan if you were to voice them aloud. It's those secret questions that Christians wouldn't dare admit, because doing so would almost certainly be misconstrued as faithlessness, rebellion or even downright blasphemy. Nevertheless, because of our shameless covenant with honesty, we treaded through those undesired titles and came up with a conclusion that was both startling and simple. Perhaps we were not the first ones to discover this, but I am quite sure that we were the first Christians to recognize it without leaving the Church over it. I would like to share it with you.

> *The purpose of this book is not to expose the faults of the Church, but to declare the truth and beauty of God.*

We have been lied to about God.

We have been lied to about who He is, what He is like, what He wants from us, and how He relates to us. We have been lied to about how He responds to us and what He expects from us. We have been lied to about His heart for us, His purpose for us, His desires for us and, most of all, His love for us. The Heart of God is basically unknown by His people. We don't know Him any more than the Pharisees and religious teachers did when Jesus walked the Earth.

That's the simple part. What was so startling was the fact that we had all believed the lie. It wasn't as though we were gloating over our newfound truth. In fact, we felt foolish over it. We felt like the woman who suddenly finds out that her husband has been cheating on her throughout their entire marriage. She now recalls all the obvious warning signs that sat right in front of her face unnoticed. She has an indescribable anguish over the lost years of her life, coupled with a sense of personal stupidity on her part for being so blind. This is exactly the place we were by the end of the service. How could we have missed it?

> *The Heart of God is basically unknown by His people.*

I suppose every Christian plays his or her part in keeping the lie covered and alive. We do it by lying to ourselves. We even lie to others about things like our faith, our victory, and our passion. We learn the lingo so we'll fit in with the others and then we just go with the flow. We follow the religious rules of political correctness by stifling the very questions that would blow the whole thing wide open, like for instance,

"Why isn't it working?"

Rather than come right out and ask the obvious question, we just wear the, it's working-mask and keep it to ourselves. I suppose it's a matter of peer pressure for most of us. Besides, who wants to face the obvious comebacks we are sure to get from anyone who hears this question? You know what I'm talking about. They're those "stock" Christian answers we give to people when we don't know what else to say. They go something like this: "Well, brother, it's because

We learn the lingo so we'll fit in with the others and then we just go with the flow.

you haven't been in the Word enough," or "You must have unconfessed sin in your life," or "You just need to spend more time in prayer," or "Perhaps it's because you don't attend on Sunday nights," or "Have you been paying your tithe?" or the ever-popular, "You just need to give it to God."

After being beaten over the head with these things once or twice, even a monkey can learn that silence is golden. They all imply personal failure or a lack of commitment. They are designed to shut you up. Why? Because the person to whom you are asking the question is also asking the same question, and they don't know the answer. It's not working for him any more than it is for you.

We have been lied to about God.

If you were to walk into a secular nightclub on a Saturday night and ask one hundred people to describe the heart of God, you would find that they would be staggeringly accurate. If you were to walk into a church on a Sunday night and ask a hundred people to do the same thing, they would be miserably inaccurate. In fact, they would contradict one another so much that you probably wouldn't even get a straight and final answer. Then after you went home and were tucked into bed, they would still be at the church having a debate over each of their theological opinions.

The problem here is that we have been taught all our lives that memorizing Scripture is the best way to "know God." We think if we know the Bible, we must know God. I am not minimizing the power of His Word or the value of memorizing Scripture. I am, however, challenging the mentality that doing so brings one closer to God's heart. I am also challenging the idea that it will be "getting the Word into your heart." Just because you read it and memorize it doesn't mean that it landed in your heart. The Pharisees knew Scripture like the back of their hand, but when God stood right in front of them, they didn't know Him from Adam. The Bible has become an excuse for many Christians. It's an excuse to not have relationship. You can read it and study it all you want, but if you have incorrect perceptions about God's heart, you will interpret it accordingly. What I am saying is that because of the lies we have believed about God, we have made up our minds about Him, therefore we cannot even benefit from reading His Word. If you think He is angry, the Word will ONLY sound angry to you. If you think He is a drill sergeant, His Word will come across that way. If you have decided that He is disappointed with you, you will only see disappointment in His Word.

> *The Bible has become an excuse for many Christians. It's an excuse to not have a relationship.*

Why do you suppose that almost ninety percent of Christians never read their Bibles? When they do read it, it's like they are meeting a quota or fulfilling an obligation. Think about this for a moment. If my wife writes me a love letter, I will plow through an army of men to get to that letter just to see what it says. Then I will read it over and over until the paper literally falls apart in my hands. Why? It's because I truly love her, and I want to know everything that is on her heart. Could you imagine if I had to have a support group of men to keep me accountable in the matter of reading my wife's letters? What would it tell you if I had to have a "mentor" in my life to encourage me every day to finish the letter she wrote me? There must be some reason why MOST OF US don't want to read our Bibles.

We have been lied to about God.

The problem is that we don't love God anymore. And who could blame us? The God we have been fed all of our lives, is simply not lovable. This, by the way, is also why we don't pray more than ten minutes a day.

Did you know that the average pastor prays only fifteen minutes a day? He doesn't love God, either. I can't say I blame him. The God he believes in is the same one he presents to you every Sunday. Who would want to talk to that God? I believe that because of the lies we have been told about the Heart of God it is virtually impossible for us to truly love Him.

So what have we resorted to? Commitments! We commit ourselves to reading our Bibles and praying every day for the next year. We commit ourselves and recommit ourselves to Christ. We honor people for being "committed Christians" and shame the others for having a lack of commitment. Truthfully, I think that most committed Christians need to be "committed" to a psychiatric ward. If it were not for the promise of Heaven at the end of their lives, I honestly think they would have

> † *The God we have been fed all of our lives, is simply not lovable.*

been better off unsaved. Religion has rendered them certifiably insane. It has caused Christians to surrender every bit of common sense to a series of jumbled and mixed-up teachings that have no rhyme or reason to them. After a while, these people lose touch with all reality and they become incapable of coexisting with other human beings. They do not know or love God, but they are "committed" to the religious slogans, clichés, and hook lines they have memorized, and they live their lives based on the ten thousand contradictory teachings they have been fed.

God is not looking for Christians to make commitments to Him. The very fact that we use terms like "committed to Christ" is proof that we don't love Him. What is a commitment? It's a way of forcing ourselves to do what we don't want to do. When husbands thunder out their boastful statements like, "I've been committed to you for twenty years," what they are really saying is that they wanted to cheat on their wife over and over, but because of their commitment, they refrained. This is not what love is. God is NOT looking for Christians to make another commitment. If you have to force it, it's not there. Please understand that this is not about making you feel condemned and guilt-ridden. This is not your fault. The God you have been given is not a God that is easy to love.

God is not looking for Christians to make commitments to Him

We have been lied to about God.

For the most part of my ministry, I have been in a state of mourning on God's behalf. I do not believe that there is a character in the entire Bible that is more misunderstood than God. Perhaps He doesn't need me to mourn for Him, but nevertheless, I do. Truthfully, I feel sorry for Him. He has been misrepresented for thousands of years. I believe the heart of God is broken over His children's lack of knowledge of who He is. This does not mean angry or vengeful, but simply broken just as your heart might break if one of your own children called you by a different name. Imagine having the very one who was supposed to know you better than anyone in the world, not even know your name. Have you ever had someone you have spent a great deal of time with mispronounce your name in public? It's embarrassing. It makes you feel hurt and unimportant to that person. This is precisely how God feels with this generation.

By now, you may be thinking to yourself that this does not apply to you. You might even feel like this book would be good for others, but it has very little to do with where you are right now. After all, you love God with all your heart. Sure, there are struggles here and there, but when all is said and done you are quite happy in your Christian walk. I want to challenge you throughout the course of this book. Look deep into your heart and be absolutely honest with yourself. I am in no way challenging your heart's desire to know and love Him. That is self-evident. If that were not so, you would not be reading this book. I want to pose a challenge concerning the truth about where you are right now. What do you believe about Him in your heart? How do you feel about Him in your heart? These are the questions to which I want you to find answers.

I do not believe that there is a character in the entire Bible that is more misunderstood than God.

As you go through this book, you might be surprised to find how many areas in which your belief system contradicts itself. You will be astonished to find the number of times your heart believes the exact opposite of what your head believes. Your head may hold to one theology while your heart holds to another and the two are as far apart as the East is from the West. It's like there are two religions battling against one another inside your mind, and you don't even know it. You have been force-fed a steady diet of lies for so long that you have grown accustomed to it, in fact, you "amen" your way through the whole meal. It's like the water in Mexico. Everyone knows that when you go to Mexico, you should never drink the water. We hear it said our entire lives. When you get there, it's easy to slip and drink it because the Mexicans are drinking it, and nothing is happening to them. Why? It's because they have developed immunity to its poison just as you have developed a resistance to the teachings you receive.

We sit through two hours of Christian television and watch six sermons in a row. Each sermon directly contradicts the other, and we don't even question it. We read book after book and get twenty different teachings on one subject that have nothing to do with one another and we don't even bat an eye. We sit through a wonderful sermon on the love and grace of God, and during the closing segment, the preacher tosses out a series of statements that completely shoot his entire message to hell, and we don't even know it happened.

For example, an evangelist will come to our church and preach a sermon on how God will never leave us or forsake us, and sixty seconds later he will insinuate that God might be thinking of leaving us because we haven't "given Him everything." We listen to teachings on God's promises and how they are a free gift, followed by a list of things we must do in order to earn them.

It reminds me of when my wife and I were in the hospital after having our first child. Every single nurse that came to our room gave us an entirely different schedule for feeding the baby. The first would tell us to feed every two hours no matter what. The second told us to feed every three-and-a-half hours, and to even wake the baby from a dead sleep in order to stick to the schedule. The third nurse told us to only feed the baby when she cried. The fourth told us to feed every three hours unless the baby was sleeping, in which case we should just let her sleep. By the time the fifth nurse came in, we quickly realized that these people don't share a table in the lunchroom. In fact, they don't share anything at all. Truthfully, I was beginning to wonder if they even had babies of their own. After four children, I have become an expert in "old wives' tales." I think I could write a book on them. The Church today reminds me of a group of grandmothers exchanging their latest "wives tale" and swearing by it to their dying day.

This is precisely what has happened to your religion. Christianity has become a series of "old wives tales." Today's preachers, teachers, and authors have become experts in the art of convincing you that the Heart of God is whatever they want it to be. They do it with beautiful illustrations and stories that sound so right, because of the way in which they are told, but when all is said and done they reek with wrongness. What is worse is that we have believed these "wives' tales" about the heart of God. We have swallowed every poisoned pill that

> *Christianity has become a series of "old wives tales."*

has been put on our tongues and now we are stuck trying to keep it all down. We are stuck trying to make sense of it all. It becomes a full time job sifting through the hype and jargon in an effort to find the slightest bit of truth.

I once sat through a sermon on "the anointing of God" where the preacher taught that the anointing was something you had to pray for and only after much fasting and interceding, God would give it to you. The very next week another preacher taught that we are all anointed of God because *the Anointed One* lives within us. The following week, yet another preacher taught on how you can lose the anointing, but Christ will never leave you. Each week, to my astonishment, the very same crowd waved, applauded and "amen-ed" their way through the entire service. Hundreds of the same people attended every service, yet no one even noticed what was happening. Not one question was raised, not one hand, not even one eyebrow.

I do not believe that these people are stupid in any way, shape, or form. I think they are extremely hungry. They will take what ever they can get. When I was a child, I was once thrown out of a petting zoo for feeding the sheep a Styrofoam cup and a paper lunch bag. To my surprise, the lamb ate it up just as if it were his regular food. I learned a lesson that day that would follow me for the rest of my life. Sheep will eat just about anything! Because of this, a shepherd has a great responsibility. He must constantly watch over them to protect them. Who among us would not eat a Styrofoam cup or a paper lunch bag if he was starving to death?

> *Any time a preacher reveals a new and deeply profound truth about God, it's probably not true.*

We have been lied to about God

Please understand, loved ones, my desire is not to bring condemnation but freedom to the Body of Christ. My heart breaks for the hundreds and thousands of precious well-meaning people who are trying their best to *tow* their spiritual lines. I do not think this has happened because of rebellion or hypocrisy; I honestly feel that it is the result of how we were raised. Please also understand that the answer here is not to cut off all respect for your pastors and leaders or to quit attending church. That would be directly out of the heart of God. I also do not believe that the answer is to pray for "power" or "fire" from Heaven to make it all go away. The answer is quite simple. We need truth!

This book is a quest for that truth. There can only be one truth and when it is found it will NOT contradict itself or confuse our understanding of God, but it will reveal the simplicity of who He is. I have come to realize one thing in my many years of ministry. Any time a preacher reveals a new and deeply profound truth about God, it's probably not true.

I am reminded of a movie I once saw where a gentleman was taking a vision test. He was asked to cover his left eye and read the top row of letters on the chart that was hanging twenty feet away on the wall of the doctor's office. To the doctor's amazement, the man read the copyright date that was typed in tiny little letters at the bottom right side of the chart. I thought to myself, "impressive, but WRONG." This man was looking too deep and he missed the biggest and most obvious thing on the chart. In my mind he failed the test. This is the problem with finding the truth about God's Heart. Too many of us are looking so deep that we miss the obvious. Unfortunately, many people would rather gratify themselves with deep thinking and extravagant imaginations than accept anything simple and obvious.

> *Too many of us are looking so deep that we miss the obvious.*

To these people, truth is a letdown and this book will frustrate them to death. Remember that Jesus Christ was a letdown to the Pharisees two thousand years ago.

My goal is not to impress you with something deeper than you have ever imagined, but to show you the "top row of letters" on the chart. I want you to laugh out loud when you read this book while thinking to yourself, "of course, how could I have missed it." For the most part, I believe that when you read this book, you will feel like you do when you are frantically tearing your house apart looking for a pencil, only to find that it's resting behind your ear. The heart of God is closer to you than you think. In fact, it's within you.

Our Father Who Ain't In Heaven

1 Corinthians 13:4-7 (NIV)
Love is patient, love is kind. It does not envy, it does not boast, it is not proud. It is not rude, it is not self-seeking, it is not easily angered, it keeps no record of wrongs. Love does not delight in evil but rejoices with the truth. It always protects, always trusts, always hopes, always perseveres.

For centuries, we have tried to identify exactly what love is. It has become the great mystery to the human race that seems to redefine itself from moment to moment. There are some who have claimed understanding, while others believe it is beyond our ability to comprehend. Love has been the subject of countless poems, songs, stories, books, movies, talk shows and sitcoms. From generation to generation, man has searched for a way to explain it, capture it, and cultivate it. Just when we think we know the meaning of love, someone else comes along and completely alters everything in an instant, leaving us feeling like we haven't even scratched the surface.

In our world, there are so many diverse definitions of love, definitions that routinely contradict themselves, making the subject of love ever more mysterious. From the moment we are born into this world, we begin searching for love. Some of us have literally destroyed our lives in our search for love. We find that our need for love is as insatiable as our need for food and water. Without it, we simply cannot survive. The problem is that we are looking desperately for something that we wouldn't even recognize if it were staring us in the face. Just when we think we might have found it, we realize that we were once again deceived and it wasn't love at all.

Many people have given up on love completely. For them, it has become nothing more than an idealistic fantasy, a pipe dream or an unobtainable lie. Even the hope of love has been dashed to the ground in their minds. For others, love has become the electric shock that the lab rat endures in order to acquire its next meal. Still, others have found love to be an addiction that never gives back what it takes away. Their entire lives have been a shattered pattern of compromise and routine letdowns, but for some crazy reason they never quit taking the very drug that is slowly killing them. I know thousands of women who would call love "the great deceiver." Ironically, because of their need for love they continually allow themselves to be swindled into giving their hearts away, only to have them put through another emotional blender and handed back to them on a silver platter.

Whatever you believe to be true about love will inevitably define your God to you.

It's not surprising that the world has defined love in so many contradicting ways. Their assessment of love is much like the Christian's evaluation of God. And why should we expect anything different? The Bible tells us "God is love." If we are ever to know God, we must first know love. Whatever you believe to be true about love will inevitably define your God to you. The reason we are so confused about who God is, is because we have been affected by the world's teachings about love. In fact, I intend to show you just how far this has gone in our thinking.

Exposing The Truth About What We Believe

This is the part where your promise to leave your head behind comes into play. For the next few moments, I want to take you on a journey to your heart. I want to uncover the truth about who you really think God is. Buckle your seat belt, because you're about to have a spiritual head-on collision with truth.

John 8:44 NIV
You belong to your father, the Devil, and you want to carry out your father's desire. He was a murderer from the beginning, not holding to the truth, for there is no truth in him. When he lies, he speaks his native language, for he is a liar and the father of lies.

In this verse, Jesus was speaking to the Pharisees and the teachers of the law. It is interesting to note that though these people did not believe that Jesus was who He said He was, *they still hated the Devil.* This is precisely why Jesus' words were so bewildering and offensive to them. These men had studied the Scriptures their entire lives. They prayed to God for hours each day. They paid their tithes and even fasted twice a week. Most of them had memorized thousands of Scriptures and had studied every piece of information that related to God. These men had created an exact science with their religion. Every religious feast was observed exactly the way Moses had commanded. Every rule and law that had been handed down to them was obeyed to the fullest extent.

We are talking about men who wouldn't even walk more than ten feet on the Sabbath because it was to be kept holy. No stone was left unturned. Never in their lifetime had any one of them bowed down to worship Satan. The very thought of such a thing was repulsive to them. These men were the religious powerhouses of their day. If there had been a religious television station in their time, they would have been center stage. The devil was the furthest thing from their minds, so when Jesus made this statement they were just as deeply offended as you would be if I were to make the same statement to you.

Get Ready To Be Offended

Our original verse at the top of this chapter contains a list of fifteen statements about love. If I were to ask you if you believe that these statements are true, you would not hesitate to answer me with a resounding "YES." Of course you do, right? If I were to ask you if you believed that because the Bible says, "God is love" this would mean that these fifteen statements are a description of God Himself, you would answer, "YES" again. You might have even heard this particular passage read with the word "God" replacing the word "Love." If you haven't, I would encourage you do to so now because it's very moving.

If you want to find out what love is, then you must know God. If you want to find out who God is, you must know love.

If the Bible is correct in saying that "God is love" then we must come to several conclusions about love and what it is. It can only have one definition and it can NEVER contradict itself. Love is what it is and that's all that it is. Just as God said to Moses "I AM who I AM," love IS what it IS. If you want to find out what love is, then you must know God. If you want to find out who God is, you must know love.

We can also come to the conclusion that our personal beliefs about what love is directly parallels our personal perception of who God is. What you believe in your HEART about love is exactly what you believe in your HEART about God. This is precisely where I want to park for a moment. *What do you believe about love?* I would like to propose to you the idea that you have

> *What you believe in your HEART about love is exactly what you believe in your HEART about God.*

bought into the world's definition of love and you believe it in your heart. The problem is that the world's ideas on love completely contradict what is written in our Scripture. The world has taught you that love is the exact opposite of everything written in this passage. Think about it for a moment.

We have been taught that love isn't patient. In fact we believe that if it's really "love" there is no need to slow things down in a relationship. Things like getting to know one another and abstaining from sexual intercourse before marriage are totally overlooked. Why? It's because we know we are in love; what's the use in waiting? Our society believes that when you truly love someone you will be impatient.

What about kindness? You would think that kindness would be attributed to love hands down. Unfortunately, there are millions of people who honestly believe that love doesn't need to be kind for it to be authentic. I am amazed at how many women go from one unkind man to another and don't even second-guess it. Many men honestly believe that women really desire to be treated badly. It sounds almost silly when you think about it, but it's shockingly true. In my years of counseling, I have been astounded at the number of people who are actually addicted to unkind people. Though there is something within them that honestly desires to be with a kind person, they routinely find themselves attracted to the total opposite. Then when they are finally faced with kindness in a person they simply find it unattractive or even boring.

Our verse also says *"love is not self-seeking."* This is precisely a one hundred and eighty degree turnaround from everything with which the world has raised us. We won't even consider dating someone unless there is something in it for us. When I ask couples why they want to get married, I have about a ninety percent chance of getting a long list of self-serving reasons. When couples are considering divorce, it's almost always because the other person *"is not meeting their needs."* Ironically, selfishness has become an attractive attribute in today's society as well. Every exalted hero of the cinema is literally dripping wet with self-centeredness. We even consider it to be a strength of sorts.

How about the phrase, *"Love keeps no record of wrongs?"* Do I need to elaborate on that one? Then our Scripture tells us that "love always trusts." We have been taught to look at trusting people as if they were foolish and stupid. You might have even counseled someone to "stop being so trusting" in their relationships. In this world, love never trusts, at least not until it's earned. How about when it says, "love always perseveres?" With a divorce rate of over fifty percent, I think we can pretty much toss that one aside. We have come to believe that people "just grow apart," and "nothing lasts forever." It even has a ring of wisdom to it when you hear someone use these excuses for their failed marriage.

The point I want to make to you is that the world has convinced us that "love" is the exact opposite of everything listed in our Scripture. Also I want to make the point that *you have bought this lie hook line and sinker.* Maybe not in your head, but you have *in your heart.* Sure, you might read this passage in the Bible and totally acknowledge its truth and power, but I don't think you believe a word of it IN YOUR HEART. Still not convinced?

I want you to make a mental list of how many times you have been hurt by love in your past, whether by someone with whom you were in a romantic relationship, or by a member of your immediate family. Take a moment and count.

If you are like most people, you may have several unforgettable instances that have already surfaced in your mind. Now I have a revelation for you; that wasn't love that hurt you! What you were hurt by was the opposite of love, but IN YOUR HEART you believe it was love. Make no mistake about it; love has never hurt you. You were hurt

It only matters what your heart believes because this is your only connection to God

by a deceptive and upside down definition of love that you swallowed into your heart and believed. Go ahead and read through our passage again and make a list of exactly which one thing it was that hurt you.

1 Corinthians 13:4-7 NIV
Love is patient, love is kind. It does not envy, it does not boast, it is not proud. It is not rude, it is not self-seeking, it is not easily angered, it keeps no record of wrongs. Love does not delight in evil but rejoices with the truth. It always protects, always trusts, always hopes, always perseveres.

Remember when I asked you to leave your head behind on this journey and only take your heart? The reason why I did this

> *If you believe IN YOUR HEART that "love" is the opposite of what the Bible says, you will inevitably attribute the character and personality of the Devil to God.*

is because I really don't care what your head believes about love. Your head may read this verse and agree completely, but if you don't believe it in your heart, you are dead in the water. This is a book about knowing God, and you can never know Him with your head. It only matters what your heart believes because this is your only connection to God. If you are like most people you probably just proved to yourself that in your heart you believe the opposite of what this verse tells us about love. So what are the implications of this?

If the Bible says that "God is love" and everything listed in this verse is a description of the character and personality of God, then I have another question for you. Who is the OPPOSITE of everything listed here a description of?

Satan

Let's go a step further. If you believe IN YOUR HEART that "love" is the opposite of what the Bible says, you will inevitably attribute the character and personality of the Devil to God. Think about this for a moment and let it sink in. I believe that this is precisely what the vast majority of us believe in our hearts about God. We basically believe He has the character and personality of the Devil.

If Jesus Christ were walking the Earth today in human form, I believe that His message would be the same to us as it was to the Pharisees of His time. He would tell us that the Devil is our father. This is precisely the point He was making two thousand years ago. The Pharisees and religious teachers had painted a picture of God that made Him look like Satan himself. They had made it impossible for the people to have a relationship with God simply because they were terrified of Him. We are no different today.

The Twenty-First Century Portrait Of God

September 11, 2001 two airplanes loaded with hundreds of innocent passengers were hijacked and flown into the twin towers of the World Trade Center. As millions of Americans watched helplessly in their homes, the towers crumbled to the ground killing thousands of terrified people. Many were seen jumping from the windows with their bodies engulfed in flames while others were crushed beneath a mountain of burning rubble. Hundreds

> † *Just listen to the way we talk about our God! It's no wonder Christians have little interest in reading their Bibles.*

and thousands of mommies and daddies were instantly taken from their families. Sons and daughters literally disappeared in the flames, never to be found again. This attack made Pearl Harbor look like a bee sting. No American will ever forget the horror of that fateful day.

Shortly after this event, many of the Nations most influential Christian leaders appeared on National television and publicly declared that THIS WAS GOD sending judgment on America for its many sins. He was not alone in this thinking. Hundreds of others followed him in this belief.

During the beginning of the AIDS epidemic, it was quite common to hear our nation's pastors explain that *this was a plague sent by God* to punish the homosexuals. Many people still hold to this way of thinking today, in spite of the fact that not all the victims are homosexuals.

Just listen to the way we talk about our God! It's no wonder Christians have little interest in reading their Bibles. Who would want to read "His" book? It's no wonder that we don't want to spend time in prayer. Who would want to talk to "Him?" I once had a man tell me that in the course of one day he was bitten by three Brown Recluse spiders. I was amazed he lived to tell about it. Then he added, "Needless to say, God got my attention." Just listen to how we describe our Father in Heaven. I have a close friend whose brother was killed in a car accident and for years his family wondered what God was trying to tell them with that. I had another friend whose brother was murdered in a drug deal, and my friend's response was that "God works in mysterious ways."

Every bad thing that happens in this world gets blamed upon God. If we lose our job, we think God is at the root of it. If we have a heart attack, God gave it to us. If we lose a loved one, it's because God killed him. If our business fails, we immediately suspect that God is punishing us for something we did. Every terrible thing that Satan orchestrates in our lives is charged to God's account. We truly believe that God has the character and personality of the Devil!

What is worse is that we rationalize it in the most perverted way by calling it the "fear of the Lord." We are literally terrified of Him, and rightly so, He is just waiting for us to make a mistake or fall into sin so He can blast us into hell. The most we can hope for is to somehow avoid the lightning bolts of His anger and try to serve Him the best way possible. Everything we do in our religion is based on fear. We give in the offering because we truly believe that He will wreak havoc upon our lives if we don't. We try our best to witness to others about this wonderful and loving Jesus Christ, but in our hearts we don't believe a word of it. We go through every religious ritual we know in an effort to gain His favor. Our prayer lives have

> *Every terrible thing that Satan orchestrates in our lives is charged to God's account*

been reduced to confessions of "forgive me" and "I'm sorry" at the end of the day. We read just enough of the Bible to say we've read it and we attend as many church services as it takes to make the guilt and shame go away.

We memorize and quote religious slogans that have absolutely no foundation for their existence. We say things like, "God won't bless you until He can trust you," and it sounds so right, but it completely contradicts the truth about who He is. God blesses because God blesses. He sends rain on both the wicked and the righteous. God is love and "love always trusts." We say that if this person or that person doesn't turn from their sin God will eventually "lift His hand of protection from them" and we don't even question where this came from. Remember loved ones, our Scripture also says, "love always protects." I couldn't count the number of times I've heard people say, "there is a time when God will totally give up on a person," regardless of the fact that the Bible says, "Love always perseveres." I challenge you in this. Every single statement about love listed in our Scripture has been turned inside out and upside down.

> †
>
> *It's impossible to have intimacy with a God you can't trust.*

I said at the beginning of this book that I believe it is impossible to love God with what we have been given. It's impossible to have intimacy with a God you can't trust. Our problem today is that we subscribe to a theology that we can't trust as far as we can throw. Can you imagine me telling my wife that I loved her and I will never leave her or forsake her, but if she ever cheated on me I would douse her with gasoline and light her on fire? Though she may never cheat on me, she will certainly never get close to me. She will do whatever it takes to survive the relationship, but I will NEVER have her heart. This is exactly to what many

Christians have resorted. We use fear to motivate ourselves to be good little boys and girls. If we follow all the rules and perform all the duties, we'll be okay when we die.

Acting On Our Hearts

Have you ever been embarrassed by the number of Christians that are just plain mean? When my wife and I were looking for a chapel to get married in, we visited nearly every church within thirty square miles of our home. After touring about 40 different places, I told my wife that if I did not already know Jesus I would totally renounce Christianity completely. It was horrifying, to say the least. I cannot remember a time, before or since, that I was treated so terribly by so many people.

Business owners who deal directly with the public will many times tell you that Christians have the worst dispositions of all. People in the restaurant business hate working Sundays because that's when all the Christians come in after church and demand perfect service and stiff the waitress at the end of the meal. These things have become public knowledge to both the Body of Christ and the world.

Have you ever heard the saying, *"Christians shoot their wounded?"* It's absolutely true! Anytime there is a public scandal involving a well-known minister, news stations don't even have to send out reporters to investigate the story. Why? Because their phones begin ringing off the hook with calls from Christians trying to expose that person with whatever information they have.

Then there is the inescapable reputation of Christians being judgmental. I once saw an episode of "The Simpsons" where the wife of churchgoer Ned Flanders said she was "going to church camp to learn how to be more judgmental." This is the number one complaint I hear from the world concerning Christianity.

We go to "gay pride" parades with megaphones and "you're going to Hell" signs. We compare war stories about how rude we were to the Jehovah Witnesses or Mormon missionaries who came to our home. We picket abortion clinics and heap truckloads of condemnation on the poor women who go to them. It's as though we don't have an ounce of grace or mercy in our blood.

Let me make it perfectly clear that not all Christians act this way. There are plenty of gentle and loving people in the Church who are just as mortified at the actions of their brothers and sisters as I am. My point is not to rebuke the Church for its infamous reputation, but to explain why this is happening the way it is. There can only be one logical reason why so many Christians in the world behave this way. *They are being conformed into the image of their father.*

Jesus was quite right when He said a son *"can do only what he sees his Father doing, because whatever the Father does the Son also does."* It makes perfect sense. If we believe in our hearts that God has the temperament and disposition of Satan, our character will inevitably be conformed to that image.

So What Is The Answer?

First of all, I want to tell you what IS NOT the answer. We do not need another service or prayer meeting where we call upon the power of God to change our lives. Power is not the answer. Truthfully, I believe we are a bunch of power addicts who are secretly dying inside. Just because we have learned to access God's power doesn't mean we know Him any better because of it. His power is available for anyone who exercises faith. Our greatest problem is that we have faith in His power and not in Him. Power is not the answer here.

Secondly, we do not need to dive head-over-heels into worship in an attempt to find an answer. The answer will intensify and authenticate our worship but worship will not bring the answer. We have all learned to worship a God we really don't love, and some of us have even learned to enjoy it. Our worship today has become a "head" experience while our "heart" numbs itself from the pain of what we truly believe.

> *We can pray for hours at a time and still not know the Heart of God.*

While the head sings the wonderful words of God's unfailing love for us, the heart tries its best to keep its mouth shut because it knows better. Over time we can't even tell the difference. Until we get a proper *heart revelation* of who our Father in Heaven is, we will always be the unhappy housewife who is repulsed by her husband's touch, but has learned to enjoy sex by closing her eyes and going somewhere else during the experience. This is worship for thousands of Christians today. Worship is not the answer here.

Thirdly, I would like to say that spending more time in prayer is not the answer. You can pray until you are blue in the face, but you will only be spending more time with the one you are afraid of. Who wants to do that? This is precisely why many of us have to "commit" to a prayer life. We don't want to do it. Most prayer is done from the head anyway, because the heart doesn't want to be there. We can pray for hours at a time and still not know the Heart of God. Though the answer will deepen and intensify our prayer life, prayer is not the answer.

Finally, I would like to make it known that we do not need to pray for Revival. Christianity has become the Harley Davidson of religions. It's a classic, and it's the most authentic, however, it breaks down every hundred miles and needs to be revived. When we stand on our stages in front of the world and pray for revival, or proclaim that revival is upon us, we are, in the same sentence, admitting to the world that our religion keeps dying on us. We have history books that meticulously analyze every historical revival that the Church has ever had in an effort to predict when and where the next one might take place. All the while, we never stop to think that if our religion keeps dying, something must be drastically wrong!

The word, "Revival" is not even in the Bible. It was never the intention of God to have a religion that routinely suffered from heart failure. Sadly, we have come to expect it. We have become addicted to the electrical shock that God has to routinely use in order to bring our religion back to life every hundred years. We preach to the world that if they come to Jesus Christ they will have life ever lasting and then we completely discredit everything we just said by laying down and dying right in front of them. We invite our friends to the revival that our Church is holding and we wonder why they don't show up.

Our greatest problem is that we have faith in His power and not in Him.

Who in the world would want to subscribe to a religion that cannot maintain its own life? Have you ever heard of any other religions that routinely need revival? Why is Christianity the only one? What is it about our religion that causes it to die over and over? Revival is not the answer!

The answer is actually quite simple. So simple, that to some people it might even be a disappointment. You see, it doesn't have the extravagance of the fire and power of God and it lacks the "holy appearance" of worship and prayer. It is just simple enough to entice the average person and absolutely confound the wise all at the same time. What this generation needs is something that will set us free from this lie. We need a revelation of truth!

Prepare Your Heart

Our journey begins here. For the next sixteen chapters I want to paint a new image on your heart. I want to take you through the most colorful passage in the entire Bible. Before we begin painting, you must first clear the canvas of your heart and wash away every stained image of God you have received. We are about to paint a picture of absolute beauty and splendor, one that will cause your Christian walk to explode with variance and life. We are about to paint a portrait of GOD.

Love Is Patient[3]

When we think of patience, there are several things that come to mind. This is perhaps the hardest word in the English language to take at face value. It has within it an implied opposite extreme. We have learned to see patience as something that must require wrath, anger and unrestraint at the opposite end in order to exist. If there were not the option of sudden violence in the midst of stress or chaos, patience would not be able to prove itself and therefore would not exist at all. Instead of just accepting patience as patience, we somehow feel that it has to be "instead of" or "as opposed to" something much worse. It's as though we have come to define patience as a holding back or refraining from expressing an anger that is begging for a release.

I can remember working with a fellow many years ago, that I thought had patience, because he would almost blow his temper over and over, but through using heavy breathing exercises he was able to calm himself down. He reminded me of a rumbling volcano that held back its eruption. He once told me that when he got angry he would clench his fists and slowly count to ten until the anger subsided. Many people at our work place applauded him for his great patience. However, there was always that feeling in the air that someday this guy was going to blow big time and God help anyone who got in his way when it happened.

Generally speaking, I think most of us believe in our hearts that patience is the equivalent of "holding back anger." It's like putting a huge plug on top of a volcano. The bigger the plug, the more patience a person has. Our understanding of patience does not go much further than this.

When we say, "Love is patient," we are likely to interpret it to mean the exact opposite of what it really means. Many of us take it to mean that love is really angry but it holds back from releasing that anger. Husbands who constantly blow their temper at their wives will often say that it is because they love their wife "too much." Our society has taught us that impatience is a sign that love is present. It's amazing how many of us actually believe this. Mothers will explain to their children that their patience is "wearing thin" with them. Fathers who have a lack of patience will reason in their minds that it is because they love their children so much they can't control themselves. Patience must not only be seen as restraining one's rage or restricting anger.

> *Our society has taught us that impatience is a sign that love is present.*

As a pastor, I find myself spending most of my time trying to convince new couples to slow down and be patient. The moment they think they have found "true love" they cast off all restraints. Some of them want to get married only three months after they meet. Others go to bed together almost immediately. They tell me that their lack of patience is a sign that they are really in love.

After all, when you know you love someone, why wait? When I try to step in and get them to put the brakes on and slow things down, I am always faced with the same predictable response. I become their mortal enemy. They can't believe that I would have the nerve to imply that this wasn't love. Suddenly in their minds, I appear to them as the stupidest person they have ever seen. They'll call me "unloving" and "controlling" or worse yet, "jealous." The very people who once sang my praises and lifted me high in the air as their leader, now avoid me in the halls of church and talk about me behind my back. These are the same people who have read my book on relationships and listened to every tape series I have ever preached. They

Love has been redefined in our hearts and most of us believe it has nothing to do with patience.

even took notes and re-preached it to their friends and family members. Everything I have ever told them rang true in their "head" but the moment their "heart" was involved the real truth about what they believed was exposed: "Love is NOT patient."

They are not alone. Our entire world has developed a philosophy that goes right along with this way of thinking. The average time that a couple waits to have sexual intercourse after their first date is somewhere between six and eight weeks. Anyone who has the guts to wait longer than that is usually accused of not caring for the person they are with. Love has been redefined in our hearts and most of us believe it has nothing to do with patience.

What is the average time span that people allow between relationships? Think about that for a moment. In my experience, I have found that people intend on being alone for a lot longer than they actually allow themselves to be alone. Some people openly admit that they need at least one year to recover from a relationship they just got out of, but when the rubber meets the road, they usually end up dating another person within forty days. The reason for this is quite understandable. They are horrified by loneliness, and being with the wrong person is better than being alone.

The problem is that instead of recognizing the truth, they almost always cover their actions with the word "love." They will tell you that they weren't looking for anyone, and it just happened. They'll even attempt to glorify God for its happening. Before they know it, they are in yet another whirlwind relationship that is strikingly similar to their last one. Why? Because they redefined love and believed in their hearts that love has no patience.

When You Ask God To Give You Patience

I think I have heard every great man of God preach on this subject, and they all agree on one certain point. It goes something like this; "If you ask God to give you patience, you'd better watch out!" Basically we believe that God will blast you with an avalanche of stressful situations in an effort to teach you patience. We call it the "school of patience."

This raises an important question: Is patience something that you learn? Is it something that can be taught? Does our Scripture say that if you love someone you will learn to have patience with them? No. If patience were something that you learned through pressure and trauma, it wouldn't be a fruit of the Spirit. What would be the point in having the Holy Spirit dwell in our lives if the fruits were something we had to be taught? If holding your breath and counting to ten was the answer, anyone could learn it.

Many people, through trial and error, have developed a willpower that enables them to hold themselves back from doing certain things they might otherwise be inclined to do. They may refrain from blowing their temper or stop themselves from jumping into situations based on their immediate lusts and desires, but this must not be confused with patience. I certainly do not want to diminish their character by minimizing this learned behavior. On the contrary, it is quite admirable, but it is not patience. Patience is not something you learn over time. It is something you either have or don't. If you don't have it, you can get it all at once, not little by little.

Patience is not supernatural willpower, either. We Christians sometimes think that a patient person possesses the anointing of God. We believe they have reached some spiritual level where God is able to flow an extra dose of patience-power to their situation. Perhaps they were just about to blow and at just the right time, the power of God kicked in and they immediately became supernaturally calm again.

> † *Patience is not something you learn over time. It is something you either have or don't.*

Remember loved ones, "love" is a commandment from God. Along with love comes patience. *There is no such thing as supernatural patience without love.* If we love, we will have patience. It's not a gift or something learned or earned, it just is what it is. We either have it or we don't. When you love, you have it, and when you don't love, you don't have it.

How Do You Get Patience?

The answer to this question may strike you as being redundant and a bit obvious, but I assure you that it is neither. I want you to prepare your heart for an idea that might surprise you. *Patience comes through love.* Remember that our Scripture tells us that "love is patient" so we need to look no further than love. If you are in a relationship that is impatient, you are not "in love." Perhaps this may offend you and for that I truly apologize, but nevertheless it's true. Impatience is not a sign that love is present, but it's a sign of the absence of love. Let me break it down for you in a way that is easier to receive.

Patience comes through understanding. Understanding comes through love. When you truly love someone, whether it is a spouse, a child or a friend, you understand their heart, and when you understand their heart you have patience.

Imagine if you worked in the emergency room of a hospital and one evening a two-year-old child was brought to you that had boiling water spilled down the front of his body. The child is screaming and wailing at the top of his lungs. As you delicately cut away his clothing, you see that his skin is literally falling off his body. My question to you is this: What are the chances that you will lose your patience with this child for screaming? Would you secretly wonder why his mother wasn't quieting him down? Would you even attempt to quiet this child down? What are the chances that you would even start to get irritated? You wouldn't, would you? Why, because you have understanding. You can see with your eyes the exact reason why this child is screaming so much. You would scream as well if it happened to you. So you don't lose patience. You don't even start to lose your patience, because you understand.

> If you are in a relationship that is impatient, you are not "in love."

Love is exactly the same way. When you love someone, you will always see the "burned baby" in everything they do. Love's eyes look beyond the flesh and into the heart. People who lack patience are blind to the heart. This is why they don't understand the person they claim to love. Love sees everything in a person's heart. It doesn't even begin to lose patience, because it understands completely why a person does what they do. When looking for patience, we must always turn to love to find it.

When my daughters Landin and Sidney were two and three-years old, I often told my wife that our children were anointed of God, because if anyone in the world could turn water into wine it was the two of them. They were in a stage of life where their whining was at an all time high. Because they were so close in age, they harmonized with each other while doing it. There were times when they cornered me and pinned me against the wall while both of them screamed and whined on opposite sides of me. Sometime in the midst of this, *I forgot that I loved them* and I started to lose my patience. It is always at the very moment that I take my eyes off of my love for them that I lose understanding of why they are crying.

People who lack patience are blind to the heart

It's as though I become blind in an instant. There is nothing more stressful than listening to screaming children when you have no idea what is wrong with them. As soon as I look at them and love them again, I suddenly see the problem. Perhaps it's because they are tired or hungry. Many times, it's because they feel insecure and they just need to be held. Whatever the reason, I have found that it is impossible to see it unless I am in tune with the love I have for them. My love for my daughters breaks through their outward actions and gets straight to the heart of everything they do. Because I can see the truth through love, I have understanding and because I have understanding I have patience.

When Patience Is Impossible

It is impossible to have patience with someone when you ultimately want to send him to Hell. I know this sounds a bit harsh, but stick with me for a moment. I believe this is precisely the problem in many Christian churches today. They have absolutely no patience for anyone who struggles with anything. Think about this for a moment.

I recently met with a group of about one hundred pastors of various denominations. In the middle of my sermon, I posed the question, "What would you do if you died today and went to Heaven, and when you got there, you found people who were Buddhists, Hindus, and even homosexuals walking around with Jesus? What if people whom you knew for a fact didn't believe in Jesus, made it to Heaven just like you did? How would you feel? Their response was unanimous; *they would be angry.* What I said to them is what I want to say to every living Christian in America. It's one thing when we have information that these people are going to Hell because of their lack of knowledge of Christ, *but it's quite another when we want them to go to Hell!*

> ✝
>
> *It is impossible to have patience with someone when you ultimately want to send him to Hell.*

Why do you suppose that for the most part the church has kicked out homosexuals? We may invite them, and they might even get saved, but the moment they struggle or fall we excommunicate them. Many Christians do the same thing to young girls who get pregnant or have an abortion. We expect that everyone quit smoking the moment they get saved, and if they don't, we talk about them and snicker behind their backs. If a couple is living together when they accept Christ, they have to either get married immediately, or move out over night. If they don't repent at once, then they aren't saved as far as we are concerned. Drug users have to stop using drugs the day they receive the Lord or we question whether or not their conversion was authentic.

The ever-popular saying, "Christians shoot their wounded" didn't come by accident. Though this is certainly not the truth for every Christian in the world, it does accurately describe the majority. This is a basic overall truth concerning the Church today. We have NO patience. Why? It's because we really want to send these people to Hell. I do not believe that we consciously feel this way, but deep in our subconscious we do. We want people to pay for their shortcomings.

> *...most people in Christianity feel that they have been called to safeguard Heaven from people whose actions don't deserve it.*

After all, it's only fair. There is no such thing as a free ride, and most people in Christianity feel that they have been called to safeguard Heaven from people whose actions don't deserve it. The result is that we have no patience with struggling people.

In about two years from now, I will be teaching my oldest daughter Landin to ride a bike. Now, because I am her father and I love her, I will be extremely patient during the process. I will be patient because I am truly concerned about the consequences that will be visited upon her if she doesn't learn how to ride a bike properly. She could crash into things or even lose control and ride out in front of a moving car. Because I love her, I will allow as much time as possible for her to get the hang of it, and I will be absolutely patient throughout the process.

If I did not love her or care about her future and safety, my patience might run a little thin. I might even pressure her to do things that she is not yet ready to do. I may even lose my temper when she doesn't catch on as quickly I would like her to. If she were to run into a tree during one of our lessons, I might even explain to her that she got exactly what she deserved because she didn't listen to my directions on steering. I would expect that she get it right the first time and I probably wouldn't be willing to stick around until she did. You see, when you don't love someone you simply won't have patience with them, but when you do love, you are patient because you care about every facet of that person's life.

Let's Talk About The Heart Of God

I recently attended a service where a well-known author and speaker preached on forgiveness. He truly had many insightful things to share on the subject. Towards the middle of his presentation, however, he took a turn that absolutely grieved every part of my soul. This gentleman began to methodically wind through his selected Scriptures and paste them together in a way that would literally strip every person present of their security in Christ. He proved beyond a shadow of doubt that unless we have forgiven everyone in our life that has hurt us, we will not make it to Heaven. In just a few short minutes, over five thousand people believed that they had either lost their salvation or were on the verge of losing it. By the end of the service, the altars were flooded with terrified men and women who were sobbing and crying out to God in repentance. It was this very night that inspired the writing of this book.

I am publicly filing a grievance with preachers everywhere on behalf of the weary and burdened.

This particular teaching was not unlike many others I have heard over the years. Let me make it clear that I am not minimizing the necessity of walking in forgiveness. The subject of this man's teaching is not the point I am bringing to the table. What I have to say has nothing to do with the subject of forgiveness. I am challenging a method of preaching that I believe causes irreversible damage and unparalleled devastation in the hearts of the listeners. I am publicly filing a grievance with preachers everywhere on behalf of the weary and burdened.

The method I am speaking of is when we systematically match sins and struggles with Bible verses that (by themselves) seem to promise Hell and damnation. Many preachers have become experts in finding these verses and delivering them to their flocks like spiritual hand grenades. They truly work at getting people to respond to an altar call, but the internal explosion that takes place is catastrophic. Whatever the subject is, there is always a verse that will send us to Hell for it. Whether it's bitterness, gossip, lust, greed, anger or selfishness, there is always a Scripture somewhere that will appear to prove beyond any question that we won't make it to Heaven if we die in the midst of committing one of these sins. So we better get right with God tonight, because we could die when we least expect it. It could be tonight,

We have painted a picture of a God who just watches from a distance, but has limited personal involvement.

tomorrow, a week from tomorrow, or even years, but no one really knows when it will be, so it's better to be safe than sorry. All we can do is hope that when our time comes, we aren't caught smack dab in the middle of committing one of our favorite sins.

The problem with this way of thinking is that it totally disregards the sovereignty of God. It suggests that He has absolutely no control over when we die. It also implies that if He could extend our life for the sake of saving our soul, He wouldn't. We have painted a picture of a God who just watches from a distance, but has limited personal involvement. When He does get involved, it is with a complete disregard for what may be taking place in our life at that particular moment. It's all by the book! Many of us secretly feel like He lies in wait for the most inopportune time to snatch us up and send us straight to Hell. We see Him as though He could care less about walking in on us in the midst of a particularly vulnerable and embarrassingly compromising episode. It's as though we believe He has no problem with humiliating us because rules are rules, and we were warned to be ready at all times, so whether our bags are packed or not, the bus leaves when it leaves.

For many of us, the Christian life has become a game of musical chairs.

This is precisely why so many Christians fear death. It has been used against them their entire lives. It's not necessarily death itself that scares us, but it's the timing of our death. We are terrified that it might happen at the worst time possible. For many of us, the Christian life has become a game of musical chairs. When the music stops, you had better be seated or you lose. What is worse is that the person in charge of the music has no regard for where you are standing when they cut the sound.

This form of teaching completely discounts the patience of God. It contradicts the truth of who He is in every possible way. It presents patience as an eye-catching, attractive attribute that holds no real value in and of itself. It's just pretty and pleasant to look at, but when all is said and done, it turns on you like a rabid dog and proves itself to be nothing more than a mirage.

The Patience Of God

My wife and I recently took our two daughters to Sea World in San Diego. We had been planning this trip for quite a long time, and had spent many hours preparing the girls for what daddy called, "the greatest experience of their lives." As the weeks and days grew closer, they were eager with anticipation. Every night before bed, my wife and I would tell the story of how two little girls went to Sea World and met Shamu the giant whale. We would show them pictures of dolphins flying through hoops and penguins playing under water. We quizzed them on all the animal names like, polar bear, sea lion, sting ray, shark and otter. They knew so much about Sea World that if it weren't for their ages, they could have both landed jobs there for the summer. At one point, we thought we might have to put the trip off another week because my youngest daughter seemed to be getting sick, but she thankfully recovered just in time.

God knows the time of your departure, and He is making sure everything will be packed and in order when that time comes.

Finally, one day at four in the morning we entered their bedroom and gently picked them up and carried them to the car. We quietly strapped them in their car seats and started down the road to California. By the time they both woke up, we were already half-way there.

Their suitcases were lovingly packed with freshly cleaned clothes that mother had washed just days before their departure. The car was filled with their favorite toys and blankets along with a healthy supply of snacks and juices for the drive. The glove box became a library of children's tapes and books. In the trunk we packed an ice chest, a video camera, extra diapers, two strollers and just about everything else we could think of.

The day of their departure took a great deal of planning on our part. Though neither of them had any comprehension of when exactly they would be going, their mother and I knew. We had been preparing everything weeks in advance. All they needed to do was believe. Daddy took care of everything else.

The heart of God is very much this way when it comes to you and the day of your death. Patience is more than just standing at a distance and waiting. It's planning and preparing along the way. God knows the time of your departure, and He is making sure everything will be packed and in order when that time comes. All you have to do is believe.

Out of the hundreds of people that have sat in my office for spiritual counseling over the past few years, I have found that about ninety percent of them share the same feelings about the state of their relationship with God. When I ask them what God would tell me about them if He could talk to me personally, they almost always reply by saying, "God is waiting for me to get my act together." It's as though they believe that God has pretty much washed His hands from their situation until they straighten up and stop making mistakes. What is perhaps the most staggering thing of all is that this is most people's interpretation of God's patience with them. Many of them will even say, "Well, He is being patient with me." What they really mean is that God is so disgusted with the way they are living their lives that He can hardly stand it, but somehow He has held back from dishing out to them what they deserve. This is perhaps the most heart breaking description of the Father's Heart that I have ever heard.

> ✝
> *When He sees you struggling with sin, His eyes see past the sin and straight into your heart.*

Loved ones, please understand this: God is patient with you because He understands you fully and completely. When He sees you struggling with sin, His eyes see past the sin and straight into your heart. He knows exactly why you do what you do. He understands every tiny facet of your heart. God even knows the things about you that you have long forgotten. He knows the very things that have made you the person you are today. The Heart of God says, "I understand why you do this or that. If I saw things the way you did, I would struggle too. I want to help you to see things differently because this sin you are struggling with is killing you." His patience with you is not a case of God holding back His boiling anger toward you, but it is simply God knowing you so well that He doesn't even begin to lose patience. Your Father sees the "burned baby" in everything you do.

You just might be surprised at how pleased God is with your heart.

You see, God is patient with you because you are "fully known" by Him. The greatest obstacle for most people to overcome is the fact that they think they know themselves. This is why we generally can't receive compliments from people. We honestly think we know better. Love is patient because love sees past everything and gets straight to the heart. What we know about ourselves is usually a set of facts about what we have done and where we have been. These are not the things that God focuses on. His focus is always on your heart. That is the part of you that He is in love with. Within the heart lies the truth about who you really are. You just might be surprised at how pleased God is with your heart.

God is patient with the speed of your personal growth. He is not like the couple that thinks that love should rush things into completion (marriage) within a few months. He will wait as long as it takes for you to complete each step in life. There is never a time when He loses patience with you because you aren't getting something fast enough. Why? God cares about the beginning and the end of your life. He has no desire to see you ride out in front of a car or crash into a tree, so He will patiently work with you for the rest of your life to see that your growth is real and everlasting. There is nothing in His heart that desires to see you in Hell. In fact, God is not even tempted to take His hands off of you regardless of what you have done in your life. He never calculates in His mind what you deserve for your failures in life. He never tallies up your mistakes in an effort to build a case against you. He is not even the slightest bit irritated at you when you repeat the same mistake over and over again. God understands and He is patient.

When your end comes, it is God's great pleasure to make it a wonderful and peaceful experience. I cannot tell you how many friends I have who passed away just after making peace with everyone in his or her life. It is truly supernatural, and it happens too often to call it a coincidence. Over and over we all hear stories about something a person said or did just a day or a week before their death that almost made us wonder if they knew they were going to die. God in His wonderful patience will do what ever it takes to make sure everything is packed and in order just before you pass on.

Love's resolve to stay forever is what gives it patience.

God has patience with you because He already knows the end of your story. He is not surrounded by the tension and stress of the unknown. This is the greatest reason for human impatience. When we are not sure of the outcome, we nearly explode with anxiety and nervous tension. This fact about us is what inspires the blueprints of most movies and novels. Not knowing the end of the story is the very thing that holds us in suspense.

God is never in anxious suspense when it comes to you, because He knows how it all ends. Love is this way, too. Because love will never ever leave or stop half-way-through – it knows the end of the story. Love's resolve to stay forever is what gives it patience. The reason why so many people don't have patience in their marriages is because they haven't decided once and for all that they will never leave. Impatience is born and bred in that atmosphere.

My wife and I attended a baby shower a few weeks ago where this truth literally beat me over the head for about four hours. I didn't want to be there. I would rather be in a prisoner of war camp than attend a baby shower. From the moment we arrived, I began concocting a plan to leave early. My mind was racing a million miles an hour, looking for the cleanest escape. I did everything short of faking a heart attack, when my wife finally looked at me and whispered in my ear. She saw the stress on my face, and what she said to me brought instant deliverance. She said, "Just decide in your mind that you are going to stay for the entire night, and your stress will go away." She was right. My impatience was brewing because I had not resolved to be there for the duration. The moment I changed my thinking, I was calm and relaxed, and believe it or not, I had a good time.

This is exactly what love does, and God is love. God has decided wholeheartedly that He will be with you for all eternity. He has patience because He isn't even thinking of leaving or sneaking away early. He is in for the long run, and because of that, He has a clear vision of the finish line. Only someone who can see the finish line possesses patience. God has it with you because He knows the end of your story, and He is pleased with it. It's a happy ending!

Love Is Kind [4]

As she walked through the door of my office, I could immediately feel her pain from where I was sitting. Her appearance could fool even the most insightful onlooker, and I, too, would have been taken if it were not for the countless times I have dealt with such a person, in such a situation. She had a delightful sweetness about her countenance that was both disarming and compelling all at the same time. Through her delicate features, I could see a spirit that was frazzled and hollow. Her eyes reflected a dimming twinkle that took me off guard the moment I looked into them. It was as if there were smoldering candles behind each eye that were on the verge of being snuffed out if something good did not happen soon. Behind an oversized handbag, her arms were folded as if to feebly hide the obvious bruises and scratches that adorned them. She appeared uneasy and nervous, like a child who was doing something wrong and was terrified of being caught.

If she had not said a word, I could have told her everything about her life. In fact, for several moments she did just that.

When the silence broke, she began to stumble through her tangled life in an effort to find a beginning place to start. I offered her a cup of coffee in an effort to cut through the tension in the room. Then, as if she had not even heard my words, she abruptly began her story. The opening was all too familiar, as I have heard it no less than a thousand times before.

"I met this guy."

What came next is what always comes next when such a woman as this sits in my office. The usual long list of terribly unkind things "this guy" had said and done to her over the past six months was followed by the tragically infamous and all too ironic, *"but I know he loves me"* statement.

I am always taken off guard the moment these words hit the air. It reminds me of the first time I heard the name, "peace-keeping missiles." The irony is so baffling, that it literally staggers my spirit for a moment, and I need a few seconds to catch my breath again. I think perhaps that this young lady's perception of love represents one of the biggest oxymorons in our generation concerning love. She is not alone, either. In fact, she is not even of the minority. There are countless women and men who have given themselves over to this pathetic system of beliefs. It's as though there is nothing better to put their hope in than the miserable pattern of unkind relationships their life always seems to conjure up.

> *Unkindness has almost become the norm of our society, and many of us have grown accustomed to its foul presence.*

What is so disturbing to me is the amount of hurting people who simply believe that love does not need to be kind. Though

The God's Honest Truth

it would be nice if it were, it's just not necessary, and it's perhaps a bit idealistic for one to always expect it. Unkindness has almost become the norm of our society, and many of us have grown accustomed to its foul presence.

It reminds me of the "starving children" commercials we have all seen on television. Precious human beings reduced to skin and bones with bloated tummies and peeling skin on their backs, crouched down in the streets waiting to die. Their faces have that same dim look of death in them that this young woman had that day in my office. Their lips are swollen with open sores and there are always flies buzzing around their mouths. The image of "the starving child with the flies on his lip" has become somewhat notorious. There must be a million of them on file.

My question is this: How dreadful must their life be in order for them to NOT brush the flies away from their mouth? Could it be that in the midst of all the bad things in their lives, this pales so much in comparison that it's not even worth spending the energy to make it go away? The very thing that turns the stomach of most Americans has become the acceptable norm for these starving children. And so it is with unkindness in relationships. It has become the "fly on the lips" of thousands of relationships. Perhaps it's because we are a generation that is starving for love. We even surprise ourselves at the polluted things we allow ourselves to endure in an effort to just stay alive. Though it's irritating to the soul, and it diminishes the spirit, it's not worth the energy to brush it away.

Unkindness has lost its stench and has become strangely compelling to many while kindness fades away into an almost unappealing persona.

Now we have a generation of people who subscribe to the "love hurts" mentality. It almost has a ring of wisdom to it when we hear it in a song on the radio. It's something we have all come to realize and accept. We can't live with it and we can't live without it.

Men have been taught to believe in their hearts that women like to be treated badly. We even say it to each other when we are together. For the most part, I think there is truth to that. This is simply the evolution of what love has become in the minds of twenty-first century Americans. Unkindness has lost its stench and has become strangely compelling to many, while kindness fades away into an almost unappealing persona. The "bad boy" gets the girl while "nice guys finish last."

We have come so far from kindness that we have even forgotten what it looks like. Much like an old friend who passed away many years ago, we struggle to remember the shape of their face and the tone of their voice, because the memory is too cracked and faded to make out. As a result of this, we become deceived easily when the counterfeit of kindness confronts us.

The Counterfeit Of Kindness

For every attribute of love, there is a counterfeit that looks like it, feels like it and even smells like it, but it's actually the opposite of the real thing. And so it is that kindness has been replaced with a horrible counterfeit that fools even the savviest person.

This is perhaps the first generation to have never experienced the real thing. We have been raised on the counterfeit so long, that we actually believe that this is what kindness really is. It would not even be accurate to say that it has been redefined because in most of our lifetimes, there has been only one definition. We have nothing to compare it to because the truth has been lost for so long. This is why many people are deceived when confronted with the phony replacement of kindness. It's the only thing they know.

The real problem with our swallowing this lie is that we ultimately perceive the heart of God to possess the same counterfeit characteristics of kindness that we have accepted in our relationships. This becomes a terrible problem, one that closes the door to ever knowing the truth about our Father's heart.

The great counterfeit of kindness is MANIPULATION.

The moment manipulation is present, true kindness becomes voided out completely. Why, because kindness MUST have nothing behind it for it to exist. There must be no ulterior motives that hold it up. It has to stand on its own for it to be authentic. This is the most important attribute of kindness, and without it, everything else is a sham. The moment a hidden motive supports a kind act, the act itself ceases to be kind and suddenly becomes manipulation.

This is precisely why most people's response to a kind act is, "what do you want from me?" We have grown accustomed to the lie. It is beyond our comprehension why anyone would do something nice without wanting something in return. It just never happens any more. We don't believe that kindness stands on its own, because it never has in most of our lifetimes. We even get nervous in the face of real kindness. We become skeptical and even angry if we can't immediately see a manipulative motivation behind someone's actions. We think to ourselves that the person who did this or said that to us must be up to something no good. It just doesn't stand to reason. In this world you don't

> †
> *...kindness MUST have nothing behind it for it to exist. There must be no ulterior motives that hold it up.*

get something for nothing. And so the authentic truth is almost more than we can bear because it mysteriously stands on its own. It needs nothing to hold it up. It is suspended by love and nothing else. There is no explanation for it. It just is.

If you understand this basic principal about kindness, you will never again be deceived by forgery. I constantly warn the women in my congregation that any time a compliment from a man is followed by a come-on, they can be absolutely certain that manipulation is present and kindness is not. The compliment may literally sweep them off their feet and lift every part of their soul, but if it came to them with an ulterior motive behind it, they may as well toss it aside and forget it ever happened. This one nugget of truth could revolutionize the lives of thousands of women in America. It could safeguard millions of people from getting blindsided and having their hearts needlessly broken over and over again.

> †
> *...until you are able to receive authentic kindness, you will never know the heart of God.*

What is most shocking about people in today's world is that most of us wouldn't have it any other way. It's actually easier to live with manipulation, than it is kindness. At least with manipulation one can learn over time to read motives and reasons behind it. Kindness has nothing to gain in return so it defies human logic. When someone in this generation experiences true kindness, they almost always look as if they have seen a ghost. There is a reason for this: kindness is supernatural. Supernatural things scare us to death. They make us feel helpless and insecure because we have no control over the matter.

At least with manipulation, you can control the situation by paying back what was done to you. You can let yourself off the hook and even up the score so you won't be indebted to that person. This is why when someone buys our lunch, we jump out and say, "I'll buy lunch the next time." That way we can cancel out the nice thing our friend just did for us by paying him back. We think this way because we truly don't like to receive kindness in its real form. If someone buys you a Christmas gift at your place of employment, you will most likely plan and plot to return a gift to them as soon as possible, simply because the humbling feeling that real kindness elicits in our hearts is unbearable. Once a gift has

Kindness must always land in the heart.

been returned, you are even and the feeling goes away. The problem is that until you are able to receive authentic kindness, you will never know the heart of God.

The second attribute of kindness that has long been forgotten is just as profound and easy to identify as the first. Kindness *must always* land in the heart. For most people, this is precisely where they fall for the lie. The counterfeit of kindness is always directed to the flesh and the head. These things pass away, but things of the heart last forever. Kindness is an attribute of love, and love lasts forever, so kindness must be aimed at the *forever* part of you for it to be authentic. We have lost sight of this mandatory aspect of kindness because we have lost sight of our hearts. Most people today don't even understand the difference between their heart and their head. This is why cheap imitations fool us so easily. Our head doesn't know the difference and our flesh loves the sensation of the lie when it hits the flesh. In the end we are fooled by something that made us feel good in the head but had little or nothing to do with the truth of our heart.

A woman will actually stay with a man who doesn't know her heart, because he makes her feel pretty. Men will be perfectly content in a relationship where they have lied to the woman about who they really are because that relationship gratifies his flesh. This is because all counterfeits are addictive. They feed the flesh and starve the heart. We become blinded to the truth because our flesh desires to be fulfilled. Truth can only be seen and understood in the heart. This is why the cheap imitation of true kindness goes undetected.

I have seen it hundreds of times in my ministry. A man compliments a woman and speaks seemingly kind words to her, just before he asks her out on a date. All the nice things he said to her immediately blind her. Something deep in her heart causes a check to rise in her spirit; she pushes it back down and agrees to go out with him. Her heart knows that his "kind words" were followed by a come-on, and most likely it was just a manipulative ploy, but her flesh kicks in and convinces her head that he really meant those wonderful things he said. Then she becomes addicted to hearing those things and she basically sells herself to someone who will never know her heart. Finally, after giving a sizable chunk of her life away, she comes to her senses and breaks up with him, only to repeat the same scenario all over again with the next guy that tells her what she wants to hear. She is addicted to the manipulative flesh-landing kindness that the world has sold her.

> ..."acts of kindness" do not necessarily come from a kind heart. Anyone can "act out" kindness.

It's important to understand that "acts of kindness" do not necessarily come from a kind heart. Anyone can "act out" kindness. Most of the time in our generation we have found that kind acts are just that, an act! They are not personalized for each individual, but they are custom-made cookie cutter acts that touch everyone's emotions but no one's heart. We are a lazy people when we buy a box of twenty-five identical Christmas cards and write the same thing on every one of them and mail them out to all our friends. Though they may touch the heart of one or two, it is certain that the other Twenty Three saw right through it and tossed the card in the trash.

The Aim Of Kindness

A kind person is an expert marksman! They hit the center of the heart every time. Their eyes know exactly where to aim because their heart loves the target they are aiming at. Kindness is an attribute of love, and love never fails. This is the clear-cut difference between *nice* and *kind*. Anyone can do a nice thing. It doesn't require love, but a kind thing ALWAYS hits the heart

> *A kind person is an expert marksman! They hit the center of the heart every time.*

because it is directed by love. Even Hitler did nice things every now and then. We must never confuse niceness with kindness. The two are miles apart. Niceness is appreciated; kindness brings you to your knees and exposes intimate parts of you that you've kept hidden all your life. This is why we would rather have people be nice to us than kind. Niceness keeps its distance, but kindness invades our personal space. Niceness makes us smile, but kindness can make us cry. Niceness pats us on the back, but kindness reaches into our heart and massages it. Niceness asks, "How are you doing?" but kindness really wants to know the answer and usually already does.

The Power Of Kindness

Because of where kindness is aimed, it always produces stunning results. Kindness has within it the power to defuse dire and sometimes deadly situations. It overrules things like: anger, rage, depression, hopelessness, gossip, envy, strife and just about any other terrible thing. There is a power in kindness that resists anything thrown its way. It topples over strongholds and crushes addictions. It changes the minds of stubborn people and deflates the pride of humanity. Kindness is more powerful than anything the flesh manifests. Nothing can stand up to it and everything turns to dust in its presence.

I am reminded of the famous Christmas program, "Santa Claus Is Coming to Town," where Chris Kringle melted the anger and rage of the "Winter Warlock" by giving him a gift that touched his heart. It's a wonderful picture of the incredible power of kindness. It can completely alter a person's feelings and emotions in an instant. It's the antidote to life's most horrible problems and personalities. Kindness never comes without leaving a trail of changed things behind it. You will know when it's authentic, because every part of you will be moved and transformed by its presence. It will leave you feeling like you've just received a spiritual blood transfusion.

> *Kindness never comes without leaving a trail of changed things behind it.*

This is a far cry from the cheap imitation we have been spoon-fed our entire lives. The problem with being fed synthetic kindness is that over time people develop a taste for it. When they are faced with the real thing, they are repulsed by its taste. Most people prefer "maple *flavored* syrup" to "*real* maple syrup." Why? It's because few people grow up eating "real maple syrup." They have been raised on the imitation for so long that they have learned to enjoy it. When you put the real thing in front of them, it makes them gag. This is precisely the problem with today's thinking concerning kindness. We would rather have something that tastes kind of like it than have the real thing. So we redefine kindness by what our tainted perception of kindness has become. It's out with the old, in with the new.

This poses a staggering problem in our relationship with God. Until we come to an understanding and develop an appetite for the authentic truth about Him, we will inevitably redefine His personality to fit our spiritual palates. In this case, we redefine true kindness to make it fit our perceptions. Before we know it, we are a generation of Christians who are addicted to "God-flavored kindness" that has nothing to do with who He is and how He relates to us.

Lies In Action

A gentleman in our church was recently on a popular game show in California where he won a brand new car. It was interesting to hear his spiritual reaction to this unexpected gift. He immediately regressed to the "what does God want from me now?" mentality. He became unsure about what to do with the car, because he was certain that something must be expected of him for having received it. Surely God had ulterior motives here. It couldn't just be for free, with no strings attached. After all, God doesn't just give us something unless we have earned it or unless He wants something in return. Surely He doesn't display true kindness, does He?

We have changed the truth, which says, "Freely you have received, freely give" and flipped it upside-down to mean, "If you give, you will receive."

Because of the fact that we have given ourselves over to the counterfeit version of kindness, we have redefined the character of God Himself to fit the lie we believe. We have been taught that the blessings of God directly parallel the amount we give in the offering plate. Everything about the heart of God has been turned upside-down in our spirits. We have changed the truth, which says, "Freely you have received, freely give" and flipped it upside-down to mean, "If you give, you will receive." This is perhaps the most horrendous deformity we have placed on the face of God in our generation. It is a direct reflection of Satan himself. The most terrible thing of all is that most of us like it that way. Why? Because we always know where we stand. We can always calculate on paper exactly where we stand with God. The problem is that this way of thinking has absolutely nothing to do with the heart of God. This mentality is not conducive to relationship.

Most people believe in a manipulative God who has something behind everything He does.

Most people believe in a manipulative God who has something behind everything He does. This is why we don't trust Him when He does something nice for us. It takes us totally by surprise because we don't believe that that is how He is. When we are in a pattern of sin somewhere in our lives, we have learned to expect nothing from Him until we get our act together. We would rather credit a blessing to mere coincidence than second guess our theology. When someone we know who isn't living a holy life, receives a blessing from God, it confuses us and makes us angry because he or she surely didn't earn it. We find ourselves concocting a mental list of spiritually manipulative reasons why God would do this for that particular person. If we can't find a reasonable explanation, we just write it off as a fluke.

We have also learned to see God as the pursuer of temporary things. The fact that God's kindness desires to touch the heart matters not in today's society. The real measure of His kindness is told through how much He rewards the flesh. Financial blessing is the name of the game. This is so much so, that we have even come to a point where we secretly judge people who are struggling financially because we think they must not be right with God. Loved ones, there is nothing wrong with expecting a financial blessing, but when we begin to define people's spirituality by the amount of temporary things they have acquired on this Earth, we have embarrassingly redefined the heart of God. When we think that a millionaire must be doing something spiritually right we are completely wrong.

Financial blessings are nice, but God is KIND. His kindness and His niceness are worlds apart. Two or three things cannot define God's kindness. One man may receive ten thousand dollars the moment he needs it, but not be touched in his heart while another man receives a stuffed toy in the hospital and is moved to tears. Remember, it's not true kindness

We have also learned to see God as the pursuer of temporary things.

unless it touches the heart. All things are temporary except for the heart of man. God's promise to you is to provide the temporary things you need to survive, but His kindness cares about your heart.

Your Father in Heaven is compelled in one direction every time He lays eyes on you. He is constantly drawn to that part of you He loves the most. Your heart! This is precisely why we think He is so mysterious. We have lost sight of our hearts. Just when our flesh cries out for one thing, God answers with another. Generation after generation, we struggle to identify the motives of our God by how they pertain to our flesh and every time we end up confused and dismayed. Until we realize what He cares about, we will always find Him impossible to understand. The moment we grasp what God's focus is, He will suddenly become real and knowable. It's the heart of you.

Out of the countless counseling sessions I have had with my people, I am always amazed at how blown away and confused people get when they find out what God really wants to say to them. It's as though they are expecting Him to confront them on every sin they struggle with. They walk in with a mental list of things they should or shouldn't be doing, and God hits them in a totally unexpected place that seemingly had little or nothing to do with their personal inventory of sins and failings. You would be totally surprised to find that your Father is not aiming at your sins and shortcomings, but His scope is directly focused in on your heart. Just when you think He is going to call you on your lust problem, He tells you that you are loved and He is proud of you. The moment you think He's about to expose your excessive gossip habit, He breaks in and whispers to your heart that you are indeed worthy of friendship and you should trust that about yourself.

> †
>
> *...your Father is not aiming at your sins and shortcomings, but His scope is directly focused in on your heart.*

Right about the time you think God is going to chastise you for smoking cigarettes, He calmly tells you about the wonderful future He has planned for you. God is this way because He knows that the cause of every sin you struggle with is found in your heart. He is not so shallow that He has to confront the symptoms of a burdened heart. He confronts the heart directly because that's who He is, and that is what He cares about. Everything originates in your heart, and your Father does not preoccupy Himself with the external manifestations of a broken heart. He keeps His eyes fixed on the prize at all times.

Loved ones, you must understand that *your heart* is the desire of His heart. It's the center of His attention. He coddles it and cherishes it; He adores it and admires it. To Him, your heart is like a beautiful diamond that entrances a young woman. He is mesmerized by its many facets and even hypnotized by its beauty. Your heart is a priceless jewel that the jeweler washes and puts under light to watch it gleam and sparkle from every imaginable angle. Everything within Him desires to gaze upon this part of you. All His actions and dealings in your life are honed in on this one place. When He speaks to you, He speaks to your heart. When He touches you, He touches your heart and when He is touched by you, it is by your heart. This is the most important attribute of the character of God that you *must* know in order to know Him.

There is a power in God's kindness that can literally carry you to freedom.

God is kind. He is always kind. There is never a point when He isn't kind or less kind than other times. His kindness drives Him to move your heart with no strings attached. He does not do it to manipulate you to do things for Him or to toe the line. He does it because that is who He is. He is hopelessly driven to the most intimate part of you.

God is an expert marksman. There is no hit and miss with God. Because He loves your heart so much, he knows it even better than you do. He has memorized it and has written it upon His heart. Every time He deals with you, it will be a dealing that will hit directly in the center of your heart and cause an explosion of change in every part of your life. He has memorized the blueprints of you, and He knows the beginning from the end. Everything within Him desires to touch you deeply. He is not preoccupied with the temporary things that surround your heart. He only aims for the most intimate part of you and He never misses.

There is a power in God's kindness that can literally carry you to freedom. It's a supernatural power because there is nothing behind it to make it stand. It stands on its own. We have been taught to believe that the fear of God's wrath is what brings us to repentance. Hell has been held over our heads by preachers who sincerely believe that fear is the greatest motivator to the human spirit. Fear has gained such respect over the years that most people would attribute more power to it than to the power of kindness. The problem with this way of thinking, is that fear pertains to the flesh, and everything of the flesh will soon pass away. It's temporary, but kindness is eternal.

We are eternal beings and we respond best to eternal things.

Our Father uses eternal things upon His eternal creations. Kindness has a force behind it that literally crushes the power of fear and stimulates the hearts of His children.

People do not respond to threats of brutality for long. It may work for a time, but eventually they get used to it and it loses its power. People do not respond to threats of abandonment. Perhaps it may work in the beginning, but over time they decide that they can live with it. People respond to the kindness of God, because we were created in His image. We are eternal beings and we respond best to eternal things. The most powerful and moving force that emanates from the Heart of God is His all-consuming kindness to us because we are like Him.

The Special Forces Of Kindness

There is a gentleman in my church that I have become quite close with over the last three years. I truly love and respect this man with every fiber of my being. I often refer to him as "my hero." The story of Mike's life is both a challenge and an inspiration to everyone who knows him personally. He is probably one of the greatest survivors I have ever known in my life.

Mike is a former Green Beret soldier who served his final mission in Desert Storm. He is one of only *two men* who were awarded a *Silver Star Medal* in that war for his heroic acts in the heat of battle. While on a mission, Mike's helicopter was shot down by a missile, and he was the only survivor. Every one of Mike's buddies that he loved and cared for was killed in the crash.

By the time the rescue crew arrived, they were amazed to find that in spite of a broken neck and back, a dislocated hip, shoulder and ankle and a bullet wound to his abdomen, Mike was miraculously unloading the bodies of his friends from the burning chopper. He was given a *Purple Heart Medal* and spent the next six "agonizing months" lying motionless in a full body cast clinging to his life. In the midst of dealing with the haunting guilt and shame of being the only survivor of his platoon, the doctors informed Mike that he would never walk again.

Not only did Mike prove them wrong, but he later went on to *carry the Olympic torch* while running through the streets of his hometown in Nebraska. He became a local celebrity who was known for never giving up. Mike's inspiring optimism is only outweighed by his transparent childlike sincerity. It's the size of this man's heart that makes him my hero. He has won the hearts of everyone in my congregation and is known as a Spiritual Green Beret by all.

Today I had lunch with my friend Mike. As we were leaving the restaurant, he told me that he had a gift to give me. There was seriousness to his countenance that told me to brace myself, because something unusual was about to take place. He told me he had prayed about what to give me for Christmas, and after a week of contemplating it, he had decided upon the perfect gift. After reaching into his car, he turned around and held out his hand. I almost fell on my face right there in the parking lot when I saw what it was that he was holding. With an excited look of sincere generosity in his eyes, Mike presented me his *Purple Heart Medal.*

This unbelievable gesture left me totally staggered and speechless. I just stood there flabbergasted and feeling completely naked. There was nothing I could say or do. I couldn't run to the nearest gift store in an effort to "even up the score," because money couldn't buy a gift that would even come close to what Mike gave me today. Nothing short of handing over one of my children could compare to this. Mike was aiming for my heart and he hit it. He hit the target in the only way it could be hit. He gave me his *heart.*

What a beautiful picture this is of the heart of God. It is His desire to touch your heart in a way that would leave you naked and speechless. The reason why God's kindness never has ulterior motives behind it is because His kindness simply cannot be repaid. All you can do is stand there and receive it. When God gave His only Son, He gave His heart! It was the only way He could *hit the target* of our hearts. His kindness is beyond the realm of *reimbursement;* it transports the human heart into a sphere where nothing but bare acceptance is possible. Only when the heart is touched can this be accomplished. Kindness is the only means to touching the heart, and God is the kindest one of all.

Love Does Not Envy [5]

The night I had waited for with such excitement and anticipation had finally come, and I wasn't holding anything back. As people began to arrive in clusters, I ran to answer the doorbell each time it chimed. In less than an hour, our house was filled with our entire church youth group of about fifty plus people. The Christmas party had finally arrived, and every room in the house was overflowing with the sounds of laughter and music. I had determined in my heart to make this the best party these people had ever seen, and I would be the master of ceremony. When it came to holding the attention of a crowd, no one could hold a candle to me. Within just a few moments, I was telling jokes, making funny faces and in full control of the entire party. Everyone was laughing and egging me on, and I loved every minute of it. As people would gather around me, I would almost lose myself and become the star of the show for that wonderful moment. I longed for it, I lived for it, and I had dreamed of this day and had even counted down the hours and minutes to its beginning.

There is a certain power that emanates from a responding crowd that I had almost become addicted to. I would feed off of their reactions to my antics, and they would in turn reap the benefits by watching me continue. It was a win-win situation and I was determined to make it last as long as I could.

About forty-five minutes into my captivating performance, an all too familiar sound began to chime from the family room. It was the haunting hum of my brother David playing the piano. Dave was several years older than me and had been taking piano lessons for most of his life. If that were not bad enough, he had also spent hours practicing and he was quite good. So good, in fact, that he stole the show every time he played.

Before I could get to my next punch line I found myself talking to thin air. The entire party of fickle friends suddenly caravanned to the family room to gaze upon Maestro David as though they had never seen a boy play the piano before. They sat in silence with wide eyes and tapping feet as Dave played song after song. I truthfully thought it would never end. The moment he finished one song, some idiot would say, "play another one," and so he did. On and on it went, like a broken record, until I thought I was going to scream. I found myself wanting him to hit a bad note or lose his place in the song just so they could see for themselves that Dave didn't deserve the attention he was getting. Of course, he played beautifully, because that same "emanating power" from the crowds' response was carrying Dave the way it carried me earlier. These people did everything but sing, "play us a song, you're the piano man" for my brother that night. He played and played and played and played until the party was pretty much over.

The God's Honest Truth

As the guests were leaving that night, they were all talking about "wonder boy" and his amazing musical talent, while my comical genius had been totally forgotten. I can remember sitting in that room just reeling with envy. Every bone in my body was sick with jealousy. It was even hard to breathe. I felt like my bones were rotting inside me. Every bit of attention was stripped from me and I hated my brother for doing that. I wanted to take that piano and smash it to pieces.

There is no question that my heart was full of selfish envy that night many years ago. Any thinking person would recognize that I was in the wrong, and my actions were not formed out of love for my brother Dave, but love for myself. I am certain that anyone would agree that *love does not envy*, but I wonder how much we really believe that.

The Evolution Of Envy

When envy is presented in its most raw form as it was in my story, it reeks with an obvious and evident odor. It's almost comical when you read about it. Surely no one would mistake its ugly presence for being love. It stands in such opposition to everything that love is about. I have found, however, that over the years we have all experienced a gradual transition from an obvious lie to a murky grey definition of truth. This ugly evolution does not just occur in a day, it takes generations and generations before it can successfully alter our perceptions and deceive the world.

When a person receives a "man-made" hip socket or kneecap, the doctors have to first fool the body, and convince it not to reject the foreign object. This is done with a variety of drugs that deceive the body's immune system and gradually convince it to accept the foreign object.

You might remember the young girl who received a baboon's heart many years ago. The world was stunned as we saw the first pictures of the living child just after the operation. There were many mixed opinions about such a procedure. Nevertheless, it was nothing short of amazing. Though the child ultimately died from infection caused by the animal's heart, the event changed medical history forever. It proved that it was possible. Scientists believe that one day it will be feasible to use the hearts of monkeys, sheep and even pigs to save lives. All it takes, is for the right drugs to persuade the body to accept the alien heart.

This same concept is true when it comes to the subject of love. It is astounding to see what many people accept over time. In a very real way we have become a generation of "pig hearted" people. We routinely accept the counterfeit. What is worse is that we have learned to live with it. Our spirits and souls are functioning with a version of love that bears a resemblance to the heart of a baboon. It doesn't happen in a day, but gradually over time. Before we know it, we are living with a heart that thinks and believes things that are absolutely hideous and unacceptable.

This is true with the subject of envy. We were all raised in a world where almost every relationship we have is born out of envy. Most people I talk to can't even imagine having a relationship with someone that they didn't first lust after. It seems that lust is the prerequisite to everything when it comes to dating. In fact, unless lust is present at the get go, most people wouldn't take a single step forward in the relationship. It seems that envy has become the prerequisite to any and every form of love in our generation. While our heads tell us that "love does not envy," our hearts believe quite the opposite.

Envy In Sheep's Clothing

Identifying envy is not always as easy as one might think. One of the reasons why so many of us are deceived is because it resembles something that is attractive to every human being on the face of the Earth: "interest."

There is a look that I give my wife that can only be described in one way. I cherish her. It's a deep, soul-piercing gaze that travels way beyond the surface level and lands deep into her very spirit. It's a stare that sees every hidden thing in her heart and adores it all unconditionally. My eyes literally scream "value" to her when she sees them. Much like a child on Christmas morning, whose eyes light

Inside every person there is a treasure chest that waits to be opened by his father.

up at the sight of the wonders before him. When my wife sees that look from me, she knows that she is being seen and appreciated. She finds her inner value because I find it, and she sees me finding it every time I give her that cherishing look.

The same is true with my children. They see that in their daddy's eyes. They need it. They find their self worth in it. They discover who they are by seeing their reflection in their father's eyes. They know beyond a shadow of a doubt that everything in me deeply cherishes their entire being. It's a look that does not say, "I would die for you," but "I have already died for you." Only in death can one accomplish such a look.

Inside every person there is a treasure chest that waits to be opened by his father. Until a person is cherished their treasure chest remains closed. The cherishing look happens when the one giving the look has discovered inner value in the one they see. Many people wait an entire lifetime for just one person to discover value in them.

I have found in my ministry that almost ninety five percent of men and women have never been cherished in their entire lives.

Because we are a fatherless generation, most of us were never cherished by the one person we really needed it from. Even as a child we all understand the created order of things. It's woven into the fabric of our spirits. We understand that the father is the ultimate authority in the home. When that "look" comes from our father, we know for certain whom we are. This is precisely why so many people today are basically lost.

Because of our innate desire and need for this powerful look, we often fall victim to the counterfeit. I'm talking about the look of seduction. It's envy in its most terrible form. Many people actually have become addicted to the gaze of seduction and lust. In fact, many people find their value in that look. Their life becomes a quest to get that from people and until they do, they don't think they have any value.

I've watched women in the clothing store purposefully buy things that will entice such a look from men. They don't even realize how obvious their intentions are to those around. They put the jeans on and immediately turn around to see what their backside looks like. They put the blouse on and check their cleavage out in the mirror. Many times they'll ask their girlfriend how certain body parts look in whatever clothing they are trying on. It's all in an attempt to acquire the counterfeit version of cherish.

Men will go from nightclub to nightclub searching and waiting for a woman to give him that seductive look. He might even spend hundreds of dollars in one night for it. It becomes an obsession after awhile, but when it finally happens it's all worth it.

We say we don't believe that love envies, but when you really think about it, most of us believe that envy is the very inception of love. Without it, love can't even begin. Another word for envy is lust. Our generation has come to believe that lust is the one element that ignites love. We flippantly say that unless we are physically attracted to a person, we won't even give them a chance. If a friend wants to introduce us to another friend who is a member of the opposite sex, our first question is "what does he or she look like?" The treasure within is not nearly as important to this generation as the flesh on the outside.

The problem with inner treasures is that they cannot be possessed by another person in a fleshy, gratifying manner. They can only be admired from afar. Selfish people have nothing personal to gain by discovering someone's inner beauty. The outer beauty is quite a different thing. That is something that can be seen by the eyes and touched by the hands. It can be taken for oneself and used for personal indulgence. It requires no intimacy or emotional closeness. Outer beauty can be used and taken advantage of. This is why so many people put the flesh at the top of their list of desires in a mate. It's envy.

> *Selfish people have nothing personal to gain by discovering someone's inner beauty.*

The Other Side Of Envy

There is another side of envy that is just as ugly and self-serving. It's jealousy. Envy, lust, and jealousy have one thing in common; they are *anti-relationship*. All three of these attributes leave a person in constant receive mode. The give-mode that is required by love becomes totally shut off and even nonexistent. Because of this fact, relationship is literally impossible to achieve.

Jealous, lustful, and envious affairs ultimately end in either death or destruction. They die because these three things are the very heart of death.

The moment a person gives their heart over to the "what's in it for me" mentality, an inner decaying begins to take place in their soul. Before long, everything in their life is infected with death. Their senses become altered and distorted. They become incapable of connecting with other human beings emotionally. Jealousy is a frantic *self-protection frenzy* that completely paralyzes a person relationally. It is born out of self-love and absolute apathy for the other person. Nothing can survive this!

Jealousy is a frantic self-protection frenzy that completely paralyzes a person relationally.

What About God?

I am always amazed when I hear some people describe the heart of God in such envious terms. Truthfully, I think most of us feel deep within our hearts that God does indeed envy. It's inevitable that we would do this because our interpretation of love allows envy in every crevice. So over time we begin to get this view of the Heart of God that directly coincides with our present perception of love.

There is one little problem that we must address before we continue on this subject. If love does not envy, lust, or get jealous, then what about all the Scriptures that say the opposite about God? In many places in the Old Testament, God describes Himself as a "Jealous God." Also, in the New Testament, the Holy Spirit is said to "envy intensely." Another translation says that He "lusts intensely." If God is love, and love does not envy, then what about these verses that seem to say the exact opposite?

It is absolutely necessary that we unravel this mystery before we continue. Entire theologies have been built on our drastic misconceptions of these Scriptures alone. I have heard preachers thunder from the pulpit that "God is a jealous God." Because we see God's jealousy and envy from a human perspective, we have created a black cloud over our religion that ultimately strangles to death our relationship with God.

What's The Difference?

I met Tammy many years ago, and I had grown extremely close to her. She became like a daughter to my wife and me. Over time, I became very protective of her and was deeply involved in every area of her life. We both loved her with all our hearts and we wanted nothing but the best for her.

Tammy started dating a guy in our church who was self-centered and egotistical. He treated her like an object and he held her at arm's length distance from his heart. My wife and I were devastated that they were dating, because we knew what her life would be like in the future if they ever married. We immediately began doing whatever we could to break them up.

One evening while Tammy was over at our house, I was doing everything I could to snuff out her interest in this man. Our conversation began to get heated, and Tammy stood up and proclaimed that I was just jealous. Without hesitation, my wife looked at me and said, "She's right, you know." My wife was not upset however, because she knew it was a righteous jealousy.

I was jealous for Tammy's heart. Not because I wanted it all for myself, but because I wanted the best for her. This man she was interested in was incapable of ever knowing her heart. My soul was tormented at the thought of her being with someone who would never see the beautiful things in her I had grown to love. I knew for a fact that he cared only for himself, and it caused a jealousy to rise up within me was that indescribable.

Tammy ultimately married this young man, and less than a year later he left her for another woman. We were not even the slightest bit surprised.

God's Righteous Jealousy

Yes, God is a jealous God, but He is jealous on behalf of you. He is not selfishly jealous like human beings are. His righteous jealousy is completely the opposite of what we understand jealousy to be. Until we understand this principal about God's heart, we will always see Him upside-down from what He really is. In fact, our entire religion has learned to see Him upside-down. We have taken the Scriptures that describe Him as a jealous God and have given them a human interpretation. It has become so common that we don't even recognize it anymore.

> *God is telling us that we need not envy for ourselves because He is doing it for us.*

When the Bible says that the Holy Spirit envies, it is being spoken of in this same context. God is telling us that we need not envy for ourselves because He is doing it for us. Selfish envy kills us. Our Father envies on our behalf, so we don't need to.

Understand that God will never tell us to do something that He Himself does not do. He will never tell us not to do something that He does. Many of us think to ourselves that it's okay for God to be selfishly jealous, or prideful, or boastful because after all, He is God. Not only is this line of thinking terrible, but it contradicts logical thinking. There are not some things that God is allowed to do, but we aren't. Remember that we are being conformed into God's image. If He can do it, we can do it. If He doesn't do it, we are not supposed to do it. This is why it's imperative that we know the truth about His image! Whatever we believe to be true about Him is what we will ultimately be changed into.

What We Really Believe About God

Unfortunately, our human perspective of a *jealous* God has attached itself to every slice of our religion. The results are catastrophic! We have become like the terrified woman who is enslaved to her husband's jealousy problem. She cannot have friends or a life of her own because everything in her world centers around her jealous

> *...our human perspective of a jealous God has attached itself to every slice of our religion.*

husband. She rationalizes to herself that he acts this way because he loves her, but deep in her heart she is confronted with the truth that he doesn't even know her. The most she can do is follow his rules and make him think he is the only one in the world that matters. Hopefully, if she proves herself to be faithful, he might release his death grip on her and give her the few remaining crumbs of her life back.

As awful as this sounds, it is astonishing how frequently I hear Christians talk about their God in this same repulsive manner. Because of our misconceptions about God, we have become just like this woman in our relationship with Him. What is worse is that for the most part, we don't even know we are doing it. We've grown up with it all our lives, so it's not really that upsetting to us.

We say things like "God wants you to give Him your life," and it doesn't even sound off to us anymore. We even encourage others to give their life to Christ because we are certain that this is what God wants.

Remember loved ones, Christ came that YOU may have life and life abundant. He never asks you to give Him your life. *It's your heart He is after.* Only an envious God would give you life and then require you to give it back to him. He gave it to you and He wants you to enjoy it to the fullest. If you give your heart to God, He can make your life wonderful.

This upside-down thinking is seen most often with Christian musicians. They are plagued with the notion that every song they ever write *must be about Jesus.* If they dare to write a song about anything other than God, they are scoffed at by the Christian community. Their faith is called into question and they are ultimately viewed as backslidden. It is heartbreaking to God that this wonderful gift of expression is never allowed to express itself completely and freely because the receiver of the gift believes that God would get jealous.

Many Christians are skeptical about listening to any secular music at all. Even if the song doesn't have any bad words in it, they believe that God would rather have them listen to Christian music or nothing at all. This mentality is born out of a belief that God envies. They think He might get jealous if they gave any part of their day to something other than Him. They see Him as a jealous husband who doesn't want them to have a life of their own.

> *He never asks you to give Him your life. It's your heart He is after.*

God Is Not Interested In "Using" You

God is not in this relationship for Himself. When we say that God wants to "use" us in some way to further His purposes, we are truly saying an awful thing about His Heart. This perhaps is the most grieving thing to me when I hear people talk this way. It's as though we believe that this is all He is in it for. We think He sees us as pawns in His big plan, and whatever way He can use us for His benefit, He will. Our prayers have become pleading sessions where we say, "Use me God; use me." I cannot accurately describe to you the level to which this grieves His heart. The very thought of it implies that God would rather have a *whore* than a wife. It is so cold and unloving, and it has absolutely nothing to do with the truth about Him.

I know people who are living in total bondage, but praise God they are being used in the ministry. Regardless of their personal suffering and anguish, they rationalize that they are at least glorifying God. The gifts He has given you are never to be used at your expense. He does not want you to be used by anyone and He will never use you. The very fact that we believe He would do this is evidence that we see Him as having the personality of the Devil. Your gifts were given to you for the purpose of bringing joy to *your* life, not for the purpose of serving Him or furthering His cause. If you have joy and contentment, the radiance of Christ will shine through you and His presence and existence will speak for itself.

The gifts He has given you are never to be used at your expense. He does not want you to be used by anyone and He will never use you.

God does have a purpose, but that purpose is not a mystery. *His purpose is for you to be His son or daughter* and this can only happen if you open your heart to the truth about His selfless love for you. The problem is that we will never open ourselves to this relationship when we think He is in it for Himself. That's repulsive to any thinking person. At any point where we veer from this truth, we will begin to see Him upside-down from what He really is.

We Were Not Put Here To Glorify God

Please understand and believe that God never gets any glory at the cost of YOU. You are His child. What is the one thing that all parents want for their children? They want them to be happy.

———— † ————
God never gets any glory at the cost of YOU.

If your child is not happy and fulfilled, it doesn't matter how clean he or she keeps their room or how well they do in school. Nothing matters to a parent except their children are joyful and content. God's heart is this same way. He receives no glory when you are in bondage or personal anguish.

God is never envious of your gifts. He wasn't thinking of what they could do for Him when He gave them to you. Your gifts were given to you for the purpose of what they could bring about in your life. He gets glory and is happy when you are free and at liberty. Your gifts were given for this purpose.

Think for a moment about the gifts that God gives his children. There are many that are listed in the Bible and many that are not. Helping, encouraging, teaching, administrating, organizing, speaking, and giving are just a few. Mechanics, doctors, musicians, managers, and accountants are some of the people who have been given gifts in these areas. What is the one thing that all of these gifts have in common? *They are all for the benefit of others.* Your joy in life comes through you helping and loving others. This is how God's heart is. God finds joy in benefiting you. The gifts He gave you are not for the purpose of benefiting Him, but YOU.

God Never Gets Jealous Of Your Gifts

God is *never* envious when others admire you and love you because of your giftedness. This is the reason He gave you these gifts in the first place. He wants people to think highly of you and respect you. He loves it when folks are drawn to you and when they are amazed at how gifted you are.

God is NEVER tempted to take a gift away from you if He feels that you are receiving glory for it. There is a mentality in Christian thinking that believes that God wants all eyes on Him and no eyes on His children. We have come to believe that if we are admired or lifted up because of our God-given talents, He will immediately become envious and jealous. This is as outlandish and shallow as me

> ☦
>
> *God is NEVER tempted to take a gift away from you if He feels that you are receiving glory for it.*

wanting to smash the piano my brother was playing because it brought him more attention than it did me. It is amazing to me how many well meaning Christians honestly believe that God thinks like this.

Could you imagine if I bought my wife a dress that complemented her and made her look beautiful, and all I was concerned about was whether or not she let people know that I was the one who bought it for her? What kind of a husband would I be if I required her to correct people when they told her how nice she looked, and inform them that she is really ugly and her husband deserves all the glory for getting her the dress? What if I were to take the dress back because people were recognizing her beauty more than they acknowledged the fact that I was the one who gave her the dress? Yet, this is exactly how we portray the Heart of our God.

I approached a little boy in our church once and told him what a good little boy I thought he was. Immediately, this five-year-old child began to inform me that he was a "bad little boy" and a "stupid little boy," and there was no good in him. I was mortified! As I walked away with a heavy heart and tears in my eyes I thought, "What kind of a father does this little boy have?" I wondered what must be going on in his home when no one is looking. This is precisely what the world thinks when they hear us talk this way about ourselves in an effort to bring our Father glory. It's morbid, and twisted. It paints a picture of our Heavenly Father that is cold and ugly. It just plain makes Him look bad.

> *God gives you gifts and talents because He loves to dress you up and impress others with His child.*

God gives you gifts and talents because He loves to dress you up and impress others with His child. He is not concerned with whether or not He gets the recognition for giving the gifts. He is truly delighted when you are lifted up and loved by others. When you publicly declare your ugliness and unworthiness, you do not impress your Father in Heaven, you are hurting His Heart. His desire is to see you lifted up and admired by everyone.

God Is Not Jealous Of Your Relationships

Several years ago, a young couple came to me for advice concerning their six-month-old baby. This child evidently had a string of reoccurring medical problems that seemed to be getting worse. I almost began to cry as I listened to them explain their theory as to why this was happening to their baby.

This poor couple blamed themselves, because they felt like they might have made their child "an idol" in their lives. Because of the fact that they loved this baby so much and had given everything over to him, they believed that God was allowing illness to attack their baby out of jealousy. Once again these people were poisoned by modern day Christianity's interpretation of a *jealous God.* They had been convinced that because they loved their child so much, God was angry with them. They even quoted a Scripture from the Bible that said God would destroy any idols that his people set up in their hearts before Him.

I've watched in amazement while people check themselves to make sure they don't love their mate too much, for fear that God will get envious and remove His presence. Some dating couples even break up because they are terrified that the person they are in love with has become an idol before God. They constantly measure whether or not their thought life is more focused on God than it is on the person they are in love with.

> *God is never in competition with your love for people!*

God is never in competition with your love for people! Understand that *anytime you love a person, you are not far from God.* It is interesting that the very avenue through which you can love God has now been attacked and called into question. This is what upside-down thinking does. It destroys the possibility of relationship. Understand that your love for people is the very evidence that *God is living inside you.* It is impossible to love God more than you do people. All people are the direct recipient of our love for God. It is impossible to have relationship with God aside from our relationship with people. He doesn't get jealous or envious of our love for His people; He delights in it because that is how He created our life to work.

For some reason, we have separated relationship with God from relationship with people. We have done this because we truly think God envies. It shocks me to see so many people who honestly believe that God desires a separate and secret relationship with them aside from their family members. Many men will lock themselves in their prayer closet while their wife is in the other room watching the kids alone. I call this adultery. It comes from a mentality that God wants His personal time with them separate from their wife. I am not putting down a personal prayer time, but I am confronting a mind-set that is directly against the Heart of God. If I stayed two hours in my office praying while my wife waited downstairs with our children that would not be called prayer; that would be called SIN.

When I see that my daughters love each other with all of their hearts, I am overjoyed. Never do I ever wonder in my heart whether or not they love me more than they do each other. As far as I am concerned, if they love each other, they do love me. The quickest way to my heart is to love my children.

Only selfish people ask the question, "Who do you love more, me or my brother or sister?" Don't ever think that God behaves this way. This twisted notion about His heart is the exact opposite of who He really is. The moment we buy into this way of thinking, we will have permanently shut ourselves out from knowing His heart. True relationship with God is impossible unless we love people. He is never envious of our love for others; He created it! In fact, GOD IS LOVE, so why would He ever contradict the very truth of what He is?

Jealous and envious people are insecure. God is not insecure. Don't ever feel like you have to prove to Him that you love Him more than anyone else. His heart is that you love people, and do so more and more. There is not one Scripture in the entire Bible that suggests anything different. Release yourself to love wholeheartedly because your Father in Heaven made you for this purpose.

Love Does Not Boast[6]

When I was eight years old, my mother had remarried, and we were living in Phoenix, Arizona. My biological father was living in Houston, Texas at the time. Every summer my older brother Kevin and I would take turns flying to Texas to spend a couple of weeks with our dad. This was a time that I had looked forward to throughout the entire school year. As summer vacation began to approach, I found myself drifting off during class thinking about my upcoming visit with my daddy. By the time school was out, and my turn to visit my dad rolled around, the anticipation and excitement was almost more than I could bear.

I can remember the day when my brother Kevin returned from Texas with a new haircut, new clothes, and a backpack full of interesting new toys. This meant that I had only a month left until I got to see my dad. I was exhilarated!

As Kevin took me into his room and displayed each new toy and article of clothing that dad had bought him, I began to notice something different about his personality. It was something that made me feel small and insignificant. I had not seen this in him before, so it made me incredibly uncomfortable. To put it plainly, he was being cocky. He had a cocky tone to his voice as he chewed on a piece of cocky gum that dad had bought him. Even his stupid haircut looked cocky. Everything about his demeanor was reeling with cockiness.

Over the next few days, my ten-year-old brother proceeded to "boast" about everything that the two of them had done together. He made it look like he and dad had something that I would never have with dad. He casually mentioned names of people that I had never heard of. He talked about places that I had never seen. He told of experiences that were completely foreign to me, and because I was on the outside looking in, I couldn't keep up with the conversation.

It was obvious that he enjoyed the fact that I was on the outside. I could see it in his eyes. There was something in him that wanted me to know for sure that I would never have the same relationship with our father as he did. It would not be as fun or intense. It would never be as close or intimate, and in just a few short days my entire perception of "how it would be" went from glorious and thrilling, to hopeless and disappointing.

The experiences that he boasted about could never be recreated. Even if we tried, it just wouldn't be the same. I'll never know, even to this day, what the two of them did together, but I will always know this; whatever they did, it was better than anything he and I would or could ever do in a lifetime. "What's the use?" I thought, "Why even try?" By the time I boarded the airplane for Texas a month later, I felt empty and worthless inside. What I had dreamt of for so many hours just didn't seem as exciting anymore. I didn't even have the energy to try to make it fun. I was officially *demotivated* by the boasting of my young brother.

Let me stop briefly here to remind you that Kevin was only ten years old at this time. His actions were not unique to any other ten-year-old on the face of the Earth. Also, I want to say that he and I are very close today. Believe it or not, I've put it all behind me. Besides, when I came back a week later, I gleefully and boastfully dished out the same meal to him.

Story Number Two

Several years ago, I was asked to be the keynote speaker for a relationship conference in Texas. When I walked into the auditorium, I was shocked to find that the place was almost packed to capacity. The other thing that took me off guard was the expression on the people's faces when they saw me walk in. It was as though they all knew me. Their eyes lit up just as they would if Billy Graham had walked into the building.

I asked the person who drove me there from the airport if I was famous in this town. He smiled and said, "Yes." Evidently, this group had done their homework for this event. They had commercial advertisements on the main television stations in that area. My name and picture had been posted all over that town. Radio stations had played pieces of my most recent sermons and as a result, it was obvious that these people thought I hung the moon in the relationship world.

Halfway through the conference a group of the "head pastors" decided to take me out to a nice restaurant for lunch. Through our brief conversations just before we ordered our meals, I could tell that these men had an extreme respect and reverence for me. Their actions and mannerisms showed me that there was a certain intimidation they felt in my presence.

It wasn't long before our food arrived, and I was graciously asked to pray for the meal. At that, I simply bowed my head and said, "God is great, God is good, thank you for this food, amen." When I looked up after praying, what I saw has made me chuckle for years. They were completely dismayed and confused. Their faces had such a look of bewilderment on them that I have never forgotten it since. It was priceless! It was a combination of total confusion and utter letdown. Every preconceived idea these men had about my spirituality and high position was completely dashed to the ground in a moment. Several of them nervously laughed while the others sat in judgmental dismay. Collectively, their view of my deep relationship with God was diminished to a level that even the least spiritual among them would not covet.

What Was I Doing?

I was diminishing myself in their eyes. I was becoming less than they had imagined. I had to do it because I knew that they would ultimately feel like I did that day my brother Kevin came home from Texas after visiting my dad. I didn't want them to feel a million miles away from their father. I couldn't stand the thought of them cowering away from their Father in Heaven, because I had boasted about my personal relationship with Him. I didn't want my bragging to cause them to feel inadequate or inferior in their spirituality.

I have discovered that the only way to truly lift hurting people up is to get beneath them.

Everywhere I go I have this standing reputation that seems to follow me. It goes something like this: "You are real." It's become the trademark of my ministry. When people say it, they're telling me that they could totally identify with me in every way. I didn't leave them feeling like I had arrived to some spiritual plane that they could never achieve. They felt like they were on my level and if I could do it, so could they.

There is only one reason why I do this wherever I go. It's because I love them, and love does not boast.

In my many years of ministry, I have found only one undisputed way of lifting people up. It may not be popular or spiritually attractive, but it always works. I have discovered that the only way to truly lift hurting people up is to GET BENEATH THEM.

The very thing that we despise as human beings happens to be the avenue that catapults others to greater heights. The answer is found in our willingness to lower oneself for the benefit of others. This is the exact opposite of boasting. Boasting is bragging about our strengths, but if we truly love, we will boast about our weaknesses for the purpose of elevating the ones we claim to love.

The Apostle Paul understood this concept and moved in it throughout his entire ministry. He said, "If I must boast, I will boast of the things that show my weakness" (2 Corinthians 11:30 NIV). And he asked this same group of people; "Was it sin for me to lower myself in order to elevate you by preaching the gospel of God to you free of charge"? (2 Corinthians 11:7 NIV)

What Is Boasting?

Boasting is bragging about the truth. It's exalting the highest truth about a person, place or thing. The problem with boasting is that it ultimately pushes everyone down around you. It leaves people feeling like failures, or at the very least, inadequate. It cultivates spiritual inferiority in the hearts of its recipients. Boasting is based on comparison. You know in your heart that people generally make comparisons between themselves and you. When you boast, you are letting them know that they don't add up. When they don't add up, relationship is impossible. Love does not boast because love is only about relationship.

I have found over the years that people generally don't follow the "unreachable." They may admire them, but when the rubber meets the road, they won't give their heart over to them. Why, because an unreachable person is not someone that we human beings can relate to. We must be able to *relate* before we can have *relationship*. People who claim to have reached a spiritual level that is far beyond the average person's ability to comprehend are usually pretty lonely people. They're lonely because there is no such spiritual level. They are living in a fantasy world. They've put themselves on an island. They are spiritual boasters, who can only be admired from a distance, but never encountered personally.

People who claim to have reached a spiritual level that is far beyond the average person's ability to comprehend are usually pretty lonely people.

This is the greatest obstacle I have to overcome when I go to a church to preach. I find myself constantly fighting people's perceptions of who or what I am. Until I can destroy their lofty religious and spiritual opinions of me, I simply can't help them. The problem is that most people immediately believe several things about a guest speaker who comes to their church. They think that he is better than they are, or he has some special powers that they don't have. They think he's reached a spiritual nirvana with God and that's why He sent them. This is a huge obstacle for me because people will never give me their hearts until they know that I'm the same as them. The moment I get those stars out of their eyes, and create an atmosphere where they don't feel "less" than me is the moment when I can do serious heart surgery within them.

At first, I'll be honest with you, I enjoyed the attention I got when I arrived to a place and everyone doted over me. It made me feel good. After all, there is a certain gratification that goes along with being famous. It feels good to have people think you're a spiritual guru of sorts. My flesh loved the entire exalted experience.

Finally though, I had to give up that "flashy prophet's dream" that I had held onto for so long. You know what I'm talking about. I had to give up that fantasy of my walking into a grocery store and healing everyone in the room, and then walking out as the people gasp in amazement at my spiritual ability. I had to give up that dream of laying hands on someone and watching him or her go unconscious because God's power was so rich in me. Besides, it wasn't happening, so it wasn't as though I really had a choice in the matter. I had to give it all up, because I truly wanted to help people.

> *...people will never give me their hearts until they know that I'm the same as them.*

"God·told·me·ism"

One of the main concerns I have after observing Christians over the last fifteen years is that I feel that "boasting" has become a way of life. It has found its way into almost every church in America. I don't believe that most people even know they are doing it, but nevertheless they are.

One of the greatest ways it is manifested is through what I call, "God-told-me-ism." Let me first start by clearly stating that I believe God speaks to His children. In fact, I think we should expect it. There is nothing more wonderful than when you know for sure that He is speaking directly to you. I have no problem believing that this happens and so what I am about to say is not derived from a lack of faith in His willingness to speak or in people's ability to hear Him. If this were not possible, where would we be as Christians?

I want to confront a general attitude that I see in people who feel that they have to boldly and bluntly announce to the world that "God told them" to do this or that. In my opinion, it has become quite ridiculous. It wouldn't be so bad if they reserved their claims of divine revelation for incredible life changing situations, such as "God told me to go to college" or "God told me to pastor this church," but it seems after talking with these people that God tells them everything all the time. He tells them what clothes to wear in the morning, what roads to take to work, what to order for lunch and what pen to use when writing a check.

> *Ultimately "God-told-me-people" do more harm than good.*

The reason why these people feel so inclined to inform the rest of us that they are hearing from God, is not because they are, but because they want to assure us that they are. The motive behind this is personal validation. They are trying to validate their spirituality in the eyes of the person they are talking to. The problem is that in doing so, they step on the hearts of everyone in the room. They leave people feeling like God doesn't love them or speak to them as much as He does that person. People walk away feeling like there is something wrong with their Christian walk, and they ask themselves why they can't hear the voice of God like this person does. Ultimately "God-told-me-people" do more harm than good.

If this is you I am talking about, I want you to ask yourself a question. Why would you ever have to use the words, "God told me?" Do you know that you could conceivably go your entire life without ever using those words again? If God really told you to do something, wouldn't the result of you doing it speak for itself?

I am not questioning whether or not He really told you, but I am questioning your motive in sharing it with others. Even if your motivation is totally pure and innocent, you need to know that you are hurting people around you. Stop for a moment next time that phrase slips out of your mouth and simply ask the person you are talking to how it makes them feel when you say it. I think you will be shocked at their response.

A Boastful Prayer

When I came to my congregation, I deeply wanted to see a group of people who sincerely prayed for each other on a regular basis. Just after worship, we started breaking off into groups of four or five and having a time where we lifted our personal requests to the Father. The people were instructed to join hands and go around the circle while each person gave their prayer request. Then they would take turns praying for one another.

The problem we started to encounter was that many people had become "expert pray-ers." They knew everything to say and exactly how to say it. It was amazing to listen to them confront the enemy, bind the demons, call down the blessing and release the anointing. These people barked out with such precision and authority that even I was intimidated. It was entertaining to watch, but unfortunately, no one was being prayed for.

These people knew exactly what to say, but no one knew how to pray. The most disturbing thing about it was the look of complete worthlessness on the faces of the poor people who were being "prayed for." When it was all over, they felt worse than they did before they came. They felt like a loser Christian whose prayers were bland and boring. They felt a million miles behind the rest of the world in their spirituality. This boastful way of praying put these precious people in such spiritual bondage, that I almost discontinued the entire practice completely.

When praying publicly, I have found that most people are more concerned with impressing the person they are praying for than they are in really praying for the person. In most cases I think we do this because of our own insecurity. We are terrified of appearing less spiritual or ignorant in the eyes of anyone. When we are placed in a position of intimacy such as a prayer circle, we tend to overcompensate by going spiritually overboard.

> *We are terrified of appearing less spiritual or ignorant in the eyes of anyone.*

Regardless of the cause, it is boasting, and boasting always has the same effect on its recipients. It causes them to cower. It shrinks their self-esteem and diminishes their spiritual confidence. Boasting has such an anti-relationship quality to it that it literally paralyzes people's hearts and forces them into emotional and spiritual seclusion.

What would cause us to pray or speak in a way that is boastful? Could it be perhaps that we are doing exactly what we believe our Father in Heaven does? Think about that for a moment. I want you to go through everything you have been taught about your God and really think about it. Does God boast?

How Does God Want You To Relate To Him?

In the Old Testament, there is the story of when Moses went up on the mountain to get the Ten Commandments from God and a great cloud covered the mountain. The Earth shook and the people couldn't even get anywhere near the mountain, or they would be put to death. It tells of the Earth trembling, thunder and lightning that accompanied that incredible experience.

Everyone present literally trembled with fear for their lives and begged Moses to go alone to approach God on their behalf.

But how does God want you to relate to Him?

Elijah had an encounter with the prophets of Baal where he challenged them to call on their gods to burn up a sacrifice and despite all their ranting and raving, nothing happened. Then Elijah stepped forward and called on the God of Abraham, Isaac and Jacob, and suddenly fire fell from Heaven and consumed the sacrifice completely. This unquenchable fire even licked up the water in the trenches surrounding the sacrifice. The people were astonished at the power of God and they fell to their faces in reverence and awe.

But how does God want you to relate to Him?

Ezekiel had a vision of Heaven, where the glory of God filled the temple, and there were creatures that were suspended in mid-air giving praise and honor to God continuously. The experience was so incredible that Ezekiel could barely stand in the midst of it all.

But how does God want you to relate to Him?

The seas roll back and leave a path of dry ground at His command, the mountains tremble at the sound of His Name, and the hills melt like wax in His presence. The glory of the Lord fills the Earth and nothing is impossible or too difficult for Him. He owns the cattle on a thousand hills and everything in-between. He flung the stars into place and positioned the planets to His liking. At the very sound of His presence everything in Heaven and on Earth falls to the ground and cries, "Holy, holy, holy." His knowledge and beauty transcends every imagination of man and His enemies literally dissolve into nothingness at the sound of

His voice. He is everywhere at once, He knows all there is to know and nothing exists that was not made by His hands.

But how does God want YOU to relate to Him?

Let me ask you this: can you relate to that? Can you have intimacy with that? Can you get close to that? How does God want you to relate to Him?

A Dirty Homeless Carpenter

Loved ones, please understand that God does not boast about who or what He is. He isn't interested in bragging about His highest truths. *Jesus Christ is God NOT boasting!*

God became something a little lower than you in order to lift you up! He not only became a man, but He became a servant of men and then He even died a criminal's death on the cross. The last thing we see Jesus doing just before He was crucified was perhaps the most astonishing example of a non-boasting God in all of Scripture. He was on His hands and knees washing dirty feet.

Peter understood fully that Jesus Christ was God in the flesh, and he tried to put a stop to it all. He refused to accept God in this way. He was very much like modern day Christians who are insistent on seeing the highest truths of His nature and nothing else. The response that Jesus gave Peter is exactly His response to many of us

Unless you can receive the simplest side of God, you will never have intimacy with Him. It's impossible.

today. You must be washed by the carpenter! You must know Me in this way if you ever want to have a part of Me. Unless you can receive the simplest side of God, you will never have intimacy with Him. It's impossible.

Many of us compete with each other in our efforts to describe the glory and majesty of God. We analyze His splendor and radiance in the most articulate ways. We meditate on His greatness and we sing of His magnificence. Most of our worship songs declare the highest truths of His being. We are overjoyed at the power He possesses and the scope of His reign. We have even taught ourselves to speak in "King James Version"

If your eyes are constantly focused on His glory you will never know Him.

when approaching Him because it feels more reverent and holy. We do this because we honestly believe that this is what God wants from us. This is how He wants us to see Him and so we feel like we are actually getting closer to the truth about who He is every time we remind ourselves of His greatness. The person who is the most poetic and articulate when declaring the majesty of God is the person who knows Him best.

HOG WASH!

Though all these things are certainly true of our God, He wants you to know the side of Him that even the angels in Heaven do not understand. He wants you to love Him for Him. If your eyes are constantly focused on His glory YOU WILL NEVER KNOW HIM.

In an ironic way, I really believe that God can relate to modern day rock-and-roll stars. These people have an entourage of groupies who follow them around everywhere they go. They exalt the musicians and dedicate themselves wholeheartedly to every song on the latest album. They cry and scream every time the band begins to play and their eyes are filled with stars the moment their favorite member mounts the stage. But in the midst of it all, the "star" himself is very lonely. Why? It's because no one knows the real him. All they see are the colored lights and the special effects.

All they know is his talent and abilities. They have become addicted to the melodic sound of his voice and his catchy meaningful words.

Many of these musicians have to leave the country to find a wife. They have to find a woman who doesn't know of their fame and splendor. Though they are adored by thousands, they are not known by any, and before they can have real relationship they have to find someone who doesn't have stars in their eyes.

This is precisely why God became a man. He wanted us to know *Him* for *Him*. Though God loves the angels in Heaven, they are basically groupies. All they can see is His glory and majesty. They can't help but cry, "holy, holy, holy." God's incredible splendor and beauty is so overpowering that anyone or anything that comes into contact with it, immediately falls to the ground in worship and awe.

There is an *inner part* of God that remains hidden and veiled behind the radiance of His shimmering glory. It's a part of Him that is tucked so deep within the blinding brilliance of His presence that it is impossible for anyone to see or understand. Unless all that is great and magnificent is stripped away, no one can ever know this inner part of God. In Christ, God became nothing so He could have real intimacy with you. Jesus is the very center core of who God is in His heart. He desires this so much that He shed all His outward glory and splendor so that we could make an honest and clear-minded choice to have a relationship with Him or not. This is the only way that God can know for sure that we truly love Him.

> *In Christ, God became nothing so He could have real intimacy with you.*

God Does Not Boast About His Accomplishments

It is not by accident that the account of the crucifixion in the Bible is about one paragraph only. Some Gospel accounts tell it in just a few sentences. This might be surprising to you because of the intense focus we have put on it over the years.

We have entire scientifically-based teachings that walk us through the pain and suffering that Jesus must have gone through during the crucifixion. We make movies that depict every lashing, flogging and beating that He underwent on our behalf. This is done for the purpose of making us feel so incredibly guilty that we just might stop sinning. We have come to believe that it is in God's heart to hold this moment over the heads of His children in an effort to get them to toe the line. If we are reminded of the pain He underwent on our behalf, perhaps we will do our best to repay Him by living a right life.

Imagine if a man broke into my home and was planning on killing my wife and children, but I convinced him to take my life instead of theirs. If he let them escape, and then he proceeded to take me into a back room and filmed himself torturing me for hours until finally taking my life, do you think that I would ever want my family to see that videotape? Absolutely not! I would want them to remember my life and my love for them. There is nothing inside of me

Guilt is not a Godly motivator.

that would ever want them to view the pain I underwent to save their life. That would break their hearts. This is exactly how God feels when we reenact the Stations of the Cross in an effort to riddle people with guilt and condemnation. It doesn't motivate; it exasperates. This is not His heart!

I cannot tell you how much this grieves the Heart of God. He never ever holds this over us. Guilt is not a Godly motivator.

There is a song that says, "I'll never know how much it cost, to see my sin upon that cross," and I want to give you the reason for that today. You will never know how much it cost because God has taken the price tag off of that gift when He gave it to you. It's not about the cost for Him. It was His pleasure. If He wanted us to meditate on the pain of the cross, He would have included it in Scripture.

He never boasts about what He went through to reconcile you to Him. The account of the crucifixion lasts only a few sentences in the Bible, but the result of the resurrection is seen throughout the entire New Testament. Relationship has been re-established and this is all that God cares about. When we focus our time and attention on the crucifixion we are missing the point. God wants us to be spiritually motivated by what was accomplished because of the resurrection. God does not boast about the cross; He downplays it and He rejoices in the possibilities of relationship with you today because of the cross.

> *The account of the crucifixion lasts only a few sentences in the Bible, but the result of the resurrection is seen throughout the entire New Testament.*

Don't ever feel like you have to re-pay God for the suffering He went through for you. This was a gift to you! Any time we attempt to repay someone for a gift they gave us, we are diminishing that gift. An attempt to repay someone for a gift is really a rejection of that gift. Just receive it and go on. It's free. Boasters always expect repayment. God is not this way. He never boasts!

Love Is Not Proud [7]

After carrying our sleeping children to bed, and giving the kitchen a quick once-over, my wife and I finally had some time to ourselves. Like so many nights before, we had rented a movie and were looking forward to snuggling on the couch and enjoying an evening of mindless entertainment.

Unfortunately, it was Angie's night to choose the movie, and so I was muscled into the grueling and torturous sentence of having to endure the latest "chick-flick." This movie, however did not appear to possess all the usual qualities I had come to expect from my wife. It wasn't a love story or a romantic comedy. It was a true story about a man who had a fatal disease and was fighting for his life.

From beginning to end, this story was a tearjerker. It took just about everything I had inside me to keep myself from just breaking out and sobbing uncontrollably in front of my wife. I found myself thinking about baseball, or work, in an effort to keep my composure. It wouldn't have been that big of a deal if it were not for my wife constantly leaning over to check to see if I was crying in the middle of the most dramatic scenes. It was like she was the "tear patrol," and I was on the run. For some odd reason, Angie was determined to see me cry, and it was becoming ridiculous and irritating.

Suddenly, I was faced with an even more difficult predicament. Though I could easily keep my eyes dry by forcing my mind to wander, my nose was beginning to run. That wouldn't seem to be such a big deal, but sniffling could give me away. What would I do? After brainstorming to find a quick and easy answer, I nonchalantly mentioned that I had been fighting a cold. This allowed me the freedom to sniffle, and so I did. Unfortunately, she didn't buy it. The moment Angie heard me sniff she immediately leaned over and arrested me. I was guilty.

What she said next, was what every man dreads. And what's worse is that she said it in a long and drawn out "baby talk" voice.

"Hooonnneeey, are you cryyyyiiiiinnnng?

"No," I replied, offended. I couldn't say much more than that because the quivering in my voice would surely give me away. I immediately broke out into a coughing spell hoping to psychologically redirect her to my earlier statement about the cold. She didn't go for it and was now more determined than ever to catch me red-handed or red-eyed. It was no use, she had caught me and there was nothing I could do.

This was humiliating! It was like having someone walk in and catch me on the toilet. It was like preaching the best sermon of my life only to learn that my fly was open the entire time. I would prefer having both my legs broken or all my fingernails ripped out. I felt like every weak and vulnerable part of my soul was being exposed. My mind was blitzed with a thousand excuses that could possibly salvage the last drop of manhood available.

While I was engrossed in my personal crusade to preserve myself in front of my wife, something extraordinary happened. It was so awesome that I shudder to think that I had almost missed it. My wife was not ashamed or letdown by what she saw in me. In fact, something quite unexpected came over her countenance. She was filled with an emotion that I had not seen since the day she first told me she loved me. Her eyes were twinkling with awe and delight and her face was adorned with a look of inner pleasure. It was as though she had finally found what she had been looking for our entire marriage.

That night, I watched as my wife fell head over heels in love with me all over again. All I could do was sit there and receive it. It was as if she needed to see me cry. It did something for her that words could not express. It touched a part of her that could never have been reached otherwise. No amount of money, gifts, cards, flowers or poems could reach this far into her heart. It took total vulnerability on my part to get there and I had arrived completely by accident.

Raised On A Diet Of Pride

Every unwritten rule associated with manhood has taught us men to show little or no emotion. Emotion equals weakness and weakness equals sissy. The action heroes we have all grown up with are stone cold in their emotions and completely independent and self-reliant. They are lone rangers who don't need anyone or anything. Nothing can penetrate their hearts because they already have all they need. Though they may help people in dire circumstances, they themselves never need the favor returned.

I can remember watching Charles Bronson when I was a young boy. He was the final word in manliness, the real thing. No one even came close. In other movies the hero always got the girl and rode off into the sunset with her at the end, but not Charles Bronson. He even ditched the girl in the end. Why? It's because he didn't need anyone. He was an impenetrable island unto himself, and not even the woman could get through his armor.

I think there is a little Charles Bronson in every man. We have been spoon-fed this disposition all our lives. We carry it into our marriages, our relationships with our friends and even into fatherhood. It's the mind-set that says, "I don't need to be touched in my heart, in fact, I won't allow anyone to even have a glimpse of it."

We may enjoy touching our wife's heart with the things we do or say, but she simply isn't allowed to ever see our hearts. We leave them feeling unfulfilled and pretty much useless.

The very core of this mentality is pride. Pride causes us to believe that we don't need anybody or anything. It closes the heart doors completely and never allows entrance to anyone. This is not the same as a person who has shut down their heart because of pain or insecurity. Prideful people honestly believe that they don't need to be touched on a heart level by anyone, and out of this attitude comes some of the most horrifying and destructive teachings the world has ever seen.

Pride causes us to believe that we don't need anybody or anything.

The Greatest Stumbling Block Of Today

I am deeply grieved at the plight of pastors and evangelists today. They are emotionally damned by a religious system that is set against them. It's a system that implies that they have "arrived" to a spiritual level in which only other pastors above them can minister to them. What is equally as devastating is that a large majority of American pastors have actually come to believe this about themselves.

A minister ministers to those below him, but he will not allow himself to be ministered to by those same people. They are beneath him and have nothing to offer. Unless someone who is in a position of equal or greater authority comes along, he keeps his heart doors closed. After all, how else could he have been given such a position if it were not for his spiritual superiority? If he admitted to having any needs, he would be admitting that he was the same as those he pastors. How could he possibly lead them if he, himself had not already arrived?

Evangelists roll into town with the same counterfeit view of godliness. They believe themselves to be there for the people and that's all. The moment the sermon is finished and they have poured themselves into all the hurting people, they hop on the next flight out and disappear into the night. They were called in because they are the experts in spirituality. They have reached the spiritual nirvana in

> † I am deeply grieved at the plight of pastors and evangelists today. They are emotionally damned by a religious system that is set against them.

which all their needs are completely met. Perhaps the pastor who footed the bill for the plane ticket and hotel could speak a word into their lives but never anyone in the congregation. It would almost be disrespectful for anyone to try.

I don't believe that every pastor or evangelist is quite this prideful, but at the very least I'm certain that this mind-set is whispering in all of their ears. It's hardly their fault. Many times they are literally pressured into such an attitude by the people they minister to. The people need to have someone to hold up who represents their ultimate dream of godliness. They want someone who is completely fulfilled and no longer has any needs of their own, someone who has reached the top and is now helping others get to where he is.

They scour him with a critical eye, being sure to point out any weakness or fault in his character. He is not allowed to be human any more. If he slips up or if the people are in any way reminded of his humanity, he is strung up and whipped with the *forty minus one* hateful letters, and he receives the flogging of their endless gossiping about his disappointing frailty. If a pastor expects to survive, he must, at the very least, present a mirage of spiritual perfection before the people. He must not have any needs of his own. After all, if he is as close to God as we expect him to be, he wouldn't have any needs.

> *We believe that true godliness ministers to people without needing anything in return.*

The problem is that most of us have the same view of godliness. We believe that true godliness ministers to people without needing anything in return. People who are godly should give but never receive. We believe this because we believe that GOD IS PROUD.

What Was He Thinking?

Have you ever wondered why God created us? If it is true that God knows the beginning from the end that seems a bit perplexing to me. Did He have nothing better to do? Was He killing time? Are we just some sea monkey experiment or giant people farm that He enjoys watching from above? Was He bored with Himself? If someone told you the ending of a movie, would you still go see it? If you already knew how a novel ended, would you read it? What was God thinking?

Most people will tell you that we were put here for the purpose of bringing glory to God. They'll tell you that we are here to

The God's Honest Truth

praise Him and lift Him up. If that's true, that sounds a bit prideful to me, not to mention self-seeking. We'll talk more on that subject later.

What would be the purpose of God creating us? Why would a God who has everything, waste His time with a bunch of measly people? What could we possibly offer Him that He doesn't already have a million times over? Surely God would be better off without the hassle that this world has caused him over the years.

The answer to this question is perhaps the most astounding fact about the heart of God that you will ever encounter. It might even offend you when you first hear it. I know for a fact that it will dash all your preconceived notions to the ground about Him. The answer to this question has within it the threat of redefining every Christian belief about what godliness is. It might even require you to "learn another language" other than the present *Christian lingo* that you have grown accustomed to. Why did God create us?

God Created Us Because He Had A Need

This pretty much goes against everything we have been taught. It seems to imply that He may not have had "everything" He needed in and of Himself. He was unfulfilled and He had a need that needed ministering to. That need compelled Him to put Himself on the line and become totally vulnerable in an effort to have relationship with us. Why should this surprise us? We were created in His image. We also have the same need. We have a need for relationship, a need to be known and a desire to share ourselves with another.

> ✝
> *We even publicly acknowledge our unworthiness in His presence so He'll be extra happy with us.*

We have come to define godliness according to our upside-down understanding of God, Himself. Pastors present themselves as being completely without need because they honestly think that this is who God is. Laymen are afraid to minister to their pastor's heart because they assume that He is closer to God then they are. They

> *"If you wouldn't be friends with a person like that, you won't be friends with a God like that."*

believe that the closer they themselves get to God, the fewer needs they will have because God doesn't need anyone. We even say things like, "God doesn't need you. You need Him." This simply is not true. God is not proud!

Remember that pride believes that it needs no one. It's an island unto itself. It is totally self-reliant. These are not characteristics that describe the heart of God; they are descriptions of pride. Our heart's belief in these things ultimately bleed over into almost every area of Christianity. Before we know it, we have developed an entire theology that supports our expectations of a prideful God.

As we say the things we say about Him, we excuse it in our minds because, after all, He is God. He should be allowed to be prideful. If anyone has the right to be prideful it should be Him, and so we paint a picture of Him with the most prideful colors we can find, and we present it to the world. Then we wonder why no one's biting.

When we worship, we do it thinking that this was the reason we were put here, as though He created us so we could remind Him of how great He is all the time. We even publicly acknowledge our unworthiness in His presence so He'll be extra happy with us. In fact, the lower we make ourselves, the more pleased and exalted He is. We proudly tell ourselves that we worship out of obedience, because that is what God requires. We pat ourselves on the backs, because at the end of our prayers we are very careful to give Him and only Him all the glory. We spur one another on to serve Him like good little slaves, and unless we do, He'll bring us to a "breaking point" where we fully submit to Him. He just might strip us of everything until we end up on our face in total compliance.

The picture we paint of our God is not only prideful, but also disgusting. There is a principal that I teach my congregation that applies to modern day Christianity in the most astounding way. It's the answer to many questions such as, why is Christianity the fastest declining religion in America, or why do people keep leaving God and "backsliding?" The principal is this: "If you wouldn't be friends with a person like that, you won't be friends with a God like that."

If we were to take the amazingly prideful things that we say about God and put them on a person we worked with, we would hate that individual with a passion. We would avoid him or her at all costs. It would take nothing less than a pure commitment to continue an ongoing relationship with that person. This is precisely the predicament that Christianity is in. We even have to have accountability partners to keep us in line because if we were left to ourselves we would slip up and leave Him. This is just humanity's natural response to an awful stench. Nobody likes a prideful person, and nobody likes a prideful God.

The Upright Truth About Our God

To say "God created us to worship Him" is as uncouth and vulgar as me telling my wife that I married her for the sex. This was the furthest thing from my mind, and God is not that way with you, either. Worship is supposed to be a beautiful consummation of a relationship that has already bloomed to eternal life. God did not create you so that you could worship Him; He created you because He wanted relationship with you. He is just like you in this respect. He desired a real two-way relationship that was mutually edifying. When you have that with Him and you worship, you are ministering to the heart of God. You are touching Him deeply because it comes out of something that the two of you share together. He is truly moved by you!

Many times when I go to preach somewhere, people will approach me with stars in their eyes and tell me what an anointed preacher I am. They'll lift me up and give me a barrage of compliments that they couldn't possibly know if they were true or not. If I allow them to, they'll go on and on in what almost seems to me like worship. Though I am always very careful to be kind in my response, I am actually kind of repulsed in my spirit. I almost feel violated. However, when I return home and my wife tells me the exact same things, I do not feel the least bit bad about it. In fact, I'm on cloud nine. Why? It's because SHE KNOWS ME. There is a difference between someone telling me things because they think they should and someone telling me the same things because they know me.

> *To say "God created us to worship Him" is as uncouth and vulgar as me telling my wife that I married her for the sex.*

This is God's heart with worship. His first and foremost desire is to be known by you. Worship is secondary. It cannot come before relationship. That would make God a fornicator. He desires marriage first! When you know Him, you worship what you know, and He does not just sit there and receive it without returning the love back to you. His knowledge of you causes Him to explode with many of the same love songs you sing to Him. Worship is not just for God. It's a time when both you and He can express your love for each other. God is just like you in this respect. He needs it and so do you. Your relationship with Him needs it. He is not proud.

Many husbands quote Scriptures to their wives that suggest that because of the fact that they are now married, their bodies are no longer their own. This is done in an effort to manipulate their wives into "giving up sex" whether she is in the mood or not, because "the Bible says so." Sadly, there are thousands of women with whom sex has become an emotional let-down, because their hearts and feelings are never considered. Their religion tells them that sex is something they are supposed to give to their husband, whether they like it or not. Mutual participation and emotional oneness is totally disregarded for the sake of their religion.

His first and foremost desire is to be known by you. Worship is secondary.

We have come to see worship in this same context. We have been taught that God is just like these selfish husbands. He requires us to lift our hands and worship Him even when we are exhausted from the day, or suffering from a headache. This generation honestly believes that their God is as heartless and self-serving as we are. Rather than knowing the truth about God's understanding heart, we have made Him out to be the husband who demands consummation on His terms, without even considering where we are at spiritually and emotionally at the time.

These tangled teachings are the result of pride. God's need for worship is not a one-sided need. It springs out of His need for true relationship. He desires mutually edifying worship that is born out of the oneness that precedes it. He is not proud, because His relationship with you is in constant need of being consummated!

God Does Not Desire To See You Break

It is true that God will bring you to a breaking point in your life, but He does not do it in order to make you submit to His authority. He doesn't do it to punish you for something you did, and He certainly doesn't do it to remind you that you are His slave.

Why then would He do it? God is looking for the same thing that my wife was looking for that night on the couch. Angie was bringing me to a "breaking point" because it moved her heart.

> *God would NEVER bring you to a breaking point unless He had already broken Himself.*

There are places deep inside of her that cannot be touched except by my vulnerability. She needs it. She needs to know that I am not impenetrable. It moves her in ways that she cannot express. God is the same way with you, and the beautiful thing is that God would NEVER bring you to a breaking point unless He had already broken Himself.

He does not ask us to be vulnerable out of principal or obedience to His supreme authority. He asks it of us because He has made Himself vulnerable to us. He knows that He can never melt Himself with you unless He opens up to you and you open up to Him completely. This is what relationship requires.

Many mornings, just after our new baby, Eva, has been given a bath, I will take my shirt off and lay her naked body on my bare chest. There is just something about a naked baby that warms the heart of a parent. For that moment, I don't want any clothes between us, just skin on skin. It's my way of getting as close as humanly possible to the one I love so much. It's all of her next to all of me. I love it!

When people have been stripped by their Heavenly Father, I am always amazed at how often they see it as punishment or payback. If they only knew that God's stripping of His children has nothing to do with that, but He does it because it warms His heart to see us that way. It's all of us on all of Him, with nothing in between. He loves it!

If you recall, the last scene of Jesus' life, He, too, was naked. This was the final picture of what God was presenting to the world. He desires complete and total vulnerability. With pride, this is impossible. God has a need, and you fulfill that need in His heart. He is not too proud to admit it.

God Is A Gentleman

Many of us have been raised with a false sense of God and godliness all of our lives. It has even affected our prayer lives to the point where we feel bad asking Him for anything. We even exalt the Christian who only thanks Him and praises Him without asking for anything. It's a sign of "spiritual maturity" in our modern day mind-sets, but nothing could be further than the truth.

There is nothing more heart warming and fulfilling to a father than to be asked for something from one of His children. It's especially touching when it is a thing that only He can provide.

Several weeks ago, I came home from work to find my three-year-old daughter Sidney sitting on the couch crying. When she saw me walk in, her eyes lit up and she ran to me with her arms out. Earlier that day, her tricycle's pedal broke, and she had been waiting all day for daddy to get home so he could fix it. There was no doubt in her mind that I could do it, and when I saw how much she believed that, I jumped into action. I was so moved by her childlike sincerity and belief in me that I literally flew across the garage to find my toolbox. Several minutes later, she was peddling around the driveway with a renewed smile on her face and I was more blessed than her.

This is God's heart with you! He is not offended when you ask Him for things. In fact, He is moved by it. He loves it. Especially when you believe that He can and will do it. It compels Him in a way that only a Father could understand. He not only loves it when you ask, but He waits with expectation for you to ask. Why? It's because He needs you to ask Him. Your asking fulfills a need in His heart to provide for the one He loves the most.

When you ask for something that only He can provide, it touches Him deeply. He is moved, because in your asking, you are showing Him that you have faith that He can do it. Anytime you admit to helplessness, God is inspired. He is not stirred because He likes proving He is better than you, He is touched from a Fatherly perspective. Your vulnerability shakes Him at the deepest, most inner part of His Heart. Prideful people close themselves off to relationship. They are incapable of reaching hearts. God would not be able to have relationship with anyone if He were this way.

> *Your asking fulfills a need in His heart to provide for the one He loves the most.*

We come from such a prideful generation where we refuse to ask for help from anyone. We think God is the same way with us. I've heard it said a million times that, "God doesn't need your help, He rose up a donkey to speak, and He doesn't need you." This is a terrible thing to say about Him. We are not doing Him any favors by painting Him in this light. This kind of talk is just foolish and ignorant of His heart. It stamps Him with a prideful disposition that doesn't even resemble the truth, not to mention it completely disqualifies Him from the possibility of ever having relationship with anyone.

Did you know that there are many things that only YOU can do? There are a host of things that God needs your help with, things that even He cannot do alone. He set it up that way because He wanted relationship and true relationship is never one way. Think about the blessing you feel in your heart when you do something for the Lord. This is the same blessing He feels, when He does something for you. Now that's relationship!

Pride Monitors

Very few people today will take the blame for something they didn't do. We all will receive the glory and praise for what we did do, but don't ever accuse us of something we weren't responsible for. Pride constantly monitors what it does and doesn't deserve. It's actually quite accurate as well. It's precise because it continually monitors, and the moment something undeserving pops up on the screen, bells and whistles start sounding.

Marriages suffer greatly because of this form of pride. The second a man feels like he is "paying for the sins" of his wife's ex-boyfriend, he callously strikes back in anger. It's not fair. Why should he be penalized for something he didn't do? It's not even something he can say he's sorry for because it wasn't him who did it.

When Jesus died for your sins, it was more than Him just paying the price. Though that was accomplished, it wasn't what made His sacrifice so powerful. Paying a debt that is not your own, is indeed a selfless act, but God took it a step further. Do you know that He not only paid the debt, but He actually took the guilt of having committed your sins upon Him? Think about that for a moment. Think of the most terrible thing you've ever done. You know

> *Love is not concerned with fair; its primary focus is to wash the one it loves, at any cost.*

what I'm talking about. That sin you committed that every time you bring it to your memory banks, you feel sick inside for having done it. Jesus actually took that to His memory banks and became guilty on your behalf. He didn't just pay for it; He actually became it.

Why would He do this? He did it because love is not proud. Not once did He complain about how unfair it was. Love is not concerned with fair; its primary focus is to wash the one it loves, at any cost.

What Inspired The Coming Of Jesus?

In Jesus' day, the religious preachers and teachers had arrived to a level of assumed spirituality that is much like many Christians today. Because of their killer prayer life, their flawless tithing records and their incredible knowledge of Scripture, they had no needs. They had truly mastered their religion. In fact, they didn't even need a Savior because they followed the law precisely.

It would seem that when Jesus came, He would be coming for these truly religious people. You would think that their spirituality alone would have been the reason why Jesus came, but this was not what inspired the coming of Christ.

Jesus even told these people that He didn't come for people who didn't need Him. He came for those who did. The very thing that compelled Him to come was "needs." *Helplessness was the fuel that drove Jesus to do everything He did. Helplessness inspired every miracle and healing that He performed.* It was the central focus of His entire ministry.

Though Jesus was a King, He had no problem becoming a carpenter. Though all glory belonged to Him, He was comfortable having no place to lay His head. Though His hands formed the entire universe, He actually enjoyed washing dirty feet. He enjoyed it, because they were the feet of people He loved. He did not require that anyone bow down to Him and give Him the respect He deserved. On the contrary, He invited them to walk with Him and call Him brother. Jesus wants you to know Him in the same way. There isn't a prideful bone in His body. It's not your fear and shuddering religious reverence He is after, it's your heart. He became your older brother, because He wanted real relationship with you. God is not proud!

> ✝
> *It's not your fear and shuddering religious reverence He is after, it's your heart.*

Love Is Not Rude [8]

While driving home from work one day, I was channel-surfing on my radio looking for something to help pass the time. After listening to several boring eighties songs that the disc jockey depressingly referred to as "oldies," I came upon a popular talk show host about whom I have heard many controversial things. He was notorious for being downright crude on the air. I stopped briefly to listen, mainly out of sheer curiosity as to why he was so well-liked. About sixty seconds into the show, I was appalled at his deliberate and calculated rudeness. Though he did have a sense of humor, it was apparent that his wit was not the reason for his massive following. The people who were calling in were genuinely entertained by this man's abrasive personality. What was even more astonishing was that everyone on the show seemed to have a real respect for this person's opinion. They actually praised him for being so "in your face" and for, "telling it like it is." He was lifted up as a picture of strength and boldness in an otherwise watered down society.

It would almost seem like a waste of time to write an entire chapter on "love is not rude" simply because one would think that this goes without saying. It's a no-brainer. Besides, this subject surely was covered in our previous chapter on "love is kind." Why restate the obvious?

In listening to this infamous disc jockey, I discovered that rudeness and meanness have very little to do with each other. He was not mean. In fact, he was rather likable. I suspect that he rose to his level of fame because he spoke the very things that were already on everyone else's mind. He even delivered his opinion with a tone and disposition that most of us secretly share, but refuse to express simply because it wouldn't seem appropriate. It wasn't as though this man was abusive to others; he was just abrasive. He was rude. His career was timed perfectly because we are basically living in a rude society.

The Attraction To Rudeness

Like many things in our generation, what was once obvious and unacceptable is now less evident and totally tolerable. You would think that things like rudeness would always be unattractive, but it seems that this characteristic has taken an evolutionary turn in the last thirty years. Rudeness has now become a desired and beloved attribute in people's personalities.

Rude men seem to attract women from all walks of life. Politeness and good manners have become a thing of the past. Thirty years ago, a man with these qualities was considered a good catch. Today, however, he would be perceived as weak and frail. I am amazed at the number of women who have redefined rudeness as strength and confidence.

Men are also fascinated with rude women. They love the fact that their wife won't take anything from anyone. I've even heard some men boast about their wife's callous response to someone who "got in her face." It's a personality trait that has won the hearts of both men and women in our generation.

Because of this transformation in our attractions, we have also transformed our understanding of love. Though it should be obvious that love is not rude, there are millions of people to whom it is not obvious at all. We have come to appreciate and even desire the very opposite of what love is. Once an attraction to rudeness takes root in someone, they become addicted to it and genuinely prefer it. Before long they find themselves being repulsed by authentic love.

Rudeness has now become a desired and beloved attribute in people's personalities.

Just as many people have become addicted to rudeness in relationships, I believe that many Christians and churches have become addicted to a "rude God." We wouldn't have it any other way. We've become comfortable with the idea of it. It challenges and motivates us to follow all the rules. We see it the same as we see it in our personal relationships; it shows strength and power. It's an attractive attribute that makes us respect and even fear Him.

We like it when it seems that God has "put someone in their place" by publicly humiliating them or raining disaster on their livelihood. We exchange stories of how God got His point across to someone by exposing their hidden sin to the world. We describe Him as having a "my way or the highway" mentality. He won't take anything from anyone. When we read Scriptures of Jesus' response to the Pharisees, we secretly insert a rude tone to His voice. We imagine Him talking this same way to people we don't like. I truly believe that we are addicted to a "rude God."

Telling It Like It Isn't

Over the years, I have watched a growing trend that has brought much concern to my heart. It seems to replay itself in almost every Christian circle at one time or another. It usually happens when a preacher is relating a conversation he supposedly had with God, and when he comes to what "God said," he presents Him as being callous and coarse in His tone.

I once heard an evangelist recall a word for word conversation where God was confronting him on a matter of personal pride and supposedly God said to him, "you make me sick." Another time the story was told that God's response to a person was, "do I stutter, or are your ears flapping?" It's usually done for effect, and it does seem to elicit a wave of chuckles from the audience, but I feel that over time it wears on the hearts of His children. We begin to expect that this is who He is and how He relates us.

> ✝
> *If we perceive God's personality as rude, we will only hear rude tones when He speaks to us.*

Have you ever had someone recall a conversation that the two of you had, and when they came to "what you said," they used an abrasive and rude tone that was a million light years from how you actually said it? It completely misrepresents your character and disposition. Perhaps they even accused you of "yelling" at them, when that wasn't what happened at all. For some reason, they perceived you as a rude person, so when recounting what you said to them, they inserted rudeness to your words and actions. Do you remember how violated and misunderstood you felt? It's almost like you were framed with a temperament that had nothing to do with the real you. This is how God feels when we do this. It breaks His heart because it not only turns the hearts of His children from Him, but it also confirms that we neither know Him nor understand Him.

The problem is that we hear whatever tone we expect to hear. If we perceive God's personality as rude, we will only hear rude tones when He speaks to us. We'll underline passages in our Bible that seem to fit our theory of His attitude. Though we may appreciate the hallucination of counterfeit strength it seems to display in Him, we will never truly give our hearts to Him. Rudeness is only attractive to the flesh, but it makes a heart relationship both repulsive and impossible.

A Deeper Look At Rudeness

Before we go any further, I want to give a few dictionary definitions of "rude." (Dictionary.com)

Rude:
1. Being in a crude, rough, unfinished condition:
   a.   Exhibiting a marked lack of skill or precision in work:
   b.   In a natural, raw state:
2. Characterized by roughness; unpolished, raw, lacking delicacy or refinement, coarse.
3. Unformed by taste or skill; not nicely finished, not smoothed or polished.

Among all the definitions I found, there seems to be one common denominator: *unfinished* or *not completed.* A piece of wood that is unfinished, and in a raw state, is rough and full of splinters. When that piece of wood is rubbed up against someone, it causes one to bleed. Rocks that have not been polished are rough and rude. This is where we get the saying: "rough around the edges." It speaks of the discomfort one might feel when encountering something or someone in this state.

The Tone Of Rudeness

In the Bible times, before communication had reached the level that we know today, the kings would use messengers to deliver their messages. These messengers were selected by their ability to not only deliver the words of the king, but to also deliver the tone in which the words were spoken.

If the king threatened to go to war against an enemy, he would send a messenger who would reenact the anger and rage that the king displayed to him. If the king was screaming and pounding his fists on the table while he gave the message, the messenger would scream in the exact same tone and pound his fists in the exact same manner while delivering the message to the enemy.

If the king invited people to a banquet and his spirits where high and happy, the messenger would act out that joy precisely while delivering the invitation. This way, those who received it would not only hear the words of the message, but the disposition of the person who sent it.

Today, however, I am deeply grieved at our present-day messengers. It seems that the words of the Bible are all they need. Understand that when the wrong tone is given to the right words, disasters happen! The only way the Bible can be properly interpreted is if the messenger knows and understands the tone of God's heart. When a tone of condemnation and anger is given to words of encouragement and love, it takes on an entirely new meaning. It lacerates the heart and causes it to cower from God. It terrifies God's children and creates fearful expectations that take years to recover from.

> *The only way the Bible can be properly interpreted is if the messenger knows and understands the tone of God's heart.*

This is precisely why the Bible says to speak the truth in LOVE. Truth ceases to be truth if it is spoken in any other tone than love. Yes, we are the salt of the Earth, but if we walk into a hospital full of people who are suffering from opened sores and rub salt in their wounds, our saltiness becomes torture. Though we are the light of the world, we must always remember

> *Truth ceases to be truth if it is spoken in any other tone than love.*

that those who have wandered in darkness all their lives can be easily blinded if we shine a spot light in their face. Salt preserves or destroys; light can either illuminate or blind. Tone is everything!

Words speak to the head. Tone speaks to the heart. Even dogs understand this principal. Have you ever spoken terrible things to a dog in a sweet voice? The dog wags his tail and licks your face with excitement. Have you ever spoken words of love to a dog in an angry voice? What happens? The dog runs away and hides.

This is precisely why so many Christians are hiding today. They have been given loving words in an angry voice. Though they have memorized the words in their head, they have also memorized the tone in their heart. A preacher can tell his congregation that God loves them every Sunday for a year, but if that preacher doesn't love them himself, the tone will always be contaminated. It's not enough to preach on a subject and cover all the points. Love must be at the heart of everything we do and say and the tone of love is NEVER rude.

The Wilderness Misconception

One of the statements I probably hear the most from people when I inquire about their relationship with God is this: "God has me in a wilderness," as though God has left them on top of the refrigerator like an avocado waiting to ripen. Many people actually believe that this is who God is. They see themselves as being in a perpetual state of unfinished growth or incompletion, and they honestly believe that God not only endorses this idea but He also participates in it.

This mentality goes completely against the basic theology of Scripture. In New Testament times, if you are a Christian, you

> *In New Testament times, if you are a Christian, you are in the Promised Land, not the wilderness.*

are in the Promised Land, not the wilderness. The wilderness time was before you were saved. Make no mistake about it; God will not put you in the wilderness! Remember loved ones, the Israelites received the entire Promised Land in one day, but they possessed it bit by bit. Just because you may have trouble accepting and possessing what God has freely given you, don't think He has put you in the wilderness. God has not left you *unfinished*, He has made you perfect forever with one sacrifice. The only wilderness in your life is the wilderness that you choose to live in, but you must know that God did not put you there. He will never leave you alone in a wilderness!

God brings all things to completion and He leaves nothing unfinished. Though you are a work in progress, He has already declared you completed! When He looks upon you, He sees only the finished product. What were Jesus' last words? He said, "It is finished." He doesn't treat *you* as anything less.

Many times we use the example of how our earthly parents were with us or how we deal with our children in an effort to describe the heart of God. This can be a beautiful example when it's understood and weighed with truth; however, this is not always the case. There are indeed ways in which we deal with our children that are similar to how God deals with us, but it is imperative that we understand that God does not treat us as children. For the most part our children are taught to respect their mommy and daddy, but because of their age and inexperience, mom and dad usually don't show them the same respect. Their opinions are not taken with a great degree of seriousness. Their choices are limited and their full submission is required for their own good. It's not until that child grows up and has a family of his or her own that their relationship with their parents becomes one of mutual respect.

Though God is your Father in Heaven, it's important for you to understand that He respects you. He doesn't treat you like a child. He understands that you are an adult and He gives you the respect that an adult deserves. When we talk as though God is "spanking" us or He has put us in "time out," we do not understand the truth about Him.

> *God will never talk down to you or treat you as anything less than an adult.*

These are things we do to our children when they are young, however, when they become adults we show them honor and respect. Adults simply don't respond when they are treated like children. Understand that God will never talk down to you or treat you as anything less than an adult. God respects your opinions and decisions. He approaches you with the reverence you deserve as an adult because relationship requires it.

Respect The Man Of God Mentality

I am not exactly sure when this popular decree started in American churches, but I am certain of the reason it began. It's actually an Old Testament thing that has been revived and reused for the purpose of getting people to do what ever the leader wants them to do. Unfortunately, it totally denies the work of Christ on the cross by implying that there are some Christians who are the "man of God" and others who are not.

In Old Testament times, this was certainly the case. Because sin had not been atoned for, God would select certain people through which He would speak. They were set apart and became "the man of God" and were called priests and prophets. In the New Testament, however, everyone who had accepted Jesus Christ into his or her hearts, instantly became the "man of God" or "woman of God." In other words, there aren't some who are *completed* and on better terms with God while others are not. This mentality is a rude and *unfinished* way of thinking. EVERY child of God deserves our utmost reverence and respect including, but not limited to, our leaders in the Church.

> †
>
> *...there aren't some who are completed and on better terms with God while others are not.*

The "men of God" in the Old Testament would give everything they had to possess what you and I have today. They were called "servants" of God and we are now called "sons and daughters" of God. The implications of that are astounding. If all the Christians in the world were gone and you were the only one left, and you walked into a Wal-Mart to buy toothpaste, everyone there would stop in their tracks and say, "Behold, the son or daughter of God." *Make no mistake about it; there is no one closer to His heart than you.* He is your Father, and everything in your life deeply matters to Him. He is as grieved and hurt when you fall as He is when the most popular healing evangelist in the world falls. Your daily walk is as important to Him as your pastor's walk. Because of what was finished on the cross, you are the person of God!

Rude And Unfinished Information

Just about every parent in the world understands what it is like to have your every move questioned by your children. With our first child, I was determined to be a super-dad and methodically answer and explain my every command. I soon learned that my three-year-old could not follow my answers beyond the first

We have built an entire religion on "because I said so."

three seconds. After giving a five-minute explanation as to why daddy doesn't want her to run out into the street I was slapped with another "But why?" After patiently telling her over and over, I finally succumbed to the ever-popular stock answer of, "because I said so." Before long, I found myself doing the unthinkable. I actually caved in and began to recite the same script that my parents delivered to me. I just cut her off half-way through and said, "You don't need to know why, just do as I say."

Though there is a great deal of truth to this "answer," it's basically a cop-out. If parents are not careful, they will ultimately find themselves never explaining anything to their children because of the "you don't need to know" loophole. What starts out as a tactic to get them to mind for reasons that they could not possibly comprehend can eventually become a rude and incomplete way of getting them to just shut up and mind even when they can understand. Many parents become addicted to giving partial information way beyond the appropriate time.

This may go over with our children, but the moment we try to use this line of reasoning towards another adult, it becomes noticeably rude. It is rude because it disrespectfully assumes that incomplete and partial information is all a person deserves to get. It's a slap to their dignity and it blatantly questions their competence. This is why I am always amazed when I hear people talk about God as though He, too, gives us the old, "because I said so" answer.

We have built an entire religion on "because I said so." It's a safeguard from anyone who dares to ask why when we really aren't sure of the answer ourselves. It has even become politically incorrect to ask why, particularly when the Bible has a verse that says to do it. Once the verse has been read, if you dare to ask why, your entire faith is on trial. You are usually met with the question; "Do you believe the Bible or not?" The verse should be all you need. In other words, "You don't need to know why, just do as it says." It has even become a language that most of us speak without even realizing it. Once a Scripture is found to back up whatever point someone wants to make, that's the end of that. No explanation required. Don't ask questions or you might be labeled a rebel.

> *I believe that quoting Scripture is the great escape of every Christian pastor, evangelist and author of our time.*

Truthfully, I believe that quoting Scripture is the great escape of every Christian pastor, evangelist and author of our time. It's something we have all learned to hide behind. It's easier than taking the time to explain it to the listener. We imagine that they have to agree and not question because the verse says it. There is an unspoken "because-the-Bible-says so" standing in the face of anyone who dares to desire a little more explanation than that. To even ask "why" after the verse has been given is borderline faithlessness. Just do as it says and don't ask questions!

Many people believe that this is true of our Father as well. They think He will only give us partial information and then command us to do what He says without explaining why. Because we have been conditioned to think He is this way, we have taught ourselves to only listen partially. This is why so many people will tell me that they don't know what God is doing in their life; it's a mystery. Most of us honestly don't believe that God will speak to us with full disclosure. We think He holds back information and blasts us with a, "because I said so" if we dare to inquire. We think it's how He tests our faith and trust in Him.

This line of thinking is preached in every "obedience" sermon in the world. Most people believe that obedience is the number one thing that God wants from us. We have come to see God as a slave master who isn't interested in our opinion; He just wants us to do what He says, when He says it. I have even heard people describe a true Christian as a broken horse who only does what he or she is told.

God never intended our relationship with Him to be like a soldier mindlessly following the orders of his Commander.

No relationship required beyond you turning right or left when the reins are tugged. When we grow up hearing these ludicrous illustrations, it's no wonder why we run from intimacy with God. Who would want a relationship with that?

When my wife and I take our daughters to the mall, we have the same talk with them every time we park. Just before we allow them to leave the car, we sternly remind them that they aren't allowed to run in the parking lot. I caution them to obey their daddy and do what he says.

I honestly believe that children are born with some weird computer chip in their brain that causes them to go crazy and run like gazelles the second their feet hit the pavement of a busy parking lot. Ironically, you can take them to a park where there are rolling hills of grass and the moment you put them down, they just stand there.

If someone were to ask my daughters to describe their mommy and daddy, we would be truly grieved if they were to say, "All they want is obedience." We do desire their obedience for the sole purpose of their safety, but to see us as only wanting their obedience hardly illustrates the motive of our hearts. It makes us look like control freaks. It makes us look rude.

God never intended our relationship with him to be like a soldier mindlessly following the orders of his Commander. If you ask "why" He will tell you why, if you don't understand He will help you to understand and if you need time to get it, He will patiently teach you until you do. Relationship is a dialogue not a monologue. Our present-day view of obedience completely terminates the possibility of a two-way conversation.

A Masterpiece At Work

God is truly an artist when it comes to you. Just like all artists, He sees the final picture long before He brings it into being. If you were to ask Van Gogh what he saw when he looked at a blank piece of canvas, He would tell you that he sees swirling stars in the night overlooking a church nestled in the midst of rocky mountains. He would describe the brilliance of each color in the picture, and the mood it would give those who beheld it. A true artist sees only the finished masterpiece.

Make no mistake about it; God will never expose the things in you that are unfinished!

Because of this amazing vision that an artist has, and because it's a unique vision that most people do not have, artists will almost always cover their project with a white veil or cloth to hide it from the world until it is finished. As far as the artist is concerned, it is finished already, because it lives inside of his heart. He covers it because he is protecting what is in his heart until it has been fully expressed.

Your Father in Heaven is creating a masterpiece in you. The masterpiece of you already exists deep within His heart. Make no mistake about it; He will never expose the things in you that are unfinished! I am startled to have met so many people who are truly afraid that God will expose them to the world.

Love Covers Over A Multitude of Sins

One evening just after our service had ended, the lobby was packed with people enjoying a time of fellowship. My daughters had just been released from their class and were full of energy and excited to see their daddy. They were running in and out of all the people searching for me, when one of my daughters lost control of her bladder and completely wet herself right there in the middle of the lobby. She did not know that I was close by and had seen what had happened. Her face immediately turned red, and she had a look of horror and embarrassment in her countenance that has etched itself in my soul to this very day. As she looked around nervously, our eyes met, and she whimpered quietly, "Daddy I, went pee pee."

He will never expose your sin to the world. From the beginning of time, God has been in the business of covering up sin.

Without missing a beat, I scooped her up in my arms and covered her from the crowd. I held her close to my body and quickly found a nearby exit. As we nonchalantly headed to the car, I could feel my suit and tie beginning to soak. Not once was I tempted to hold her out away from me, but I squeezed her tight and spoke gentle loving words in her ear and reassured her that no one saw what happened.

I was covering a masterpiece that was still growing. This is what fathers who love do. This is how God is with you. He will never expose your sin to the world. From the beginning of time, God has been in the business of covering up sin. He soaks it up into Himself and away from you. Believe it or not, He will also cover up embarrassing sins and struggles that you secretly deal with.

> *The only exposing God ever does in your life is when He unveils the beautiful things about you to others.*

Do not fear that God will ever humiliate you in order to humble you. Exposing an unfinished person is rude. He is great at keeping things just between you and Him. You are His masterpiece and He will protect you and cover you until you are complete.

The only exposing God ever does in your life is when He unveils the beautiful things about you to others. Just as my wife and I prod our children to recite the alphabet in front of dinner guests, He wants others to love you and be as proud of you as He is. The moment the guests leave, your Father returns to you and begins sanding out the blemishes, ironing out the wrinkles, and bleaching out the stains that only you and He know about. All that is rude and unfinished is covered with a veil of perfection.

I am not telling you that others will never find out your sins. Sin has a nasty habit of eventually exposing itself. All of us have been exposed once or twice in our lives, but make no mistake about it; God was not the one who did it. This is never in His heart. Love is not rude.

Today's Unfinished Mind-Set

Love does not date someone for ten years and then break up with them. There is a point in every relationship where a consummation MUST take place. Consummation means to bring to fulfillment. Love marries. Jesus didn't just date the Church; He married the Church. We come from a generation of dating with no purpose. Many people live their whole lives in a continuous state of incompletion because they are with someone who has no intentions of marrying them. Even in many marriages, there seems to be a rude

Entire theologies are built on a rude God who hasn't resolved in His mind to stay with us forever.

attitude where one or both people haven't resolved to be there until death parts them. Divorce is always an option if things get bad. Until any couple has decided in their hearts that they will never leave the other, they will both experience rudeness in that marriage. It manifests in the midst of arguments when divorce is threatened at every turn. Over time this "unfinished" mind-set rubs the soul raw and causes the spirit to bleed internally.

We believe that God is this same way in His marriage to us. We think He threatens divorce if we don't do everything exactly the way He wants us to. We search the Scriptures to find the perfect scenario where God would for sure leave us if we did this or that. We debate heatedly with anyone who would suggest to us that God would never leave us. Entire theologies are built on a rude God who hasn't resolved in His mind to stay with us forever.

Something happens in a person's mind and behavior when they decide once and for all that they will never leave. They don't interact the same way with their spouse from that point on. They weigh their words and the tone of their words very carefully before they speak them. Why? Because they know that they'll have to live with whatever mess they create with their partner. When you have a "*forever*" mind-set, you take great care of your relationship.

Have you ever stayed in a hotel for over a week? How did that place look and smell by the time you left? If you are like most people, it probably resembled a crack house. There is no reason to keep it clean when you know your days are numbered. If you spill grape juice on the carpet, you'll clean it up with a dust buster. Every towel and washcloth is used and thrown on the floor. All the sundries like shampoo, conditioner, soap, toilet paper and Kleenex have been removed from their place and lovingly packed in your suitcase, and once the place has been properly pillaged you leave. This is a rude mentality. It's evidence that you're not planning on sticking around.

Many people know that God will never leave us, however, they depict Him as one who acts and behaves in a manner that resembles one who has not resolved to stay forever. Make no mistake about it, loved ones, not only will God never leave you, He will also treat you in a way that is consistent with His personal promise to be with you forever. He will never create a thoughtless mess in your heart by speaking coarsely or abusively to you. He knows quite well that He will be spending eternity with you, and every word He speaks to you is with that in mind. Though many people may recount to you "scripted" conversations with God in which He did the opposite, be assured that they are only relating their misguided perceptions of His heart. His words were tainted by what that person expected to hear based on their religious upbringing, but it has little to do with the truth.

God is never rude to you for one basic reason; He has resolved to be with you forever in a marriage relationship.

God is never rude to you for one basic reason: He has resolved to be with you forever in a marriage relationship. Divorce is never in His mind when it comes to you. He will never leave you, and because of this fact, He treats you in the same way He desires to be treated by you. That's right. The author of the "Golden Rule" not only wrote it for you, but He follows it Himself. It was created *for* relationship by the One who desires to have it with you.

Love Is Not Self-Seeking [9]

My parents had been acting strangely for a number of months and there seemed to be a tense unfamilier thickness in the air. At night, I could hear my mother crying in the other room when she thought my brother and I were asleep. I can remember hearing whispering arguments spoken in between each stretch of uncontrollable sobbing and weeping. From my room, I could only make out bits and pieces of their conversation. I could hear my mother pleading with my father to think about the kids and how this would affect us. He was quiet. If I had not seen his car lights through my bedroom window an hour earlier, I might have been tempted to think he wasn't there at all. I waited for his response. I waited and waited. Nothing. Again the sounds of my mother's pain came leaking through the walls of my room. I felt weird inside of my heart. It was like I was doing something wrong by hearing all this. I knew for sure that this sort of thing was not meant for my ears. I kept it to myself.

Several weeks later, my parents called us into their bedroom. First my brother Kevin went in and they shut the door behind him. I sat on the living room couch with my eyes fixed down the hall and on the bedroom door. What could be happening? My six-and-a-half-year-old brain was trying to piece everything together as quickly as it could. I felt like I was waiting in the principal's office to receive punishment for something I did. My heart was pounding and my palms were wet. Finally the door opened and out came my brother. He had a stoic look on his face, like someone had brainwashed him. My mother's face was red and her eyes were swollen. She had a Kleenex in her hand and her hair looked as if it had not been washed in a few days. Then she motioned for me to come to her.

The walk from the couch to the bedroom has been with me for almost thirty years. I remember every single step. The air got bulky and moist as I approached the room where they were. It was an overcast day, so the lighting was dim and unusual. My father was lying on the bed in the fetal position with his back to me. From behind me, my mother picked me up and laid me in between them. He did not roll over to see me; he just lay there motionless. For about ten minutes, I laid with them and listened to them cry. I waited for an explanation as to what was happening, but it never came. For the remainder of the day I would leave and return to this room only to find them in the same position with the same look in their eyes.

One short week later, I finally got the answer to my question when I watched my father drive away to start a new life. I stood there sobbing and calling his name as he got into the car. As he backed out of the driveway, I tried to make eye contact with him in hopes that he might change his mind. Hysterically, I screamed at the top of my lungs when I realized he didn't see me. As he pulled forward and drove past the front of our house, I waved my hands in the air to try and get his attention. He never even turned his head. I could hear my mother from inside the house calling for me to come to the kitchen. What could be in the kitchen that would matter more than what was happening on the porch? Shutting her voice out of my mind, I continued to call my father back to me as he drove further and further off into the distance. After standing there for what seemed like an eternity, I made my way to my mother who was standing in the kitchen with a peanut butter sandwich in her hand. She handed it to me with tears in her eyes and left me alone.

In the three minutes it took for my dad to get into his car and drive out of my life, something horrible happened deep within my heart. It was a pain that is indescribable. It felt like my heart had been put through a meat grinder. My spirit was shattered and my very soul was crushed in a way that I have never been able to put into words. Things that I had never given much thought to such as breathing, standing, walking and eating suddenly became torturously difficult to carry on. I did not even have the strength to hold my head up or keep my eyes open. Perhaps it was because there was no real reason in my mind for anything at all. A cloud of hopelessness covered my eyes and mind, making it almost impossible to endure each minute of the day.

Six-and-a-half-year-old boys are not equipped to wrestle emotionally for a sound mind or a will to go on living. These things are taken for granted. Having been stripped of both, I became numb and incoherent. I ran a high fever and began throwing up violently. My mother rushed me to the doctor.

Diagnosis Murder

The doctor gave the explanation that all doctors give when this happens, "This child has just suffered a traumatic event and it's not unusual for such a reaction to occur." He told my mother to take me home and make sure I got plenty of rest.

In recent years, I have often pondered looking that doctor up and suing him for malpractice. You see if he had taken the time to check my pulse, he would have surely found the cause for my fever and vomiting. If he had put his stethoscope to my chest and listened, he would have known for certain why breathing was so difficult for me. You see, if he had of done these things he would have found that I was dead.

I was dead before I came to meet my mother in the kitchen. I was dead on the way to the doctor's office and I was dead on arrival. In fact, for the next twenty years I was a walking dead man. The only two emotions that my physical body comprehended were anger and depression. Though my body continued to grow, my heart had perished within me. At the age of twenty-six, I reasoned like a six-year-old boy. My emotions were unstable and out of control. When things didn't go my way, I threw temper tantrums and annihilated anything and anyone standing in my path. My actions and reactions resembled those of a small child. Six-year-old boys destroy toys and demolish trinkets, but twenty-six-year-old men with six-year-old hearts destroy worlds and demolish lives.

You see, the doctor had made a ghastly mistake in his diagnosis. It was not rest and relaxation that would make the difference. I needed to be raised from the dead.

A Deathly Decision

On the day my father left me, I made a decision that would ultimately keep me in a state of death for the next twenty years. I decided that I didn't need love in my life. Year after year, I followed this covenant I had made with myself and year after year, I became more and more empty.

By the time I turned eighteen, I was in a continuous state of deep depression. Many of my days were spent alone in my room staring at the walls with a hopelessness inside me that is beyond explanation. Waves of loneliness swept over my soul and swallowed my spirit. Getting out of bed in the morning was not only difficult, but useless. There was no purpose in my life. Nothing mattered to me. I was just waiting to die.

One day, I remember hearing my mother talking to someone on the phone about me, and she told this person that I just needed to find someone to love me. Perhaps she was right, I thought. Maybe I did need love. Maybe that decision I made so many years ago was the cause of all my pain. I was lonely, and if I were to find the right girl, everything could change for me. I envisioned what having that special someone would be like. I dreamed of how my life would finally have fulfillment and purpose. The pain of my life had brought me to rock bottom and I was finally willing to renounce my decision about not needing love.

I began searching for the perfect girlfriend. I wanted a girl who would love me for me, a girl whose heart would be solely dedicated to me and no one else. The problem was that the moment I found a girlfriend who truly loved me this way, I only felt better for a few months. Once the newness had worn off, I was back to my same old depressed and empty self. I went through several more girlfriends before I realized that it just wasn't working. Nothing I did was able to make this desolate feeling go away.

Before I knew it, I was on an all-out quest to find love. I began searching for it in everyone I met. The problem was that I didn't really know for what I was hunting. I had never really encountered love before. In fact, I wasn't even sure what it was that I had renounced twenty years ago. How would I know if I found it? What did it look like? How did it feel? Where should I look for it?

It wasn't as though I didn't have love in my life at all. My mother loved me, and I knew that. I had friends who loved me, and even some of my relatives, but I still felt the same way inside. Perhaps love wasn't all it was cracked up to be. If I had it and I still felt the same way, something wasn't working. Truthfully I found the *experience of love* to be a huge let-down. Once again I was faced with my earlier decision to scrap love altogether. What's the point?

After several years of this agonizing expedition, I came to a point of total surrender. I gave up. I threw my hands in the air and let go of everything. It was on that day that I opened my heart to the very thing that I had avoided all my life. It was a mixture between revelation and desperation. Alone in my Los Angeles apartment while lying in my bed late at night, I asked Jesus into my heart. I can remember the feeling of absolute fulfillment flowing through my spirit. I knew then, that I had found the answer to life, and in that very moment everything changed! Suddenly I felt fulfilled and not alone. The emptiness drained away and it was replaced with the creator of the universe. My life suddenly had purpose and my future was bright. All the hopelessness I was saturated in slowly trickled away and for the first time in almost twenty years I was ALIVE.

For about two months.

Then, believe it or not, in just about eight weeks I was right back in the same boat. A title wave of hopelessness and emptiness rolled in and covered my heart. Other than the knowledge of where I would go after I died; nothing had changed. I was still living in darkness. I was still plagued with the same sensation of uselessness that followed me all my life. Only my afterlife was affected, but my *now-life* was completely unchanged. Though I had found Jesus, I hadn't found love, or at least I hadn't found the side of love that I was missing.

I knew that the Bible said that "God is love" so I began a long and exhaustive search of the Scriptures in an effort to find what I had overlooked. I wanted to experience love more than ever before, and I was willing to do whatever it took to find it. After many months of meticulous study, I finally began to uncover the truth about love. What I found was unexpected and surprising.

Love Is Not Self-Seeking

The Bible rarely, if ever, talks about receiving love. The *experience of love* is not when you receive it, but when you GIVE IT. There is nothing honorable about me admitting that I needed someone to love me. Even a baby knows that. Having someone to love you is NOT the equivalent of you living in love. The only way to live in love is to be the lover. True joy and fulfillment come through loving people, not through finding someone to love you.

Because of the fact that our world has turned this extremely important aspect of love upside down, we have become a generation of dead people. We have taken the most beautiful and indispensable gift in life and turned it into the exact opposite of truth. We have turned it into an instrument of death. This tangled and distorted viewpoint has soaked its way through every crevice of our religion as well.

> ✝
> *The experience of love is not when you receive it, but when you GIVE IT.*

We shop for churches that will feed us, and the moment we don't feel full, we leave. We can't even decide whether or not to attend a service unless we know for sure that there is something in it for us. If we drop out for a few weeks, we become angry because no one called us to see where we were on Sunday. When we visit a new church, we judge it by how nice everyone was to us. Did they talk to us? Did they invite us back? Did they follow up with us after we filled out the visitors' card? Churches have now begun to advertise that they will "love you" if you show up. It's become a slogan for success in the ministry. If you want to build a church you have to make people feel that they are loved.

> ✝
>
> *True joy and fulfillment come through loving people, not through finding someone to love you.*

The Greatest Deception Of All Time

I believe that this subject is one of the greatest deceptions concerning love. Selfishness is not only incapable of loving but it's the cause of every terrible thing on Earth. It's the root of every problem and struggle in our lives. Selfishness is the cause of depression and suicide. It's the reason for divorce and child abandonment. Every crime ever committed has selfishness at its very core. What is even more astonishing to me is that we now say "until you can learn to love yourself, you can't love anyone else." This is preposterous! Jesus Christ said, "No man hates himself." The problem is that we already *do* love ourselves.

The pimply-faced teenager who stands in the mirror and cries uncontrollably is not crying because he hates himself, he is crying because he loves himself. If he hated me, and I had pimples, he would be tickled to death about it. People don't commit suicide because they hate themselves, they do it because they love themselves so much that they want to put themselves out of their misery. If they truly hated themselves, they would endure the hardship as a self-imposed punishment.

People who are considered "high maintenance" because they get offended easily are the most selfish people of all. The reason they get offended is because they are more concerned with how *they feel* about what someone said, then they are about what was said and why. Anytime someone's life is about them, they constantly take offense at everyone else. Their entire heart, mind, and soul are focused on themselves.

This is the most lustful generation America has ever seen. Love gives. Lust takes! The nature of lust is selfishness. Most people can't even fall in love with someone unless there is an initial lust in the air to begin with. It's the prerequisite to love for millions of people today. Unless we have sex with a person we can't even begin to have feelings of love for them. I am amazed at how many people have never fallen in love without first sleeping with the person. Most people don't even think it's possible.

A Self-Seeking God?

At every point where our perception and understanding of *love* is desecrated, we can be certain that our view of God will be affected in the exact same way. Whatever we believe about *love,* we ultimately believe about God. Over the years we have redefined the heart of God in a way that depicts Him as being the ultimate self-seeker in the universe. Then we rationalize to ourselves that it's okay for God to be like that, because He is God. It

Nobody likes a selfish person, and nobody likes a selfish God.

has grown out of control in our thinking and ultimately is the reason why so many people just won't give their hearts to Him. Nobody likes a selfish person, and nobody likes a selfish God.

In the next several pages, we are going to cover some topics that might make you feel a bit uneasy. You might be surprised at how saturated your thinking has become with this vision of a selfish God. The good news is that the revelation of truth that you are about to receive has the power to set you free forever if you decide in your mind now that you'll read this with an open heart. Buckle your seatbelt and get comfortable.

God Does Not Demand His Own Way

One of the most basic principles that we have to understand when it comes to the heart of God is that He has given us choice. Choice is the very thing that separates us from the animal kingdom. It's the part of us that is truly in His image. Not only has God given us this wonderful gift, but He also values and respects our choices. He waits eagerly to see what choice we will make and He has promised to go with us and bless us along the way. Our choices belong to us, and there is no part of Him that is tempted to take them away.

Our choices belong to us, and there is no part of Him that is tempted to take them away.

Many Christians are terrified of making a choice for fear that the choice they make will not be the "GOD CHOICE." It's as though they believe that whenever they are faced with a menu of options in their life there is only "one" that is in God's will and all the others are not. This is why so many people simply don't make choices at all. They pray and fast in an effort to get God to reveal *His choice* to them and until they are certain that they've heard right, they just do nothing.

Understand, loved ones, if God wanted you to always go with His one perfect choice, then you really don't have choice at all. When Adam was naming the animals, the Bible says that whatever he named them, that's what they were called. God gave that choice to Adam, and whatever Adam decided, God went with it, too. There was not one perfect "God choice" when it came to a Zebra or a Giraffe. Adam could have been afraid that He might miss God when naming the Buffalo, but Adam knew that the choice was his and the only wrong choice was to not make a choice at all.

Obviously, when it comes to sin, that is a bad choice. I am not talking about things like that. I'm talking about whether or not to stay at your job, or buy a used car, or what outfit to wear in the morning. These things are up to you and God likes it that way. He will not decide these things for you. He waits on you to choose and then He promises to bless you once you do.

Do not think that God must always have His way in everything. While there are certainly things that are in His will, He never demands to always have His own way. There are millions of things that He leaves completely up to you. Remember that when God does have a will, it's not because He wants you to submit to it in order to make Him feel superior or to prove to Him that He is God. His will is always with your best interest in mind.

In spite of what many people might believe, God will never "take control over you." There is never a point when the Holy Spirit will overpower you and your choices. Though thousands of people claim that this is what is happening, you can be certain that it's not. Don't waste your time praying for God to do this because it will never happen. You were created in His image and part of that image is "self-control." In fact, it's one of the fruits of the Spirit. When you have His Holy Spirit living inside of you, you'll know it by your own self-control and not by Him controlling you. He isn't self-seeking, He is YOU seeking.

...if God wanted you to always go with His one perfect choice, then you really don't have choice at all.

Did you know that God's Spirit has even subjected Himself to your control? I am not saying that you can tell Him to do this or that and He will do it, but I am saying that He will wait for you to give your personal approval before He does certain things in

He waits on you to choose and then He promises to bless you once you do.

your life. He won't force Himself on you. This is why Paul told the Corinthians that only one or two should give a message in tongues at the most. He was telling these people

that the Holy Spirit's working is subject to their control. They are responsible for their own actions. God doesn't just move on someone and cause someone to uncontrollably spout off a message in tongues against their will. They are the ones that decide when and where to do it.

The "If You Love Me, I'll Love You" Mentality

Many people believe that the moment they accepted Jesus Christ into their hearts, God extended His love to them and began to work in their lives. It might interest you to know that God was working in your life long before you ever opened your heart to Him. He loved you before you were even created. He doesn't wait for you to love Him before He extends His love to you. It's always been there and it will always be there. His love is never dependant upon your reciprocation.

God even works in the lives of people who hate Him. He gives gifts to people who completely deny His existence. You did not receive your gifts when you came into the body of Christ; you received them when you were created. Though you might learn to use them best after knowing the giver Himself, you still had them from birth. A gift is a gift. Nothing is required in return. It's given out of love and not out of a desire to receive something back.

Though your love for God is very important to Him, and He values it from every part of His heart, you also need to understand that God is not a needy love junkie. Many people try to bargain with Him by holding out their devotion like a carrot in front of His face. They will use their love for Him as a negotiation tool to get what they want. He will never be moved or manipulated by promises of dedication and adoration. Your love must always be free just as His is. We do this because we believe in our hearts that He is self-seeking. Make no mistake about it, God's love is not for what He can get, but it's for what He can give.

> *He will never be moved or manipulated by promises of dedication and adoration.*

God is not in competition for your love. I am always mystified when I hear people boastfully say, "I love God more than my wife." The only way to love God more than your spouse is to love God through your spouse. Your husband or wife would be the direct recipient of that love. Don't ever think that He will even raise such a question. He is quite all right with you giving all of yourself over to your mate. He isn't insecure.

Many people try to make God out to be an adulterer. They do it by carrying on a separate secret affair in their prayer closets while their marriage partner sits alone in the living room. There is nothing wrong with alone time with God, but when it becomes a wedge between you and your spouse; it's not what God desires. Everything about Him is found inside of your husband or wife. If you want real relationship with Him, you must find it in them.

God Is Not Affected By Your Sin

God also does not wait for you to repent before He loves you. Repentance is always in your best interest because all sin destroys your life and depletes your joy, but it's important for you to know that God doesn't hold back His love for you until you repent. In other words, He is not waiting for you to get your act together. He loves you now regardless of where you are in your life. His love never stops the moment you hurt His feelings. Believe it or not, He is hard to hurt.

He is not waiting for you to get your act together. He loves you now regardless of where you are in your life.

Jesus forgave a woman caught in adultery before she even asked for forgiveness. His love for her was not dependent upon her repentance. Because He loved her, He told her to "go and sin no more." He didn't wait to see if she would sin again before He loved her. He loved her before, during and after she sinned. What a wonderful message!

Many of us have been taught that when we sin, God is personally offended. We have come to believe that He sees all sin as how it pertains to Him. That's pretty self-seeking, if you ask me.

Understand that God's loathing of sin has nothing to do with how it affects Him. He despises sin because it destroys His children. When we come to Him begging for forgiveness for something we did, His forgiveness is not even the issue. The real issue is whether or not you can forgive yourself for sabotaging your own life. Don't think for a moment that He is offended and mortified because of what your sin *did to Him*. It's not about Him. He is in anguish because of what your sin *did to you*!

My wife and I have written an easy to remember poem for our children, "No doors, no drawers, no chairs, no stairs." In a way, it's a law in our home. I came up with this because I have found that the four most dangerous things to a child are doors, drawers, chairs and stairs. Ninety percent of the time, when one of my children get injured it's because they were playing with one of these four things.

When they get hurt playing on the stairs, do I get personally offended? Of course not, because it's not about me. I'm really not even angry at the stairs. The pain in my heart is born out of a sincere selfless love for my children. I hate what stairs do to kids when they fall down them. This is God's heart when it comes to your sin. He paid for and destroyed the power of sin because He loves you, not because He was so selfishly concerned with how it affected Him.

> ✝
> *God is not concerned with how He looks when you fail.*

I am amazed at how many of us try our best not to sin because we are representing Jesus. It's as though we think that Jesus' primary concern is how He looks. We mourn when famous Christian figures fall into public disgrace because we think it makes Jesus look bad. This is the furthest thing from God's heart!

God is not concerned with how He looks when you fail. His concern is ALWAYS about you. He is never personally embarrassed by your faults and shortcomings. His reputation means nothing to Him. It's *you* He cares about. He is just as grieved when you fall, as He is when your pastor falls. It's not about Him.

If God were so worried about His reputation why would He take all of your sin upon Himself and actually *become sin* in order to set you free? Think about that! God is never self-seeking.

God's Plan and Purpose For You

There is a mentality that many of us have adopted in which we believe that everything God does in our lives has to do with some mastermind plan He has to

God is not looking for servants and messengers; He is looking for sons and daughters!

further His kingdom. Unless we can connect the dots to some sort of Christ advertisement or promotion, we just aren't pleasing God. This misguided mind-set is deep in the hearts of thousands of Christians today, and I truly think that it's born out of our belief that God is self-seeking.

This is the reason why so many people go into the ministry. They sincerely believe that their life means nothing unless they are somehow serving Christ. We even define the Christian walk as, "Serving God." We do this because we think that this is ultimately what God is in this for. We think He wants an entourage of personal slaves and servants. We have been conditioned to think that God wants us to put all our personal desires aside and become His butler. If that's not self-seeking, I honestly don't know what is!

Have you ever stopped to think that God's plan for your life has to do with YOU? His first concern is your happiness and fulfillment. Everything He does is so that you can have life abundant. Every gift He gives you is to enhance your life and bring the most joy possible to you. His kingdom does not benefit one iota until that happens. Understand that God is not looking for servants and messengers; He is looking for sons and daughters! Out of that relationship, you will *become the message.*

There are many pastors in the world who were created to be math teachers, accountants, ski instructors, and fireman, but because they believed that God's main concern was finding people to serve Him, they gave up their purpose in life and joined the ministry. This perhaps is the most grievous thing to the Heart of God because it strangles any possibility of real intimacy. Slaves can only respect their masters, but they never eat with them and share their heart.

Our Acknowledgment Of Unworthiness

When I watch this attitude displayed during a worship service, I can feel the heart of God bleeding deep within me. This mind-set is absolutely devastating to Him. There is no part of His Heart that desires to hear us acknowledge that, "we are not worthy," or "we are filthy and wicked." This is upsetting to Him for several reasons. First of all, the very fact that we believe He gets a *personal rise* out of us recognizing the lowest parts of ourselves is downright cutting to His character. Secondly, it hurts Him deeply because we are literally telling Him that everything His Son accomplished on the cross

There is no part of His Heart that desires to hear us acknowledge that, "we are not worthy,"...

was for nothing. We are denying the righteousness that He freely gave us and we are choosing to wallow in the mud of our past. This is catastrophic!

It is interesting that every place in the Bible when someone fell on their face in the presence of God and declared their shamefulness, God's first words were almost, always, "GET UP!" This behavior doesn't do anything for Him. He can't have relationship with us when we keep doing this. He made you perfect for a reason. Every time we glorify self-loathing we completely miss the Heart of God.

Unfortunately, this attitude has become the politically correct way of thinking in the Church today. People refuse to even receive a pat on the back for a job well done for fear that it will somehow be stealing glory from God. All kind words and compliments are religiously rejected and redirected

> *Every time we glorify self-loathing we completely miss the Heart of God.*

to God. We have come to believe that God expects us to never receive anything without reminding ourselves that it wasn't us but it was all God.

Believe it or not, every time you reject someone's compliment of you, and "give all the glory to God" He doesn't receive an ounce of glory. In fact, God is complimenting you as well. He doesn't need to hear that it was "all Him" especially when you participated. He is proud of you when you accomplish something great and there is no part of His heart that wants "*all the glory.*"

The idea that God always wants all the glory is one of the most self-seeking perceptions we have of Him today. We end our prayers by telling Him "we will be careful to give Him all the glory." Sadly, we believe that this is all He cares about. Nothing could be further from the truth.

Moses came down off the mountain after spending time with God and his face shone with GLORY. God had no problem with that because Moses was His boy. Loved ones, please understand that the Heart of God desires that all His glory be upon His children. He is not in competition with us; He is our greatest promoter. When His glory is on us, He twinkles with delight. I want every wonderful thing about me to be on my children and

God is the same way with you. Though He may never share His glory with someone outside of His family who seeks to possess it for selfish reasons, He is pleased to bathe you in it.

Ask yourself how close you would allow yourself to get with a friend at work that always desired to get all the glory. Would you even talk to such a person? If you wouldn't be friends with a person like that, you won't be friends with a God like that. God's desire is to lift you up, not push you down.

People think this way because they haven't crossed over into the new world of what was accomplished on the cross on their behalf. Everything is different now because of what Christ did! We are now family members. Until this foundational New Testament fact is swallowed by Christians today, they

...the heart of God desires that all His glory be on His children.

will always be stuck in an Old Testament "hired hand" way of thinking. It is imperative that God's heart be viewed as a Father now and not a dictator. Fathers are not self-seeking!

Love Is Not Easily Provoked[10]

As the garage door was closing, and my parents could be heard backing out of the driveway, the excitement in the air began to rise. My youngest brother Brian was peeking through the living room window ready to give the signal the moment they drove out of sight. As soon as the coast was clear, the fun began.

The six of us had created a game with our family dog that I am almost embarrassed to tell you about. His name was Pierre. He was a French Poodle, and he had the nastiest temper I had ever seen. Because of the fact that he was a poodle, it made it all the more fun to provoke him to anger. I guess it was just an oxymoron. The last creature one would expect to act so bold would be a French Poodle. We found it hilarious.

I suppose if he had of been a German Shepard or a Rottweiler, we wouldn't have played such a game, but Pierre could do nothing more than chase us around the room and snip at our heels. French Poodles can't even snap; they snip, and Pierre was the worst tempered, snippiest dog on the block. If dogs could have a short man's complex, he definitely had it.

In the corner of the living room, we had a crushed velvet chair that had flaps that draped to the floor. Pierre would hide under the chair (in absolute fear) while one of us would go around behind the chair. The other five would run around in circles in the middle of the room screaming like maniacs. The kid behind the chair would tilt it backwards without warning and Pierre would dart out and snip the heels of whoever was closest. It was kind of like "musical chairs" only with an angry poodle instead of chairs.

Over and over we did it, and every time that dog came snipping, the sounds of children screaming filled the house. We were careful to give each child a turn as "chair tilter" so that everyone could experience the exhilaration of provoking Pierre. By the time we heard the garage door opening again, this poor dog was on the verge of a heart attack. Seconds later my parents would walk in to a living room full of children diligently doing homework and playing a quiet board game. I thank God to this day that Pierre couldn't speak English. Our parents would have put us in therapy for years for doing such a thing. Actually, if Pierre could have spoken English, I'm quite sure he would have been in therapy.

Love Is Stable

Though human beings are not animals, the similarities in our behavior sometimes make the divisive lines run a bit thin. I'm quite sure that most thinking people would agree that my brothers and sisters and I were clearly the animals in this story.

This illustration, however, is a stunning picture of many marriages in our generation. We call them "*love-hate*" relationships. It's a relationship where one or both people are provoked from one emotion to another in just an instant and for the most ridiculous and shallow reasons. The tension in such a relationship is so thick that you can cut it with a knife, and when the couple is asked why it is this way, they will usually tell you that it's because of their "intense love" for one another. They share the same opinion of love that millions of broken people share.

Giving up self-control is the very essence of addiction.

They believe that true love explodes with waves of emotions that overtake a person and drive them to do things they would not otherwise do. They believe that love is easily provoked.

It would be too easy to reduce the subject of this chapter to "anger" alone. Though it is true that love is not easily provoked to anger, the fact is, love is not easily provoked to anything. Love cannot be moved from one emotion to another. It cannot be content and happy in one moment and be hurled into anger, depression, offense, or lust the next. Love is stable and real and it cannot be controlled.

The issue here is really "control." There is a term in our society that baffles me every time I hear it spoken. It's a label that we put on people who constantly seek to control others. We call them, "control freaks." While there are many people who are controlling and overbearing I am amazed that *they* are the ones being called such a name. If you ask me, the person being controlled is the real freak. It seems to me that a person who willingly gives up their self-control is the person with the real problem. Why would anyone want to do this?

There is something about losing control that becomes strangely addictive. This is a common thread that runs throughout every addiction known to man. Giving up self-control is the very essence of addiction. This is why it is so hard to recover from things like alcoholism, pornography and drug addiction. Having no control becomes a convenient pattern of life and the prospect of regaining self-control feels almost unnatural. It takes too much personal responsibility. It requires us to stand on our own two feet and be accountable. It is much easier to lie back and allow others to control us. It doesn't take any work.

Our view of love in this generation has been so distorted that we actually expect a loss of control. We even measure love's authenticity by how much control is lost in the midst of the relationship. In fact, love has been turned, tied and twisted around so much that we now call it, "*falling*" in love. We actually relieve ourselves of all personal responsibility. It's looked upon as an accident that was unavoidable.

...love has been turned, tied and twisted around so much that we now call it, "falling" in love.

It's not surprising to see that people who subscribe to this mentality often "*fall*" out of love as quickly as they "*fell*" in love. After all, accidents happen, and whom can you blame when love is involved?

Provoke:

To move a person to action or feeling or to summon something into being by so moving a person. To incite to anger. To stir to action or feeling. To give rise to; evoke. To bring about deliberately, induce, provoke a fight. (Dictionary.com)

It is amazing to see how often my own children test the waters with me in an effort to routinely re-evaluate the stability of my love for them. To put it simply, they provoke me. They purposefully edge their foot across a line that I've set for them while glancing my way to see my reaction. Will I lose my temper? Will I scream at them? Will I just sit there and do nothing? What will I do? They are testing me to see exactly what my limits are. What they are really doing is checking to see if there is any point of control that they might gain over me. They want to know if their actions can manipulate my behavior. If I blow my temper, they are the ones who gain that control over me. If I sit there and do nothing, they have established that they can override my rules for their life without having any consequence. From the day they were born until the present, they are always testing me to see where I stand.

I have watched families where a three-year-old child has complete control over his mother and father. It's almost comical to observe. Psychologists tell us that it's just the child starving for attention, but I don't think it stops there. I honestly believe that the child is starving for control. Many children play their parents like a fiddle. The parents are so provoked by them that the child literally decides the mood of the home from moment to moment. The parents become like a couple of puppets in the child's hands. Whatever the child wants to happen can be manipulated into existence simply because mother and father are easily provoked. At the end of the day both parents blame their love for their child as the reason why they were provoked by him so easily.

> *Children will not give their heart to a mother or father that they can control.*

The downside of this little game is that while "little Billy" may be able to control his parents, Billy also has an unavoidable inner sense that parents who are provoked are parents who don't love. Children need stability in their parents. They have the truth of love written on their hearts, and that truth is that *love is not easily provoked.* Ironically, they test it and try it in an effort to gain control over them, but every part of that child needs his parents to stand strong and not be controlled. The very moment that the parents cave into manipulation, intimacy is strangled to death. Children will not give their heart to a mother or father that they can control. There is no security in that. They need something bigger than a *screaming, angry daddy* or a *sobbing, worried mother.* Children are looking for something bigger than they are, and until they find it, they will never share their true self with their parents. This is precisely why kids who can provoke their parents are always blatantly disrespectful to them.

If you were to see a house teetering back and forth every time a slight breeze brushed up against it, would you consider moving into that house during a storm? Of course you wouldn't. Children will no sooner put their hearts in the hands of teetering parents who are emotionally blown and tossed back and forth. True love is never provoked!

The Provoked Eventually Provoke

Children are not really the ones to blame in a scenario like I've just described. For the most part, this is a learned behavior. Their parents taught them, and their parents learned it from their parents. The upside-down belief that love *does* provoke has been passed from generation to generation.

Parents try to provoke their children in a number of ways. They'll use fear or shame to get their children to obey. Threats of pain and punishment are always waved in the child's face. Many times guilt is the great provoker, and with some parents; the threat of withholding love and affection does the trick. Whatever the technique, the mentality behind it is the same. It all comes from a heart that doesn't understand the truth about love.

> *The upside-down belief that love does provoke has been passed from generation to generation.*

Before long, we become an entire society of broken people who have mastered the art of pushing the right buttons in people to get what we want. Unfortunately, we never feel a sense of security in any one relationship and without that, we are empty and alone.

Eventually we build up walls to defend ourselves against other people who might attempt to *push our buttons.* We learn to introduce ourselves in a way that warns people not to get too close. We boast about our nasty temper and brag about how we sometimes "*lose it*" and "*see red*" when someone makes us mad. We let people know up front that we get offended easily because we are very sensitive. Many of us use the *martyr syndrome* to introduce ourselves. The suffering victim of life usually gets what he wants from anyone because everyone is terrified of putting yet another straw on the back of an emotional camel.

> *Some people become experts in provoking others. They are known as being "provocative."*

Some people become experts in provoking others. They are known as being "provocative." We are all familiar with this term. When we hear it, we immediately associate it with someone we know personally. We might even have a list of people that fall into this category. Just pick up any one of the thousands of women's magazines that promote this way of living. Even department store catalogs are laced with it. Turn the television on and watch it for five minutes and you will see provocativeness in every commercial, sitcom, and movie. We are truly a generation who not only believes that *love is easily provoked* but we are a nation that wants it no other way.

My heart grieves deeply for the women in this generation. They have been taught that *love is provoked* from the day they were born. To thousands of women, it becomes an addiction. Their entire life is surrendered to this false understanding. Many get caught up in the world of exotic dancing, because it feeds them a false sense of power over men. The power of provocativeness becomes a drug that eventually poisons their hearts and eats their souls.

Sometimes we make the mistake of thinking that only the "Barbie" looking women are the ones who have believed this lie. I have found, however, that this tangled way of believing exists in just about every woman alive, to some extent.

Women who are overweight or who just don't meet the physical standards that this world has set for them are also victimized by the *love is provoked* mentality. They are victimized by it because they constantly feel like they can't compete. This feeling alone is evidence that they too believe that love is provoked. Many times they feel like they don't have anything to offer anyone unless they could somehow lose the weight or get plastic surgery in an effort to become more provocative. If they find themselves attracted to a man who isn't interested in them, they often wish in their hearts that they could be sexier in order to provoke him into a relationship.

> *We are truly a generation who not only believes that love is easily provoked but we are a nation that wants it no other way.*

Once perhaps the weight is lost and the makeover has been completed, the woman finally feels good about herself. She stirs with excitement when a man at the mall stops to check her out as she walks by. That look gives her validation as a woman and she suddenly feels beautiful for the first time. The irony of all this is that the man's look has absolutely NOTHING to do with her.

I wish that I could explain to millions of women that when they wear a high cut skirt and a low cut blouse and a man approaches them for a date, THAT IS NOT LOVE! It is simply a man being provoked by their provocative attire. His response has absolutely nothing to do with her as a person. Nevertheless, she feels good about herself, because someone was successfully provoked by her. She feels this way because she is no different from anyone in today's world. She believes that love is easily provoked.

What Are We Provoked By?

We are provoked by what already exists in our heart. If we are lustful in our heart, we are provoked by sexually provocative things. If we are angry, we are provoked to anger. If we are selfish, we will be provoked to taking offense at everything. Whatever already exists within us is the very thing that we will be provoked towards.

People who are not lustful, are rarely provoked to having an affair on their spouse. People who do not burn with anger, rarely, if ever, blow their temper. People who always put others before themselves are almost impossible to offend.

Back To The Heart Of God

By now, you are probably wondering why we have gone on such a long journey into the world of provoking. It is important for us to understand the level in which we have been deceived when it comes to *love*. Remember that at whatever point we are misled concerning love, we will also be misled concerning the Heart of God. If we see love through a cracked lens, we will ultimately see our God through that same lens.

I want to confront some common Christian notions that I believe have evolved straight out of our heart's belief of an easily-provoked God. You might be surprised at how much of our religion has been poisoned by our misguided perceptions of love.

God's Heart Is Not Provoked Or Controlled

At first glance, I would suspect that most, if not all people reading this book would totally agree. When we read it or hear it spoken, it sounds so solid and true, but when we reflect on our behavior and our actions in daily life, our heart reveals something entirely different.

Many people, without even thinking about it, pray with a phony religious tone to their voices, hoping that it will somehow have the ring of holiness that God is looking for. They might even speak in "King James Version" because it sounds righteous and dignified. When they talk that way, they feel like they are reaching God in a language the He simply cannot resist. Perhaps God will hear them and mistake them for one of the apostles, and accidentally give them what they are asking for.

> ✝
> *We act out what we think God wants to see and hear, and hopefully He will be fooled into doing what we want Him to do.*

I want to say that I completely understand that with many people this is a matter of culture. They are simply approaching God with the understanding that they have been given of Him. This is their way of showing God the respect that they genuinely believe He deserves. I am not poking fun at or disrespecting anyone who sincerely falls into this category. I am, however, confronting those of us who have developed an *attitude of acting*. This attitude is the direct result of our twisted perceptions of the Heart of God.

God is not provoked by the Shakespearean dialect of the King James Bible. He is also not moved by religious tones of holiness that many of us conjure up in an effort to spur Him to action. Thousands of us have been taught that this is how we get answers to prayers. We *act out* what we think God wants to see and hear, and hopefully He will be fooled into doing what we want Him to do.

I cannot recall how many times I have watched people add that *quivering-weepy-wailing* sound to their voice during an intercessory prayer meeting. They will literally *act out* their prayer with a fake animated cry and a phony whimper before the Lord. It's as though many of us have come to believe that if we perform passion and mourning, God will be stupid enough to fall for it. If someone walks up behind such a person in the midst of their provoking *episode* and taps them on the shoulder, the "sobbing prayer warrior" looks up with a *straight face* and *dry eyes*.

> †
> *...many of us have come to believe that if we perform passion and mourning, God will be stupid enough to fall for it.*

There are many beautiful and authentic times when people sincerely wail and mourn during their prayer. When these times come in the context of real life, we should embrace them and let ourselves go. When it comes from a broken heart that is calling on God to bring healing and comfort, it is truly moving to Him. However, when we find ourselves faking it in an effort to manipulate God, we are declaring our belief in an easily-provoked Heavenly Father.

Unfortunately, many of us today have become expert actors on a quest to control the hand of God. We read that God desires us to enter His presence with boldness, so we act out boldness the best we know. Though we are actually under guilt and condemnation and our heart is terrified of Him, we do our best to portray the character we think He wants to see. Then we learn that God desires us to have a humble heart so we do our best to depict humility when we come to Him. Some of us have heard that God is a God of passion, so we throw our hands in the air and strain ourselves in an attempt to create counterfeit passion. When all else fails, we do what we all have learned to do as a last resort. We quote Scripture to God in an effort to force Him to follow through with what He "said He would do." We might even remind Him that, "we know He is not a liar" so He has to do it.

Loved ones, please understand that all of these little methods we use in our religion are nothing but pure manipulation. We know it when we do it, but until we are actually confronted with the truth of what we are doing, most of us will just go on acting out a play for a God we believe is easily provoked. This is exactly why we do these things. Our perception of who He is has been turned upside-down in our hearts. Because of the fact that we believe that love is easily provoked, we naturally believe that God is easily provoked. The moment we fix that lie, we will be free to be ourselves in His presence because we will know that He always hears us because He loves us.

> *We quote Scripture to God in an effort to force Him to follow through with what He "said He would do."*

Sinners In The Hands Of An Angry God

I wonder how much of your heart believes that God is angry. Most of us were raised with a God that was either angry or just plain disappointed. I have found that an astonishing number of Christians truly think that God is fuming with anger at them. They are terrified of ever meeting Him.

Not only was our generation raised with an angry God, but, we were raised to believe that God is *easily angered*. It doesn't take much to set Him off. We quote Old Testament passages that seem to depict Him as a volcano waiting to erupt. We study every incident where people were put to death in the Bible and use it as evidence that God is easily angered. Then we hold it over the heads of anyone who might be thinking of leaving the Church or doing something sinful. It becomes the dark cloud that follows American Christians around wherever they go.

Not only do we believe in an angry God, but we depend on it. He *has* to be short tempered, or we might just go out and sin. It may not taste very good when we are alone and imagining it as it pertains to us personally, but when someone crosses us or betrays us, it sure comes in handy. Christianity in America truly believes that we need an angry God in order to keep people in line.

Fear has become the glue that holds the Church together today. We depend on fear for everything. If ministries were to eliminate fear from their midst, I believe that they would literally cave in upon themselves. The entire infrastructure of Christianity in our nation is held together by it.

> *Fear has become the glue that holds the Church together today.*

Everything we practice in our religion is laced with the poison of fear. Offering sermons, altar calls and even salvation sermons rely on fear to motivate people. What is worse, we now teach people that it is right and good to be terrified of God.

I have watched in amazement while pastors will preach a sermon on the love of God, and just before the altar call they will switch horses in the middle of the stream and toss out a few terrifying statements about how God will bring disaster upon you and your family if you don't repent. Though it makes for a great altar call, it guarantees that people will never open their hearts completely to Him. They are terrified of a God who is easily angered.

Love Is Not Easily Provoked

Remember that we are provoked by what already exists within us. My question to you is this, what is the point of the death and resurrection of Christ? If God's wrath is still churning and fuming, what was the point of the cross? Evidently nothing has changed through the death of His Son.

I want you to understand something before we continue on. The wrath of God was quenched at the cross! He is NOT angry with you. There is nothing IN Him that burns with anger, so He is not provoked to anger. You can stand securely on this fact.

God Will Never Turn His Face From You

The idea that there is a point where God will turn His face from you if you do something wrong has been held over the heads of almost every Christian in America at one time or another. Make no mistake about it. *God will NEVER turn His face from you*! His eyes are constantly on you.

It is true that God cannot look upon sin because He is so Holy. This is why He turned His face from His Son when Jesus was on the cross. All the sin of the world was on Christ at that time. God turned His face ONCE, and then NEVER AGAIN.

If God is still turning His face from us, then the blood of Jesus didn't take away our sins. To even say that God will do this is an anti-Christ mentality. It denies the work of Christ on the cross. If anyone tells you that God will do this, you can know for sure that it is a lie from the pit of Hell. It will simply never happen. Don't ever worry that God is not watching over you. His eyes are on you constantly. You are everything to Him. Nothing you ever do will cause Him to be provoked in a way that He would turn away from you.

If God is still turning His face from us, then the blood of Jesus didn't take away our sins.

God Is Not Provoked By Your Giving

God will not love you any more if you give everything than He will, if you give nothing. Many times we confuse *consequence* with *blessing*. In the spiritual realm there are laws that have been set up that apply to every living human being on Earth. Just like the law of gravity applies to Christians, but also Buddhists, Hindus, Muslims and even Atheists. The laws that govern

> *...our entire religion has painted a picture of an easily provoked God who can't control Himself every time we give.*

giving in the spiritual realm are not *blessing*, they are *consequence*. When you or anyone gives, it does come back to them. It's true with everyone, not just Christians. If you jump off of a building you are not being *cursed* when you hit the ground, you are experiencing the *consequence* of the law of gravity.

It's important to understand these things about giving, because our entire religion has painted a picture of an easily provoked God who can't control Himself every time we give. It's just not true. I have found that most modern day Christian philosophies are based on the belief that God can be provoked. God is not provoked by your giving.

God is more grieved by those who try to provoke him through their constant counting of every dollar in an effort to make absolutely sure that they gave the exact required amount of 10%. He is also grieved by those who beat themselves up because they just fell short of 10%. Any time our contentment in God is based on whether or not we are caught up on our tithe, we are not only depersonalizing God but we are declaring that He is easily provoked. We have been taught to expect nothing from God unless we first "pay" our tithe. Many of us have been told that "God can't bless us" unless we pay our tithe. This is preposterous!

It's interesting that God, Himself says that He sends rain on the righteous and unrighteous alike. He provides for the sinners as well as the saints. Even those who are wicked and unbelieving receive blessings from God. It's funny that once a person becomes a Christian, they suddenly can't ever receive blessings from their God unless they are caught up on their giving. If this were true, then we would all be better off if we just stayed wicked.

God is not provoked by someone who stupidly gives his whole paycheck in the offering, and then leaves his family with nothing to live on. People are encouraged to think this way, because they have been taught that such action will provoke God into giving them a miracle. It is otherwise known as "Tempting the Lord."

When Jesus was in the wilderness being tempted by the Devil, Satan took Him to the highest point of the temple and quoted a Scripture to Him that said God would command His angels to guard Him, and not allow His foot to strike a stone. Jesus was being tempted with the exact same thing that modern day Christians are tempted with in the Church. We are tempted with *making it happen*, rather than just having faith that if it did happen, God would provide.

The verse that Satan quoted to Jesus was saying that if Jesus ever fell off or was pushed off of a high place, God would send His angels to protect Him from harm. Satan was suggesting to Jesus that He JUMP off the temple. This is precisely what 95% of offering sermons do today. They encourage poor well-meaning Christians to "tempt God" by jumping off of their monetary temple to their financial death. We teach people this because we believe that God is provoked by it. We believe that God is forced to come through

> ✝
> *God will not love you
> any more if you give
> everything than He will,
> if you give nothing.*

because He did for the poor widow who gave all she had to the prophet. IF He did it for her, then He must do it for us.

God is not provoked when people purposefully put themselves in financially dangerous positions in the name of "faith." There are many accounts in Scripture where someone was down to their last penny and when they gave it, God created a miracle. The moment we *create* such a situation by sabotaging our own lives in an effort to force the hand of God to perform a miracle, we are basically "jumping off the temple." This grieves His heart because it assumes that it is in His will that we always live on the edge of total destruction. The heart of your Father is that you are stable in every area of your life. Ironically, many people truly believe that God gets a kick out of seeing His children between a rock and a hard place. Strangely, we have come to believe that this is the only time when God can work in our lives.

> †
> *God is not provoked when people purposefully put themselves in financially dangerous positions in the name of "faith."*

Sometimes life brings you to a place of devastation, and the promise of your Father is, when you get there He will hold you up and deliver you. Manufacturing that situation on purpose is "tempting" or "provoking" the Lord. Why take something that is so beautiful and natural and force it into existence before its time? Your Father doesn't need to be provoked into helping you. He is there all the time for you.

God Is Not Overly Sensitive & Easily Offended

There are two connotations for the word *sensitive*. Ironically, each one is contradictory to the other. They stand at opposite ends of the universe. One person gets personally offended so easily that everyone has to walk on eggshells when they are in the room. The other person is sensitive to the needs of others. Amazingly, we call both people *sensitive*. The first person is so

—————— † ——————
We have become
absolutely petrified of
"grieving the Holy Spirit."
—————— —————

self-absorbed that they can't see anyone else but themselves, so everything that happens in their presence either hurts them or offends them. The second person is so *others-absorbed* that they rarely get personally offended, because their eyes are focused on the hearts of others and not on how everything pertains to self.

For the most part, I think that the majority of Christians honestly believe that the Holy Spirit of God is like the first person. We have become absolutely petrified of "grieving the Holy Spirit." In fact, most honest people will admit that they secretly feel like they have hurt the Holy Spirit more times than they can count.

I can personally remember a time in my life when I was petrified the moment the preacher said those infamous words; "The Spirit of God is in this room tonight." I felt like the audience was being encouraged to be sensitive to the Spirit because the Spirit was so sensitive. It seemed like if anyone stepped out of line or said something wrong, the Holy Spirit would run, lock Himself in the bathroom and cry His eyes out.

When I took an honest look at my heart, I came to one conclusion. If the Holy Spirit were a person I knew at work or met at a coffee shop, I wouldn't even like Him. I try not to purposefully surround myself with people with whom I feel like I have to walk on eggshells. It's just too mentally exhausting.

Understand that God's Spirit is the second definition of sensitive. He is sensitive to your needs. He knows everything about you. He waits for the perfect time before speaking to you, and when He does, He speaks in the perfect tone and

The God's Honest Truth

says the perfect thing. Every part of the Holy Spirit is focused on your heart.

Don't ever worry that you have hurt His feelings. In fact, He doesn't want you to. Believe it or not, the Holy Spirit is extremely hard to hurt. He is an amazingly secure person, and He has patience with you because He knows your heart better than you do. People get hurt when they don't understand. He understands everything because He lives inside of you.

You cannot provoke the Holy Spirit to grief easily. His emotions are stable because He loves you and love is not easily provoked. Stop worrying that you've hurt Him and just know that He loves you. You can rest in that knowledge.

Love Keeps No[11] Record Of Wrongs

Before I tell you this story, I want to make a few disclaimers. I feel the need to explain the situation, before I just waltz into the meat of this family chronicle. At the risk of sounding chauvinistic or typical, allow me to tread through the details that preceded this event in an effort to fairly show all sides of what took place.

Our first two children are about sixteen months apart in age. When we had Landin, our oldest, my wife had breastfed her for about six months. We switched her to formula because we had planned a trip to London for our anniversary and it wasn't practical to take the baby. We weaned her several weeks before our departure and left her with her grandmother.

Before we left for London, we found out that we were pregnant again. Ten months later, Sidney was born. My wife had breastfed Sidney for one year, before introducing her to a bottle.

I said all that to say this:

If we add ten months for the first pregnancy, plus six months of breastfeeding, plus ten months for the second pregnancy, plus another twelve months of breastfeeding, we get a little over three years. This is three years and two months of not having a menstrual cycle for my wife. She had forgotten what it was like to experience this, because it had been so long. We both forgot that there was such a thing, until about two weeks after we weaned our second child.

Now the story begins.

One day I was in my office at the church, counseling a married couple. I was dazzling them with my "relationship wisdom" and they were visibly moved. In fact, it looked like I was going to save their marriage in one short hour. As I colorfully described the very essence of marriage and the beauty of *becoming "one,"* I could see that I was getting through to each of them. Little did I know, back at the homestead "*there was a storm a-brewing.*"

Both the man and his wife were already in tears and had made incredible breakthroughs in the short time they were in my office. Just as I was giving a heartfelt discourse on "how to live in the heart of your spouse," my phone rang. Usually I have it on "do not disturb," but occasionally I forget. I immediately apologized for the distraction. They were both understanding and encouraged me to go ahead and answer it.

It was my wife.

The first words out of her mouth were, "I WANT A SEPARATION!" I said, "Excuse me?" She replied, "I've been thinking about it, and I'm not happy in this marriage and I want a separation."

I have heard of the term, "poker face" before, but it wasn't until this very moment that I actually understood its innate purpose and value. With this couple sitting only three feet in front of me, I kept the straightest dignified face I could muster. Because of the fact that I know my wife so well, and this was one hundred percent out of her character, I knew immediately what was happening. I nonchalantly answered back, "Yeah, okay, we'll call you later then, bye-bye," and I hung up. I continued the counseling session (with a bit less enthusiasm than before) and respectfully sent them on their way.

By the time I got home that night, my wife was laughing at herself because she knew what had happened. She apologized several times and explained that she was in the middle of her first menstrual cycle in three years and it came upon her like an unexpected emotional hurricane. I had already figured out what had happened, and we both had a good laugh about it, and then the incident was dropped.

Disarming My Bazooka

It would have been so easy to hide that episode away in the back of my mind until the perfect moment to pull it out and blast her away with it. There were many times where she did something that upset me and the record of this incident would have come in very handy. There have been several occasions where she flat out had me backed against the wall during an argument, and I could have come out firing in her face that mistake she had made. It could have been like owning an atomic bomb. It's a sure win, the moment it has been dropped.

This even gave me the right not only to bring it up, but to also do it myself. Now that she mentioned *divorce* when she was in the midst of an emotional breakdown, I could do the same to her. Every time we had a disagreement I could threaten to leave her or tell her "how unhappy I am in this marriage." After all, I should be allowed to do it, if she did it.

I made a decision that very day that I would never bring this up for the rest of my life. I knew the future possibilities of destruction and separation that could visit us if I had not made that decision. Our entire marriage could have entered a world in which we could have started a countdown to divorce. It was completely in my hands, and by the grace of God I did the right thing.

There were several reasons why I let this go. First of all, *I knew that she didn't mean it.* She was speaking out of an emotional frenzy and not from her heart. I knew that! I knew it because I know her. It wasn't worth holding on to something that we both knew she didn't mean. Secondly, I dropped it because I love her so much and *I didn't want her to continuously feel the regret and shame* of having said what she said. The very thought of that makes me sick in my heart. I wanted instant freedom for her, from that incident. In fact, I put that fire out so fast that we now remember it as being one of the funniest things that has ever happened in our marriage. It's not even looked upon as a dark moment. Finally, I knew that if I had held that episode over her head, *she would have continued doing that very thing* every time she got the slightest bit emotional. It was imperative that I kill that thing immediately, or it would eventually kill both of us.

The File Cabinet Of Today's Love

If I were to ask anyone in today's society if love keeps a record of wrongs, they would unanimously say "YES." Most likely everyone would agree that it shouldn't, but the majority of people would admit that it does nonetheless. What is even worse is that most of us have relieved ourselves from all personal responsibility of doing it. We even say that we can't help it. We tell our spouse or friend who wrongs us that we can forgive them, but we can't forget what they did. There is no point in trying, because we are human and it's not our fault. It's expected. Because we expect it, we continue to do it.

Any time we keep a record of something wrong that someone did to us, we are imprisoning that person in a world where they will be caught in a continuous cycle of doing that same thing over and over again. This is the biggest reason why most people persist in their grinding routine of sin. They have never been set free from the things of their past. The only way to set someone free is to throw away the records and give them a clean slate.

A young woman who had been married for about two years called me one day for advice. Her husband was struggling with a nasty temper, and it seemed to be getting worse every time he blew it. She explained to me that the previous night they had gotten into a disagreement and he started screaming and yelling at her. This time it did not stop with just words, he actually slapped her leg. Never before had this man gone so far as to strike his wife. They were heartbroken. It was apparent to both of them that they needed intervention.

When I sat down and spoke with this young man, he tearfully began to tell me about his mountains of failures. He felt like he had done so many wrong things to this woman that it would take years to wade through them in an effort to reclaim her heart. He honestly didn't know where to start because everything was such a tangled mess. It reminded me of my kitchen just after our family has cooked and eaten Thanksgiving dinner. Every plate, utensil, cup, glass, pot and pan is filthy and stacked on the counter. It's the messiest our kitchen ever gets. The thought of cleaning it makes me instantly depressed. I don't even know where to start. It's so taxing that I usually just leave it for the next day and go to bed.

The next day I become like McGyver. I create a plate out of a Tupperware lid and I use an old pair of chopsticks that I found in a junk drawer to eat breakfast off of it. A tin can (rinsed out with water) makes a great drinking glass, and a T-shirt becomes a napkin. Before I was married, I might have lived a month or more like this because the mountain of dishes was more than I could handle.

This is how this poor gentleman felt in his marriage. He felt like he couldn't do the right thing, until all the wrong things were cleaned up. Because he didn't know where to start, he just did his best to hold things together just one more day. He ultimately found himself repeating the same behavior towards his wife, and slowly getting worse.

This man's wife eventually made a decision to *clean the kitchen* of their marriage herself. She did this by permanently destroying all the records of his past behavior. She never brought up his past again. She spent all her time encouraging him for the good things he did rather than reminding him of the wrongs he committed. Once his slate was wiped clean, he knew his wife welcomed his intimacy. Once he was allowed to reestablish that closeness with her he felt like he could make the changes he knew he needed to make, and that is exactly what he did. He was literally driven to change through a wife that didn't keep a record of his wrongs.

> *Every marriage that ends in divorce has one thing in common. One or both people kept a meticulous record of the other's wrongs.*

Every marriage that ends in divorce has one thing in common. One or both people kept a meticulous record of the other's wrongs. When the records are kept and counted, there comes a time when there is just too much on record to continue the relationship. Eventually, the record keeper can only see what is in the past, and they become blinded to the things that they used to love about their partner. Record keeping causes us to look only at the records and over time we will ultimately define the person by their past.

When one of our daughters was an infant, she became ill. Our doctor asked us to keep a record of how many poopie diapers she had in a twenty-four hour period. We were religious about it. Every time she had a bowel movement we saved the diaper and put a slash on a note pad along with the exact time she did it. After about three days of precise documentation of her bowel

> *Record keeping causes us to look only at the records and over time we will ultimately define the person by their past.*

movements, I came home one evening and asked my wife, "Where is the poopie machine?" I immediately realized that I was defining my baby girl by the very records I was keeping on her.

Obviously I was joking when I said that, but the principle is true in all of our relationships. When I talk to divorced people, it is interesting to hear the titles they put on their former spouse. The husband will say, "Well, she was a liar" or "She was a nagger" and the wife will tell me, "He was a workaholic" or "He was a controller." They both kept such careful accounts of the other person's faults, that they ultimately saw that person in the light of their mistakes. They gave that person a new name and completely forgot the name of the one they used to talk to on the phone for hours, and couldn't wait to see again. Our world has taught every one of us that love does keep records of wrongs.

Many parents can't even receive a compliment about one of their children in a public setting without stepping in and correcting the person who gave it. If someone in a restaurant comments on how well behaved their children are, they feel the need to *set the record straight* by informing them that their children are really out of control, bickering brats. It's usually done in a humorous way, but to the listening children it resonates in their hearts for years. The children become even more out of control because that's what the *record* says about them. They behave and become the name that their parents call them by.

Is it really shocking to find that a child who is called a "bad little boy" acts like a bad little boy? Anytime a parent defines their child by his or her actions, they are ensuring that their child will continue in a pattern of the actions that they have defined them by. Only a *record of wrongs mentality* defines a person by what he or she has done in the past. Most of us have grown up with this and as a result, our hearts have come to believe that love always keeps a record of wrongs.

It's not surprising to find that any time a person is in the midst of real change in their life, their immediate family is usually their biggest discouragement.

> *...any time a person is in the midst of real change in their life, their immediate family is usually their biggest discouragement.*

Convincing mom and dad that we are not the same person who made all those mistakes growing up is almost impossible. Usually I counsel people to create a sizable distance between them and their family during their personal change. Mother and father have become a constant reminder of past mistakes. They are many times the last people to quit calling us by the name of our past.

What Do We Believe About God?

Because of our learned perceptions about love keeping records of wrongs, we ultimately believe that God keeps an account of our wrongs. Most of us know in our *heads* that this is not true; however, our *hearts* believe the exact opposite. We toss around the "I'm forgiven" slogan on Sundays but I have been hard-pressed to find more than one or two people in any Christian circle who actually knows it in their heart. How could they when their entire life has taught them exactly the opposite?

I think the greatest evidence that most people believe God keeps records of their wrongs, is the fact that *most people religiously keep records of their own wrongs*. If we really believed in our hearts that our Creator did not keep such records, then it would stand to reason that we wouldn't do it either. However, many and most people do exactly this.

Like an internal tax auditor, they never allow themselves to overlook or forget one mistake they've made in life. It eventually becomes a habit of the soul that won't allow any undeserved comfort to creep inside and give them a dose of freedom. Forgetting personal wrongs seems irresponsible or even inwardly fraudulent. Before they know it, they

People believe in their hearts that God is proud of how abusive they are being to themselves.

begin calling themselves names that correlate with the sins they've committed. People do this because they believe that in God's eyes they deserve it. They even believe in their hearts that God is proud of how abusive they are being to themselves. Eventually, they start to believe that when they are on a personal bashing binge, it is actually the voice of God talking to their heart like that.

It is heartbreaking to encounter the thousands of people who nervously live their lives watching and waiting for God's wrathful payback to visit them. You would think that a mafia leader is after them by the way they talk. Eventually, they become so paranoid that they begin to confuse *consequence* with *payback*. Anytime something bad happens in their life they sheepishly look towards Heaven and say, "I know I deserved that, Lord." Even silly things like a flat tire on the freeway, or a bladder infection strangely become "God paying them back" for something they did in their past.

Make no mistake about it; there are consequences to our actions. Sin always has a consequence that follows it. If we stick our hand in a meat grinder there will be an immediate consequence to that action. The heart wrenching thing is that what used to be an obvious consequence for sin is now redefined to be God's fury giving us what we deserve. Once a person feels like God is punishing him and giving him what he deserves, he will cower away from intimacy with God. Once he cowers from intimacy, he has no power to stop his self-destructing sin. Again the consequence for that sin comes ripping and grinding through his life and again he blames God for it. Entire theologies are based on a false view of our Father's heart and actions.

> *At any point where a person feels condemnation, it is because that person believes that their God has kept a record of their wrongs.*

Condemnation is devastating to human hearts because it renders people spiritually paralyzed. At any point where a person feels condemnation, it is because that person believes that their God has kept a record of their wrongs. God does not save back every sin we have committed for the purpose of using those mistakes as future ammunition when He decides to pay us back! I believe that this line of thinking has tortured the majority of Christians for most of their lives.

Why Doesn't God Keep Records Of Wrongs?

Your Father doesn't keep a record of your sins for the same reason that I didn't keep a record of what my wife did many years ago. *He doesn't want you to live with the shame and regret of having done it.* Shame is deadly to the spirit. He wants you to let it go. This is why He says in the Bible "there is no condemnation for those who are in Christ." The only

The only ammunition that God needs against your sin is forgiveness.

ammunition that God needs against your sin is *forgiveness*. It's the only weapon that works! It's the only way God can clean your heart of the shame of your mistakes. It is imperative that you know this. He will never require you to pay penance for something you did wrong. What would be the point in Christ dying on the cross if we were expected to pay God back every time we sinned?

Your Father doesn't keep a record of your sins because *He knows that if He did, you would be caged in a cycle of repetition.* This is the biggest reason why people continuously repeat the same sins over and over. They believe in their hearts that God has written it down somewhere in Heaven and He won't let it go. Because they believe this lie, they continue to behave according to the records they imagine God is keeping.

Condemnation is an enemy of your Father. It denies the accomplishment of Christ's death and resurrection. It completely bypasses and rejects everything God freely gave us, and supposes that it somehow didn't work in our situation. Condemnation is the power of sin. At any point in your life, if you are under condemnation you need to know that God has nothing to do with it. It is NOT the Spirit of God speaking to you; it's the spirit of the enemy lying to you!

Your Father doesn't keep a record of your sins because *He doesn't want anything ugly being held over your head.* You are precious to Him and when He looks at you He sees only a picture of perfection. He doesn't want anything unholy or unattractive to appear in that picture.

If you think about the literal meaning of "holding something over a person's head," it is cold and unloving. Imagine writing down the sin that one of your children committed against you on a piece of paper and then holding it over their head whenever they walked into the room. It's labeling your own child. When you love, this is the last thing you would ever want over the head of one of your children. God is this way with you. He is the loving parent who is constantly wiping your face clean and fixing your hair before a family picture. He wants you to always look your best regardless of where you have been or what you have done. He would never hold something repulsive against one of His children. That is unthinkable to Him.

> ✝
> *Condemnation is an enemy of your Father. It denies the accomplishment of Christ's death and resurrection.*

Religious Mindsets That Believe The Opposite

Though most churches teach the truth concerning God not keeping records of wrongs, there is overwhelming evidence that our religion doesn't believe a word of it. Our tangled understanding usually surfaces through the things we repeatedly do and say in the midst of everyday church life. I believe that for the most part these things are small and unintentional, but over time they begin to add up to a whole new theology.

Before we know it, we live in a religious society that speaks one thing and believes the very opposite of what it just spoke. We have become so accustomed to this through the years that when it does happen, we don't even notice it anymore. Most of these mind-sets even have a ring of truth to them because we have heard them so often. Though they directly contradict what we claim to believe about God, they have been with us for so long that we just don't question them anymore.

I want to list a handful of ways in which I believe that our religion has turned this truth upside-down. Understand that this is not for the purpose of bashing our religion or complaining for the sake of complaining. It is essential that we take an honest look at what we really believe in our hearts. It has everything to do with how we see God. You might be surprised at what your heart really does believe about Him.

God Doesn't Force You Into A Ministry

There is an unwritten understanding in the Christian world that says if a person came out of a life of drug and alcohol abuse, God will most likely call that person to minister to ex-drug addicts and alcoholics. If someone was delivered from prostitution, God will give her a ministry to hookers. If God freed a person from homosexuality, He will then use them to preach the Gospel to homosexuals.

The very core of this perception about Him comes from a belief that God associates our past with our future. Though many people may have a special heart for others who have come from their previous lifestyle, this does not mean that everyone is called to have a ministry that pertains to their past.

When I met the Lord I was singing in a rock-n-roll band in Hollywood, California. Immediately, I assumed that God had called me to preach the Gospel to the rock-n-roll world. I changed the name of my band, wrote some Christian songs, and began booking myself in clubs all over Hollywood.

The problem was that once I began to know the Heart of God, my heart began to change. I no longer felt the anger and rage that fueled my performance on stage. I was uninterested in the rebellious spirit that drew me to the rock-n-roll world in the first place. Eventually, I couldn't even relate to the culture and I became depressed and confused.

This was one of the biggest obstacles I had to overcome in the early years of my walk with God. I was certain that He would call me to save the people in the culture I came from, but I was totally miserable doing it. Finally, I just quit everything and did nothing for a very long time. Little did I know, God had a plan for my life that was in a completely different direction than what I had ever expected. It wasn't until I understood that God never keeps a record of my past that I was freed in my spirit to go a completely different direction.

> *Your calling may have absolutely nothing to do with the life you used to lead, because your Father has no record of it in Heaven.*

It is small-mindedness that sees a person's future through the lens of their past. Our God can do anything! He took a Pharisee named Saul, and changed his name to Paul, then sent him to the Gentiles to preach the Gospel. Don't ever feel trapped by your past! Open your heart to the possibilities of what God can do in your life. You are not bound by the things you have done or the places you've been. Your calling may have absolutely nothing to do with the life you used to lead, because your Father has no record of it in Heaven.

True Testimony

A testimony is not about where you have been versus where God has taken you and what he has *done* for you. A testimony is about WHO GOD IS. This, and this alone, is powerful enough to win the hearts of the most pagan people in the universe. The problem is that for the most part we don't believe this. This is precisely why we tell and retell our story of how God saved us from our wicked past. We are trying to sell Him to people

God is not excited about what you came from; He is excited about having a relationship with you today.

because we don't know Him ourselves. We don't think He is sellable on His own, so we capitalize on the level of wickedness to which we were enslaved, in an effort to make God look stronger and more attractive.

Please understand that we do not glorify God by showing the world the level of wickedness from which He saved us. In the beginning of you Christian walk when that is all you have go ahead and tell it. There must be a time, however, when your testimony shifts from "back then," to something even more beautiful; it's a testimony of WHO GOD IS in the context of a personal relationship NOW. Try to remember that because of the fact that God keeps no record of your past, He is pretty much unfamiliar with your past. When we get stuck in the rut of just telling our original story of salvation, we are basically not involving God with our testimony. God is not excited about *what you came from;* He is excited about having a relationship with you today. Out of that relationship, you *will become a testimony!*

I am sincerely grieved by Christianity's constant assumption that we have to "*sell God*" to a dying world. The fact that we feel we have to do this is evidence to me that we really don't think anyone would want Him for who He really is. We don't care if they *know Him*; we just want people to get saved. This marketing mentality has become the preferred line of thinking for an entire generation of Christians.

Most mainstream ministries today won't even allow someone to hold a microphone unless they have a wicked and sinful past. The problem with this form of *advertising God* is that it overlooks the people who have known God their entire lives. They are left thinking that they don't have a testimony. In fact, many times these poor people find themselves wishing they had sinned in some terrible way in their past so they could be "a witness for Christ."

The bottom line reason why people aren't interested in hearing from people who have walked in relationship with God their entire lives is because most people aren't the least bit interested in knowing God. It's not God's heart we are selling. How could we? We don't even know His heart. It's SALVATION we are selling. It's Heaven at the end of our lives as opposed to a burning Hell. We wear

God's heart for you is because of your position in His family, not because you follow the rules well.

T-shirts that say, "Turn or burn," and we arrogantly say things like, "I know where I'm going," and this is what is supposed to convince the world to become a Christian. It's like God has taken out a million dollar life insurance policy on Himself, and once His children got wind of it, all they do is talk about what they are going to do with the money when good old Dad kicks the bucket.

Understand that this decline in Christian thinking is the direct result of our false belief that God keeps a record of our wrongs. It causes us to over-focus on where we are going when we die and under-focus on relationship with Him. We have become so terrified of the record-keeping God we believe in, that we find ourselves doing whatever it takes to promote Him. The problem is that in the midst of our promotion, our actions prove that we really don't like Him at all.

Have you ever found yourself worried about what a new convert might be thinking during an offering sermon? Do you find yourself hoping that the preacher tones it down and doesn't say the things he usually does for fear that your unsaved friend you brought to church might be turned off? Think about this for a moment and ask yourself what this should tell you. It says to me that people who aren't used to the terrible things we say about God are more likely to get up and walk out, than someone who grew up with it. Perhaps they know something we don't.

It is God's desire that you let your past go. He doesn't need you to make sure that everyone knows how bad it used to be in relation to how good it is because of Him. God is no more glorified by your past than you are. He has truly let every wrong thing in your past go. In fact, He has cast it in the sea of forgetfulness.

Your Walk With God

God is not proud of you because you have come so far in your walk. God is proud of you because you are His child. He loves you because you are His child. His heart for you is because of your position in His family, not because you follow the rules well.

He will always encourage you in your walk because He knows you need it. The further you get from the things that destroy your life, the better off you are. God truly loves putting distance between you and death, but make no mistake about it, it is not that distance that makes Him look at you with adoration. You are loved by Him for one reason and only one reason: you are His child.

God Doesn't Need To Have A "Second" Plan

No matter who you are or what you have done wrong, God's original plan for your life still stands! God is not the least bit surprised by anything in your life. He is the builder who has counted the cost long before He began a good work in you. You can be certain that He will bring that work to completion.

Most people I talk to think they are on plan #768 because they have disqualified themselves so many times from what God had originally designed for them. This mind-set comes from the thousands of teachings that imply this terrible lie about God. They leave people feeling like they are no longer eligible for God's best in their lives. This is a lie from the pit of Hell!

Loved ones, you can rejoice in the fact that your Father can do anything! What is impossible for man is possible for God. Don't ever worry that you have thrown God a curve ball in your past that has knocked Him off balance. The promises He gave you are the same as the promise He gave Abraham. God said to him, "It has been done."

God Does Not Label Divorced People

God is in the business of restoring people, not labeling them. Divorce has been referred to as the "unpardonable sin" in the Church. It's amazing to me that someone can come out of a life of sexual promiscuity where they had ten to fifteen different sexual partners in their dating history, but the moment someone gets a divorce they are labeled for life.

The fact that it is this way is perhaps the most impressive and overwhelming evidence that as a whole, we do not believe *God keeps no record of wrongs*. My heart breaks for divorced people in the Church today. Even a former murderer finds more grace and acceptance than these people.

When we understand that keeping a record of wrongs, ultimately catapults people into a cycle of repeating the same sins over and over, it's not surprising to find that some statistics show that the divorce rate in the Church is higher than it is in the world. This is grieving to God because we are proving to Him that we haven't the slightest idea what marriage is in the first place.

Please understand that it is not the *physical act of divorce* that God has a problem with. It's the *divorce from intimacy and oneness* that couples allow to happen in their marriage years before the legal papers are ever filed. God hates emotional walls that shut others out and willfully decide to be internally unknown by everyone. God hates apathetic hearts

> *God is a hundred times more grieved for divorced people than He ever was for divorce.*

that are uninterested in pursuing intimacy with a spouse. Understand that it is the closing of the heart doors that God is against. He hates these things because they kill people inside.

Having said that, there are millions of self-righteous "un-physically-divorced" people in the Church who don't even have a clue that they are as guilty as the people at whom they point their fingers. What is even more repulsive is that they honestly think they are earning brownie points with God because they are following the law of marriage by not "physically separating." That attitude is as heartless as their decision to live that way.

Heartlessness *is* divorce! It is heartless to encourage a woman who is being physically abused by her husband, to stay with him, because "abuse" is not listed as "Biblical grounds" for divorce. When we damn a woman to live day in, and day out with an alcoholic husband who can't keep a job and ultimately has his wife and children living out of the back of his Chevrolet, *we are the ones* guilty of divorce. It takes complete and utter emotional divorce on our part to say such a heartless thing.

Forgive me for using such strong words, but this topic has crucified the spirits of millions of precious people in our generation. God is a hundred times more grieved for divorced people than He ever was for divorce. It's people He cares about. Not religious rules!

I made up my mind years ago that I would be a father to the women in my congregation. Fathers think differently than pastors. Fathers think with their hearts, while pastors many times go by the book. God is a Father.

God Is Not Santa Claus

He is not "making a list and checking it twice." I find it humorous to see how gleefully we sing that song to our children. I'm guilty of it, too. I remember hearing the words of that song as a child and immediately going into a state of fear.

God does not bless us for being good little boys and girls. God blesses us because God blesses. That's what He does. He blesses

He doesn't need a reason to love you and bless you.

and redeems. When you receive a blessing from Him, just accept it and know that it's because you are His child. Believe it or not, God doesn't even keep records of rights. He doesn't need to. He doesn't need a reason to love you and bless you. Your position in His family is reason enough for Him.

God Does Not See A "Sinner Saved By Grace"

We commonly call ourselves "sinners" because we are convinced that God calls us by the name of our wrongs. It's kind of like when I called my daughter the "poopie machine." I did that because that was the record I was keeping. Once I quit keeping records, I didn't even consider calling her that. Yes, it is true that we WERE sinners, and God did save us by grace, but NOW God sees us as PERFECT! Though we may still sin from time to time, He still doesn't see us as a "sinner."

This is perhaps the biggest misconception with the most devastating consequences to Christians' lives today. Remember loved ones, you will always live up to the name that you are called by. This is why so many people still struggle in sin daily; they believe that God is still calling them a sinner. It's not true. God keeps no record of wrongs. He doesn't see you this way, so stop seeing yourself this way.

"The Unpardonable Sin"

Ironically, this will be popular with few and decidedly unpopular with many. The teaching on the *unpardonable sin* has been used against Christians for hundreds of years. It is perhaps the most frequent fear that is brought to me in my ministry.

I want you to understand something right now. *You will never commit the unpardonable sin.* You haven't committed it, and you never need to worry about accidentally committing it. Don't let anyone tell you differently! Jesus was talking to UNBELIEVERS when He warned them of this sin, NOT BELIEVERS. Because you are in the family, you never need to worry about this subject. If there were such a thing that applied to believers, you would think that at least one of the New Testament writers would have mentioned it.

> *There is nothing a child can do that is unpardonable by his or her father.*

That's a pretty big subject to just casually forget to write about. They didn't cover it because it has nothing to do with believers. There is nothing a child can do that is unpardonable by his or her father.

Most people don't even know what the unpardonable sin is. I've heard about a thousand renditions of what it could be, and they all have one thing in common; they are used to manipulate and put fear into the hearts of precious people. This is terrible, and it has nothing to do with the Heart of God.

If you read the text concerning this subject, it is self-explanatory. Jesus was talking to the Pharisees who were trying to discredit Jesus' ministry. They were *knowingly attributing the works of God to the Devil* for the purpose of influencing those who might come to God and leave the Pharisee's evil grip. It has nothing to do with you, so please don't ever be anxious about this again.

While we are discussing this subject, I want to make another statement about something that has been traditionally viewed as unpardonable. Brace yourself. Suicide does not guarantee people a one-way trip to Hell. I am not minimizing the horror of suicide. I think that is self-evident. Clearly, it's a selfish act that devastates those left behind. I'm just stating the fact that not everyone goes to Hell that does this. I think that the traditional teaching on this subject came about as a deterrent to people who might be thinking of suicide. The problem is that it has one nasty side effect.

> † *Suicide does not guarantee people a one-way trip to Hell.*

Now the family who is left behind, not only has to deal with the loss of their loved one, but they are also confronted with the pain of their Christian friends informing that their loved one is burning in Hell. I'm not sure the trade off is a good one here.

Why not rather preach on the Heart of God. If you know the Heart of God, suicide will never be an option. Everything is found in His Heart.

You Are Not MARKED; You Are SEALED

Understand loved ones, that you are not marked by your past. God hasn't kept any record of it, and He is not about to start now. When you die, there will not be a videotape in Heaven that plays everything wrong thing you did while on earth. God has made you perfect forever!

When you approach Him in prayer, don't wonder if He is still angry about what you did the day before. Just know that His eyes light up the moment you speak to Him. You are free to get as close as you will with Him. All is forgiven and it's time to come home.

I was fully relaxed, lying in my bed in pitch darkness listening only to the sound of a gentle breeze running through the tree outside my bedroom window. My mind had settled to a comfortable numb, and I was moments away from a deep sleep. Suddenly my bedroom door was kicked open with a loud bang. Someone holding a flashlight shined it directly into my face, almost blinding me. Just as my eyes regained their focus, there was a man dressed in black coming down on me with a twelve-inch French knife. I screamed in horror as adrenaline rushed through my entire body. There was nothing I could do. There was no time to respond. The feeling of fear was more powerful than any drug I had ever experimented with in my life. When my brother got up off of me, and turned the bedroom lights on, we laid there together and laughed hysterically.

"Ok, it's my turn now" Brian said, as he handed me the knife and the flashlight, "make sure you wait a long time before you come in."

"Get real relaxed, and try to fall asleep," I said as I turned the lights back off and closed the door behind me.

After about fifteen minutes of silence, I would kick the door in and reenact the same murder scene he played out on me. Over and over we took turns playing the helpless victim and each time we found it more thrilling and exhilarating than the last.

Playing the part of the attacker wasn't what was so charging about this. It was the rush of fear that we got when we were being attacked. This is what we were after.

Believe it or not, this was a little game my brother and I stumbled upon almost fifteen years ago when we lived together in Hollywood, California. We were two single men (is it any wonder why) who were bored out of our minds, looking for something to pass the time with. Since we had already bought BB guns and destroyed every drinking glass, coffee cup and dinner plate in the apartment, we were quickly running out of options.

It wasn't until days later that we realized we were actually flirting with a spirit of fear. We were taking Hell's biggest weapon formed against people, and using it to get a cheap adrenaline rush. This was the first and last time we ever played that game.

Delighting In Evil

It's difficult to imagine anyone delighting in evil and then calling it love. The only way this can happen is if someone's perception of love was completely the opposite of the truth about love. Real love has nothing to do with evil, so it would take a pretty tangled understanding of what love is for a person to believe that it delights in evil.

Our society, however, is indeed twisted in their thinking when it comes to the subject of love. Because we have all grown up in this culture, it would stand to reason that we have bought into some of its misconceptions. It is amazing to see the level of blindness that we have learned to live with in this generation. The things that we consume and call "love" remind me of the documentaries that we commonly see about distant countries where people eat maggots and roaches and refer to them as a delicacy. When a person grows up in an environment like that, they get used to it over time. In fact, they learn to crave it over normal food. This is precisely the level of deceit we have given ourselves over to concerning love. We have exchanged the true authentic taste of love for maggots and roaches, and we don't even know we've done it.

Political Correctness At Any Cost

Our world has taught us that not only should we accept a destructive lifestyle that is deadly to people, but we should also delight in the lifestyle itself. If a person dares to speak against homosexuality, they are beaten to death by the mallets of political correctness. Over the last ten years, our nation has convinced itself that "love knows no sex." We have not only accepted this way of thinking, but we now promote it, advertise it and even respect it.

There is no question that we should love the people who struggle with homosexuality. It is my contention that the only reason why America has embraced and delighted in the evil of this destructive lifestyle is because they truly DON'T love the people who have this struggle. If we did love these people, we would never in a million years agree that this is an okay way for them to live. It kills them internally. If we loved these precious people, we would do whatever it took to help them break free of this, rather than condemn them and excommunicate them from our churches.

Homosexuality depletes people of all joy and destroys their inner soul. It is a dark and grey world even when full acceptance is given to it by society. If we truly loved people, we would not delight in the very thing that strangles them to death, we would help them escape this terrible lie that devours their identity and purpose.

This is perhaps the most extreme example of how this generation believes love delights in evil. We believe it in this instance only because we have believed it in every other area concerning relationships.

The Lust For Evil

We truly have become a generation that delights in evil. Most people have never even had a relationship without it. In fact, evil is ninety percent of the initial attraction in many relationships. Thousands of women describe to me an unexplainable magnetism that they feel for a "bad boy." They will pray and pray that God reveals His perfect choice in a man to them, but God knows that He can't because if He did, they wouldn't even be attracted to that man. They find godliness, repulsive. Their heart cries out for maggots and roaches. It cannot understand milk and honey.

> *...evil is ninety percent of the initial attraction in many relationships...*

Most people cannot even conceive of falling in love with someone unless there was an initial lust at the onset of the relationship. We have come to believe that love and lust are inseparable. Our world has taught us that love comes from lust and love needs lust in order to bloom.

One of the most vulgar examples of our upside-down thinking is when a person has sexual intercourse with someone they barely know and then call it "making love." Remember, love does not call evil love. Because of the fact that our world doesn't even know what love is any more, it's very easy to accidentally confuse the two.

If a married couple is still able to lust after each other after several years of being together, they are looked upon as having a "healthy" sex life. The problem with this way of thinking is that all things of the flesh eventually die. Lust comes from the flesh, and it must be fed more and more for it to survive. There is a point when nothing will appease its appetite and it will ultimately destroy a marriage.

Love and lust are complete opposites. *Love gives, and lust takes.* Love comes from the heart while lust is of the flesh. Most people cannot tell the difference between the two because the mechanics seem to be the same. The difference, however, is worlds apart. A couple who lusts, eventually loses interest in their partner and a couple who loves, never loses interest. Lusting people think about how they can please themselves, while loving couples are in it for the other person.

> *Until we are able to rightly divide evil from love, we will always unite the two.*

The lines have become so fuzzy and faint that married couples are publicly encouraged to try new things in the bedroom to spice up their sex lives. The very fact that this is such a common suggestion is proof that their entire sex life is based on dying self-serving flesh. Christian couples are so confused today that their most common question is, "What is legal in the marriage bed?" Sadly, most Christian marriage counselors give them the exact same advice that the world gives. There are entire "Christian teachings" that promote evil sexual practices under the covering of marriage. I speak more in depth on this subject in my book, *The Relationship Code*.

Until we are able to rightly divide evil from love, we will always unite the two. As long as the lines are blurred in our minds, our perception of the Heart of God will follow suit. This is exactly what has happened in our theology today.

God Does Not Delight In Carnal Giving

The only way to understand God's Heart for giving is to love people. When I give my daughters eggs in the morning, I don't walk around the corner and ask God to bless me because I gave. When I present my wife with a new dress, I don't tell her that I'm "giving it to her in faith" as she holds it up to herself in the mirror. That would break her heart. She wants to know that I gave it to her because I love her.

> *The only way to understand God's Heart for giving is to love people.*

The subject of giving is without a doubt the most misunderstood topic in Christianity today. God finds absolutely no delight in our present day teachings on giving because they are just plain evil. They appeal to the flesh of everyone listening.

We have all heard the infamous stories about the guy who gave his whole paycheck in the offering and just three hours later someone presented him with a check for ten thousand dollars to cancel the debt on his house. I am not denying that this happens, and I'm not even suggesting that it wasn't the work of God, but it's interesting that NOT ONCE in New Testament Scripture do we hear of such a story. Not because it never happened, but because the *focus* in the New Covenant times is now on *love*. When you love, giving IS the blessing.

In the Old Testament times, spiritual things were played out in the physical realm. In New Testament times, spiritual things are played out *in the heart.* People in the Old Testament times got a physical blessing *after* they gave because God was preparing their hearts for a new time. He was teaching them to associate giving with blessing, because the day was soon coming when giving *would* be

> †
> *All New Covenant theology must be understood through the eyes of Love!*

the blessing *in the heart.* That time is now, if we love. If we don't love, however, we will always be drawn back to the "what's-in-it-for-us" Old Testament mentality. All New Covenant theology must be understood through the eyes of Love!

God does not delight in us giving for the purpose of getting something in return. That is heartless. He delights in watching His children express their love through giving. Jesus said, "Where your treasure is, there your heart is also." Money and love go hand in hand. We give from our hearts because that's where our treasure

> †
> *When you love, giving IS the blessing.*

is. The only way to replenish that treasure is to give. Remember, we are being conformed to His likeness, and God never gives for the purpose of receiving. He gives because He is love.

God does not delight in the belief that He is all about money. He doesn't charge for His blessings. They are free. Anytime we insinuate that there is a price attached to God's blessings, we are making Him out to be selfish.

God never wants us to give for the purpose of paying Him back for what He did for us. This mentality diminishes the gift of salvation He gave us. If you gave someone a gift, only to have him hand you a fifty-dollar bill the next day, it would be his way of rejecting your gift. Don't ever feel like you have to pay God back for your salvation. Just receive it.

God Does Not Plunder The Unsaved

Once again, the Old Testament stories where we see this happening was God *playing out spiritual principles in the physical realm*. Today it's about the heart. God does not rob the wicked; He blesses them. When we pray for Him to take from the unsaved and give it to us, we are declaring our belief that God is a thief. We are also making it impossible for us to ever love the unsaved. Obviously we don't believe that God loves them if we think He would do this, so why should we?

> *When we pray for Him to take from the unsaved and give it to us, we are declaring our belief that God is a thief.*

When we tell stories that seem to prove that God has done this, we are radically misrepresenting the truth of His heart. He will never do this, and He is truly grieved that we would think such a thing about Him. He loves the unsaved as much as He loves you. He sent His Son to die for the unsaved. When you were still a sinner, Christ died for you! He didn't plunder your household and business, He gave to you. This is His heart.

How God Gets Your Attention

I am always amazed when I hear someone pray for God to bring disaster and tragedy into the life of a "backslider" or an unbeliever in an effort to get them to realize how much they really need God in their lives. Does this sound a bit off to you? People who pray this way truly believe that God has the heart and personality of the Devil.

Besides the fact that this is just downright silly, it displays a total and complete misunderstanding of who God is. The kindness of God leads people to repentance! He will never bully anyone into doing what He wants him or her to do. God does not delight in evil and He certainly doesn't delight in prayers that suggest that He, Himself, will perform evil.

Yes, God does work through life's tragedies, but He is never the one who caused them. His promise is that in the midst of life's hardships, He will be there to comfort and heal. Even when those hardships were caused by our own actions! God never delights in people getting what they deserve. His entire ministry is about saving us from what we deserve.

God Does Not "Get Revenge" On People

We have all heard someone use the old, "Vengeance is mine, saith the Lord" at least once in our lives. Perhaps you might have even said it yourself. We commonly use this when someone sins against us, and we want him or her to pay dearly for it. It's our way of thinking that God will pay them back in full

God's vengeance is NEVER on people; it is on HELL!

for what they did to us, and all we need to do is just sit back and wait patiently and faithfully. It's as though we believe that God is a mafia leader who brutally takes care of His own.

If a man who is addicted to drugs, breaks into your home and steals your television set for drug money, then gets away scot-free, how does God get vengeance? He does it by sending someone to witness to that man and eventually bringing him to salvation, then delivering him from drugs. God's vengeance is NEVER on people; it is on HELL!

God does not delight in getting *revenge on people* and He never participates in it. God delights in forgiveness, and when you forgive someone, you are freeing that person to receive a touch from God that will release him from Hell's grip. This is how God gets His revenge. Remember loved ones, our battle is not against flesh and blood, and neither is God's.

Lying Testimonies That Glorify Wickedness

God is not interested in looking like the super hero that saved you from the bowels of your wicked past. Some people's pasts get more and more wicked every time they give their testimony. It's as though they believe that God delights in that evil or He is somehow more glorified when they build it up.

Nothing about the evil of your past glorifies God. He desires what is true and only what is true. He would much rather you talk about what you have with Him NOW. Unfortunately, thousands of people never experience a NOW relationship with God because they are too busy talking about THEN.

Even our movies end with the hero riding off into the sunset with the lady he saved. We never get to see how the relationship turned out. It's as though that part really doesn't matter in our minds. There is something in the human spirit that desires a "happily ever after" ending over the honest to God truth middle.

God does not delight in us skipping over the middle part of our testimony. "Rags to riches" testimonies are only enticing to the flesh. Truth is found in the middle. God *wants* us to tell the story about the in between time. He is not secretly hoping that we will skip over the raunchy details of how we stumbled and fell over and over BEFORE our life was eventually changed by Him. Leaving out those details for the sake of making God look good is false advertising. It hurts the "consumer" because when they get the product home, they are perplexed as to why it's not working for them as quickly and easily as it did for the people at church who sold it to them.

God Does Not Delight In Fear Tactics

Understand that in *no way does the end justify the means!* When we use fear to either get people saved or to get them to toe the line, we are partnering with evil. ALL FEAR IS EVIL. God does not delight in the use of evil to manipulate His children into salvation or repentance. When we do this, we are not acting according to His heart, because we are openly declaring that God delights in evil.

Hell was never supposed to be the force that drew people towards God. The Bible says that the Holy Spirit draws us to God. Threats of Hell bring fear and condemnation. Only a loveless generation would even think of doing such a thing. If someone told our children that we might pour gasoline on them and light them on fire if

> *When we use fear to either get people saved or to get them to tow the line, we are partnering with evil.*

they didn't mind us, we would be enraged. This is unthinkable because we love our children, yet it's a common practice among many Christians. It's not the Heart of God!

God finds no delight when we tell people that He might take one of their children from them or destroy their business if they don't give their lives to Him. The darkest point in Christian history is still very much alive today. There is an underlying "crusades era" mentality in thousands of Sunday sermons nationwide. This is Evil! While it may cause people to physically run to the altar, it causes them to spiritually shrink back from God's heart. God did not create man to save their souls from Hell. He created us to have relationship. Fear tactics make that impossible. The end does NOT justify the means.

What if I were to send someone to my wife before I married her and have them tell her that if she didn't marry me she would lose her job, gain a hundred pounds, have her house repossessed and come down with a severe case of shingles. She may agree to marry me out of total fear but she will NEVER give me her heart. What kind of a marriage is that? God wants people to love Him for Him, not for the purpose of saving their souls from burning in Hell. He will never threaten our families or our health in an effort to coerce us into a relationship. God is love.

> *God wants people to love Him for Him, not for the purpose of saving their souls from burning in Hell.*

When we win people with the power of Hell, we make them "sons of Hell," and not sons of God. Jesus tried to explain this to the preachers of His day when He said, *"You travel over land and sea to win a single convert, and when he becomes one, you make him twice as much a son of Hell as you are." (Matthew 23:15 NIV)*

The goodness of God outweighs the badness of Hell a trillion times over. Using fear only proves that we haven't personally experienced His goodness to a degree that exceeds our faith in Hell's badness. It is impossible to experience something that we don't believe in. We only see what we put our faith in.

God Never Uses "Left Behind" Tactics

Several years ago, I was at the park with my children, watching them roll around in the sand and climb up and down the Jungle Jim. When it was time to leave I began calling their names and waving my arms at them. My oldest daughter just kept swinging, because she didn't want to leave.

When we win people with the power of Hell, we make them "sons of Hell,"...

After calling her several more times, I began walking towards the car and I said, "See ya' later Landin; we're leaving." I will never forget the sound of absolute horror in her voice as she screamed and ran to me. Just then the Lord reminded me of all the times that was done to me when it came to my Heavenly Father. I have never done that again to either my children or my congregation from that day forward.

All New Testament references to the Rapture were for the purpose of encouraging Christians who needed something to look forward to. Never was the Rapture used to terrify people into repentance. Only in this generation do we do this.

When preaching at a conference in Texas, I asked the audience of several hundred people to close their eyes and answer a question for me. I asked them to raise their hands if they were afraid of the Rapture. Every single hand in the auditorium went up! I almost started crying. What was supposed to be the most beautiful day of all to a Christian has been used against us so much that we have now come to live in fear of its arrival.

I would like to give you the first accurate prediction concerning the timing of Christ's return that will actually prove to be right. There are thousands of authors and preachers who have tried to predict the timing of the Rapture and so far, all of them have been completely wrong. My prediction goes something like this...

"Jesus Christ is not returning any time soon!"

Imagine being a groom on your wedding day, and just before you went out to meet your bride, someone came to you and informed you that they found her hiding in a broom closet in absolute terror of your coming. Would you want to come to that? There is no doubt in my mind that until we get a right revelation of who God is, Jesus Christ will not be coming. He wants His bride to rejoice at the trumpet sound, not scream in terror.

I cannot accurately describe to you how much it grieves God's heart when this glorious day is used against His children. The return of Christ is His long awaited wedding day, and we have turned it into something that is used as a tool of terror.

You need to know right now that you are completely safe. Nothing you do will make you any more ready. You are going with Him when He comes because you are His child. Nothing you do will ever cause Him to leave you behind. Don't let anyone tell you anything different. The Rapture was never meant to be used against you; its purpose is to encourage you.

I remember as a child I never had any friends at school. Many of the kids would make fun of me and call me names. Even the teachers would publicly humiliate me in front of the class. One day, in the midst of that Hell on Earth I remember thinking to myself, "My daddy is picking me up today, and then it will be all better." This is God's heart for you when it comes to the Rapture.

The Possible Loss of Salvation

God wants you to know that you are totally secure in Him. *You* don't ever have to worry whether or not you will go to Heaven when you die. You belong to Him and He will NEVER let you go. Insinuating that God might go back on His promise to you is insinuating that God is loveless and evil.

Could you imagine if someone went to one of your children's elementary school and stood up in front of hundreds of kids and told them that their parents might abandon them or disown them if they stepped out of line? How would that make you feel as a parent? This is precisely how grieved God is when we do this to His children.

The only way anyone could do such a thing is if they had not love in their hearts. When you love, it is inconceivable to even think of something so awful. Yet this is an every day experience in many Christian circles.

The Importance Of Security

Couples who live together without getting married are killing themselves, because they are forced to hold back places in their heart and not allow them to grow. Without a "forever" covenant, they would be stupid to just let themselves go completely, and give every part of themselves. They can't because of the way they were created. This is why the divorce rate for couples that live together before they get married is shockingly higher than it is with couples that don't. They suffocated their hearts before they got married.

> ✝
> *The moment you lose sight of your security you will cease to grow spiritually.*

The nature of love is that it expands. All things of God expand. Living together without a promise of security requires an intentional constraint on the heart. Because love comes from the heart, non-secure relationships ultimately restrict the heart from growth until it dies. It's very much like putting a can of soda in the freezer. It eventually explodes. It's important to understand that as a Christian, if you don't believe in eternal security, you are basically just "living together with God". Eventually your heart will experience an explosion that comes in the form of anguish, resentment and even death of faith.

If you keep a boa constrictor in an aquarium, he will stop growing at a certain point. He will only grow in ratio to the size of his surroundings. If you let him loose in the house, he will get much bigger, but again, he will stop growing at a certain point because your house is only so big. If you let him free in the wilderness, he will grow to full size and live many years. Relationships that do not have a "forever" covenant are like a boa constrictor in a fish aquarium. Their growth is stunted and they die early.

Anything less than ETERNAL security is no security at all.

Security is the number one thing that all relationships need to grow. You have it in God. Don't ever allow anyone to confuse you in this matter. Heaven will never be taken from you. It is imperative that you know this. You will never go to Hell if you have asked Jesus into your heart. The moment you lose sight of your security you will cease to grow spiritually. God calls it a "promise" and a "guarantee" for a reason and the promise is to you.

I want to emphasize this point to your heart. Until you believe this, *you will never know the Heart of your Father*. It is vital that this one point is swallowed completely by your spirit. This is the starting point for you. It's the starting point of all true relationships. Even earthly marriage begins with a "forever" covenant. If you have been a Christian for twenty years, and you don't know this one point, you may as well tear down everything and rebuild. This is the foundation of Christianity.

It is astonishing to find millions of Christians who haven't even crossed the starting line of their faith. There are entire denominations that diligently fight against this one imperative aspect of truth. I've preached to all of them and I can tell you that *without a doubt*, their people are miserable. I know this because I've asked for a show of hands, and *every single time*, over ninety percent of the congregation raises their hands admitting that they are unfulfilled.

It is not my purpose to come against any denomination; however, when something that is directly against the truth of God's heart is being taught, I will always take a stand. God is not a denomination! God is love and everything about Him must be seen through that lens.

You must cross this line if you want true relationship with God! There will NEVER be any security until you do this. Ask yourself what other kind of security there is if it's not *eternal*. Anything less than ETERNAL security is no security at all. Without eternal security the human heart will hold itself back. There will always be a spot of agony in the heart of a person who can't trust implicitly. We give this to our children without even thinking about it so why should we expect anything less from God?

Love Rejoices [13]
With The Truth

She had watched him with a secret crush for nearly a year before they first spoke. Their first conversation was nothing more than a simple hello, but to her it meant the world. Though it really wasn't a dialogue, but more of a verbal acknowledgment she had waited patiently for this moment, and it proved to be everything she dreamed it would be. Explosions went off in her heart as she returned his salutation. "Finally," she thought to herself, "he knows I exist."

Now that the door was open, she made it a priority to find herself in his company as often as possible. If a group of people were going to dinner after the church service, and she knew he would be there, she was sure to attend. It didn't really matter if they sat together, because just being in the same room with him was a delight in itself. Perhaps they might exchange a glance or two, and if she was lucky, he might tell her goodbye at the end of the night.

Over the next several months, another milestone was crossed in their relationship. This time his greeting to her had something special attached to it, her name! He actually remembered her name! "Why would he take the time to memorize my name if he were not interested," she thought to herself. He had never asked her personally what her name was. Did he investigate it and find it out through a mutual friend? Who could he have talked to? Perhaps he heard someone else call her by that name and he just remembered it. "Nevertheless he did remember it," she reasoned, "and that must stand for something."

On one occasion, they were both hiking up a mountain while at a church retreat together and he turned to her and asked her about a specific situation at her workplace that she had mentioned in a group setting almost six months ago. "He was listening," she thought to herself. Now it was becoming downright obvious that he, too, was interested. When you take this, and set it along side the fact that he picked up her napkin when she dropped it in the dining hall earlier that day, things were looking pretty positive.

Now she sits up all night with her best friend and begins counting and recalling every specific incident where he showed interest. There was the time he laughed at a joke she cracked, then there was that time he said he would keep a family situation of hers in prayer. There was also the famous "poke-on-the-shoulder incident" when he wanted her attention, and who could forget the time he told her he thought he saw her driving on Bell Road and Greenway? He obviously must be thinking of her when he is out and about during his day.

At any moment, he was sure to ask her for a date. Even if he didn't, she was okay with that because they were already "kind of dating." She talked about him obsessively. Her friends got tired of hearing his name in every conversation, but she just couldn't stop herself. She knew they were supposed to be together, and it was just a matter of time before it happened. If they knew him like she did, they would surely understand. Even her best friend was starting to come around and see "the signs," so it must not all be in her mind.

After her sister frantically encouraged her to come into my office to meet with me, she reluctantly agreed. In the first few seconds, his name came spilling out of her mouth, and I began to ask her about it. Her eyes got that far-off look to them, as she swooned over every dazzling moment they had shared together. I had not heard that they were seeing each other so I was taken by surprise. When I asked her how long this had been going on she began to give me a carefully constructed step-by-step explanation about what they had together. It was instantly obvious to me that this was all in her mind.

I asked her straight out, "Does he like you?"

"Oh yes, it's obvious," she said, "I can't believe you haven't heard."

I took a more direct approach and said, "Did he tell you that he likes you?"

"Well, no, not in those exact words," she replied, "but I know for a fact that he does."

"Has he told anyone else that he likes you?" I fired back.

"He doesn't really talk to a lot of people about his feelings," she said, while starting to appear a bit nervous, "but if you ask my best friend, she will tell you."

As I reached over my desk, I picked up the phone and said, "Better yet, I'll call him personally and ask him myself."

"NO!" She shrieked back. "Just forget it, forget I said anything."

I promised her that I would ask him in a way that he would never in a million years expect that she put me up to it. I even suggested that we call a friend of his that was sure to know the truth, but she adamantly refused over and over.

My heart broke for this precious woman, because I knew her world was about to crash in on her. She had lived in the most extraordinary fantasy world for almost two years, and today it was being exposed for the lies it had told her. This is not easy for anyone who has gone through this. Living a lie sometimes feels a thousand times more comforting than facing the truth, especially when so many thousands of hours have been spent concocting that lie. It becomes an entire world where everything mysteriously fits together to create the greatest romantic story in the world. This particular young woman walked out of my office and proceeded to put herself back in the very same fantasy world for the next year and a half until the guy she liked finally married someone else.

> *Living a lie sometimes feels a thousand times more comforting than facing the truth.*

Upside-Down Love Despises The Truth

This story is perhaps the most common story I get in my office. In fact, this young woman was about the fiftieth person in this predicament I've counseled in the last three years. It is grieving to me because it represents millions of people who have been convinced into an upside-down version of love. It's a version where nothing real and true exists, but only a dreamy set of made up situations and fantasies.

The problem is that this pattern of behavior does not stop when the woman finally gets married. Ironically, her new husband can TRUTHFULLY proclaim his love to her over and over, but she will retreat into an emotional world where she imagines that it isn't true. Every move he makes will be misconstrued as evidence that he is thinking of leaving her. It's not so much the fantasy of the wonderful that she is addicted to; it's the loathing of truth. Truth, to a fantastical person, appears boring and simple. Its plainness is a complete disappointment.

> †
> *Truth, to a fantastical person, appears boring and simple.*

Women are not the only ones who do this in the context of relationships. There are many men who behave the same way. The only difference is that we don't call them "dreamers," we affectionately refer to them as "stalkers."

Our society's entire infrastructure is held together by lies. Authentic truth poses an awesome threat to our way of life in America. It slaps us in the face with its boring simplicity and raw practicality. We are harshly reminded of our appetite for lies every four years during the presidential and political campaigns. It has come to be known as a fact of life. We've learned to expect lies. In fact, we embrace them. Whoever is the better liar gets our vote.

Every form of advertising makes promises to our flesh that cannot possibly be fulfilled. They do this, because they have learned the art of telling us what we want to hear. We are all like this young woman in my story. We will believe anything if we like what it tells us and if it makes us feel good inside. We have become addicted to the way a lie makes us feel. It's euphoric and soothing when just the right thing is said. Whether or not it is true, is not the issue. It all has to do with whether or not we like it.

If a commercial implies that their shampoo will make us look thinner, we'll buy it without even thinking. If a car commercial insinuates that members of the opposite sex will become suddenly interested in us if we pull up in their new sports car, we will sign our life away. We are literally looking for something soothing to believe in. We seek for something to take us away from the ruthless reality of real life and personal responsibility and hurl us into a world of dreamy licentiousness.

Make no mistake about it, we know for a fact that these things will never deliver what they have promised us, but we choose to overlook the truth and focus on the lie. The woman in my story was not blindsided by these lies. She knowingly made them up herself. She knew the truth, but she refused to focus on it. The fantasies she had created in her mind were much more fun to live with than the truth. They were deep and thought-provoking, while the real truth was unexciting and ordinary. At the very threat of having to put those colorful things down, she stormed out of my office and returned to her self-made Fantasy Island.

Our world has taught us to despise the truth and rejoice in a lie.

She did this for the same reason we all do this. Our world has taught us to despise the truth and rejoice in a lie. The very word, "love" has been associated with this, for many decades. We have come to see it as an escape from reality. Our television programs and movies all support this fantastical viewpoint when it comes to love. We are fascinated by its apparent mystery and its sharp teeth. We have become addicted to a perception of love that feeds our senses and charges our soul. The lies alone are what make it so enticing and desirable. To rid our relationships of them would be like taking the thrill out of a rollercoaster ride. It's unthinkable!

Weeding Out Lies

The only way to accurately tell if something is love or not, is to take the lies away. Almost always, when we do this we will find that what we believed was *love*, wasn't *love* at all. Once the evil is eliminated, the relationship literally disintegrates into nothing.

Women will come into my office confused as to whether or not the man they are living with is truly in love with them. My suggestion to them is that they stop sleeping with him until they are married. Almost always the woman embarrassingly refuses to take this advice because she already knows in her heart that he probably will leave

Most people would rather think that something evil is love than find out the truth.

her. She would rather rejoice in a lie and continue living in darkness than know the truth and be set free. The risk of losing what the lie gives her is far greater and more powerful than the prospect of freedom that the truth could usher into her life.

A man once came to me for advice concerning a married woman he was in "love" with. He had rationalized his way into believing that this woman was already going to leave her husband before she even met this man. I interrupted him and asked him if he would like to discover the truth about that. He hesitated for a moment, and then asked me how. I told him to break up with her and tell her that even if she *did* leave her husband she could never be with him. If three months went by and she still left her husband, then he could go back to dating her with my blessing. Needless to say, this man did not take my advice because he preferred the lie over what he knew was ultimately the truth. About six months later, he did finally break up with her, only to find that she went back to her husband and is with him to this day.

The moment lies are taken out of the picture, truth will shine through. Most people would rather think that something evil is love, than find out the truth. We would rather be dating the wrong person than not dating anyone at all. We delight in lies because they tell us what we want to hear. Though we know it's a lie, it still feels good for the moment. When it all blows up in our face, however, we are not really surprised, because if the truth be known, we knew it in our hearts all the time.

A woman who finally leaves her alcoholic husband, will tell you that their relationship began when they met at a bar. Marriages that end because of a husband who has a lust problem, usually began with that same obvious lust problem and it's never surprising that the man who wanted to get married after knowing his wife for two months, now wants a divorce after two months of marriage. Every relationship that ends in a break up has one thing in common: The reason for the break up came about because of something that was seen in the beginning, but consciously overlooked. We are never surprised when our world of lies blows up. We knew it all along, but we willfully chose to overlook the truth because it was too inconvenient.

> *We are never surprised when our world of lies blows up. We knew it all along...*

The Greatest Lies Ever Told

Many years ago, I met with a young couple for emergency marriage counseling. Evidently Tamara had caught David looking at pornography on the Internet. She was devastated. Every part of her felt violated and rejected. For all intents and purposes, it was adultery as far as she was concerned.

As Tamara was describing her heart to her husband, David just sat with his head down in obvious embarrassment. I could tell that he was truly sorry for the incident, and he was willing to do whatever it took to reconcile.

Every time we began to go down a road to recovery, Tamara would interrupt and give David a few more emotional lashings. It was clear that she was not ever going to let this man live it down. I could tell that this was going to be a bigger problem than I had imagined.

The one thing that Tamara continued to say was, "I just can't understand it." She must have said that twenty times or more in less than an hour. Finally, in an effort to help her understand, I asked her if she enjoyed romance novels. She said that she had collected them since she was a little girl. I asked her if she liked romantic movies, and again she told me about her collection of all the greatest hits. Pretty much every night of the week, Tamara would relax on the couch and either read one of these books or watch one of her movies.

Romance is pornography for the woman's heart.

My next question to Tamara stunned her into complete silence. I asked her, "If your husband knew what was going through your mind when you were watching one of these romantic movies, how would he feel?" Her eyes looked to the ground in shame, and she quietly said, "He would be devastated."

Tamara was getting the same rush when she encountered *romance* as David got when he encountered pornography. Romance is pornography for the woman's heart. It is as much of a lie as pornography is; it tangles social perceptions in the same way and it is many times just as devastating to a person's life and relationships.

Without even knowing it, we have been blindsided by a seemingly innocent yet inherently evil notion of what love is. Because of the fact that lies were able to masquerade themselves in a way that would bring delight to the average person when they associated it with love, we have been fooled into accepting a terrible counterfeit in place of the real thing. Unfortunately, as in every previous chapter, we find that our misguided impressions of love directly disfigure our mental picture of the face of God.

Romance:
-A strong, sometimes short-lived attachment, fascination, or enthusiasm for something.
-A dreamy, imaginative habit of mind; a disposition to ignore what is real, a girl full of romance
-Not based on fact; imaginary or fictitious
-Fanciful; marvelous; extravagant; unreal; as a romantic tale; a romantic notion; a romantic undertaking
-Not sensible about practical matters; unrealistic
(Dictionary.com)

It is surprising to find that what we consider to be at the very heart and foundation of love in today's thinking is actually an outright lie. We have been taught to long for untruthfulness at the very conception of our relationships. This is catastrophic!

When women desire a romantic man to sweep them off their feet, they are literally saying, "I want a man who will lie to me." It's a lie because the person is behaving in a way that is not the least bit consistent with who they are. Their actions make promises that they personally never intend on keeping. The entire world of romance is just a game of fantasy and manipulation. In reality, we all know this; however, we still delight in it because it feeds

The God's Honest Truth

our flesh with a fantastical rush. Romance always feeds and appeals to the flesh. Truth feeds and appeals to the heart.

A man who is charming can just about get anything he wants from most women. Women dream of being charmed by a knight in shining armor. Every love story, and romance novel in the world is chock full of charming men who seduce their women. It seems innocent enough, but when you look at the actual meaning of the world "charm" it takes on a whole new significance.

Charming:
-To cast or seem to cast a spell on; bewitch
-To use magic spells
-To subdue, control, or summon by incantation or supernatural influence; to affect by magic.
-To subdue or overcome by some secret power, or by that which gives pleasure; to allay; to soothe.
(Dictionary.com)

There is an addiction that many women have to this form of manipulation. It provides them with a *high* that is hard to beat. Just as with most addictions, the end result of that person's relentless quest to get their *high* is usually a tattered and torn trail of failed relationships and broken hearts. It's not surprising that such devastation comes from something that is ultimately rooted in witchcraft.

Our relationships today delight in romance and charm. We dream of it, expect it and do whatever it takes to harness it. All in all, it is an escape from truth. It is role-playing for the purpose of gratifying the flesh. This way of thinking has clearly bled over into the way we see God. Our entire religion has been transformed to parallel the world's version of love, and it is ultimately the cause for Christianity having the most dramatic decline in recent American history.

God Does Not Delight In Hype

God is not delighted when we romanticize Him to people in an effort to get them saved. Some of the promises we make people concerning the Christian life are just plain lies. They are lies that appeal to the flesh of the individual listening. Instantaneous deliverance, a life without struggle, and financial prosperity are just a few of the charming things I've seen presented to desperate people. We think God wants us to tell them what they want to hear in order to win them over, so we give Him a French accent, a dozen roses and a stack of winning lottery tickets then put Him up on stage and sell, sell, sell.

God is not delighted when we romanticize Him to people in an effort to get them saved.

When we promise people that they will never feel lonely again, and all their problems will go away the moment they ask Jesus into their heart, we are setting them up for disaster and disappointment. In my twenty years of ministry, I have yet to find someone with this testimony. God does not delight in it because there is no truth to it at all. It completely voids real life experiences. Remember loved ones, evil is the absence of truth. God does not delight in lies. A lie is a lie, even if we think it makes God look good. When we promise instantaneous victory by the power of God to anyone who answers an altar call, we are publicly declaring to God that we don't believe that the TRUTH is enough to set people free. God never said His power would set us free. He pointed us to *truth* for that. If we do not know or understand the simple truth about Him, we are left grasping for a drop of His power to do the job. Christians seek power, because they know not the truth. They are in bondage without truth, so they feverously search for power to free them, but in the end they only become powerful prisoners.

Though I rarely if ever hear people say that they regret having started a relationship with Jesus, I have found that most Christians will admit that they felt charmed into a religion that never lived up to its promises. It usually takes people years to recover from the guilt and condemnation of not acquiring what was promised to them in the sales pitch before they can ever begin a real relationship with Him. Though we may be convincing people when it comes to signing their name on the dotted line, we are ultimately setting them up for disillusionment and failure.

There is no need to hype up what is already perfect.

We do this because we honestly think that if people knew the truth (in the upside-down way we see it) they wouldn't want anything to do with Him. The sad thing is that we are exactly right. If we had a right-side-up understanding of His Heart, we would find that the truth of *that* is enough to win the entire world. There is no need to hype up what is already perfect.

God does not delight in craftiness and deviousness. When we shrewdly invite our neighbors over for dinner and show a phony interest in their conversation for the purpose of weaving in an invitation to church, we are not acting in the Heart of God. This is literally impersonating the Devil himself. It's a mentality that completely side steps love and relies on cunning wit. We become as deceitful and calculating as the prowling wolf at a singles bar searching for the perfect one-liner.

The *love* in our hearts is what is supposed to win people to Jesus. This, and only this, is what God delights in. He delights in it because it's the most powerful force in the world. If we want to invite people to Church, GREAT, but just come out with it, and don't be sneaky about it. Their response will be directly linked to the love you have already shown them. If they turn you down, they are turning down the representation of Jesus you have already displayed to them. Believe me, if you love them, they will follow you anywhere.

God Rejoices With Jesus

If God is love and His Son Jesus is the Truth as the Bible says, than another way of saying "love rejoices with the truth" is to say "God rejoices with Jesus." God rejoices in the bare bottom facts about the simplicity of who Christ is. He is not embarrassed by the plainness of Christ. He even proclaimed several times that He was very pleased with His Son. Christ later praised His Father for

God rejoices in the bare bottom facts about the simplicity of who Christ is.

finding pleasure in revealing the truth to little children and keeping it hidden from the wise and learned.

God is pleased to reveal Himself to the world in the most common and easy to understand way. He rejoices in the fact that everyday people can connect and relate to Him. God has made the truth so basic and clear that even little children can know Him personally. This is the truth in Jesus that God was so pleased with. Love rejoices in truth being ever so basic and uncomplicated.

Having said that, I want to *hit* you with this next statement:

Super Spiritual People Will Never Know God

You know the kind of person I am talking about. They are a dime a dozen. Every facet of their humanity has been burned up with their mystical ideas of true spirituality. They commonly float through life acting as if they are on a higher spiritual plane of existence than the rest of the world. Their eyes have a distant glassy look to them as if they are peering into an invisible realm. All normalcy and common sense has been abandoned to their philosophy of supreme Christianity. Super spiritual people truly believe that the truth of God is found in the absolute abandonment of their humanity and the embrace of the mystical.

This is the number one reason why so many people miss God. They are just looking too deep.

These people I am speaking of simply *cannot* know the heart of God. Though they would tell you that they have received all the deep revelations of God, they are actually missing Him completely. The fact is, if they were confronted with a drop of truth about Him they would reject it with every fiber of their being because it would bore them to death. It would be a total let-down if they were to really know the truth. The sheer simplicity of it would be offensive to them. It might even sound blasphemous and disrespectful.

This is the number one reason why so many people miss God. They are just looking too deep. They want something huge and spectacular, and they won't accept anything less. Their hearts crave revelation beyond a dirty homeless carpenter. They find themselves studying the Greek and Hebrew words in the Bible and looking carefully in between each line in an effort to find something deeper than what is plainly stated. They will read it over and over waiting to receive something profound to explode and until it does, they feel like they are spiritually starving to death.

The Pharisees were exactly this way in their time. They were the experts in deep revelation about God; however, when God came and stood right in front of them they didn't recognize Him. Instead of rejoicing with the Truth (Jesus) they despised Him. They couldn't fathom accepting anything less than their lofty super spiritual fantasies about who God was. Surely, He was more profound than a simple carpenter! Jesus Christ was a complete let-down to the religious leaders of His time, and very little has changed today.

Anytime someone gives you a *new deep and profound spiritual truth* about the Heart of God you can pretty much count on it not being true. With Jesus Christ, what you see is what you get. You either accept it or you reject it. Jesus IS the mystery revealed. He is NOT a mystery that is still being revealed. He plainly said that if we love, we will know God; if we don't love, we won't know God. Don't ever look deeper than that. This is the very truth that God rejoices in. People who truly love, never question the truth of this. However, people who don't love, almost always reject this theology, and begin probing the Scriptures for something more flavorful and filling for their spiritual bellies. To the self-proclaimed super-spiritual Christian, the truth is impossible to see.

> *If you want to know the heart of God you must think simple. The deeper you look, the farther away you'll get from understanding.*

Keep this in mind. All truth must pass the "little child test." If a child can understand it, it's probably truth. If it's so deep that we need years of theological training to understand, *it's a lie*! If you want to know the heart of God you must think simple. The deeper you look, the farther away you'll get from understanding.

God Rejoices With The Truth About You

One of the biggest reasons why we avoid the truth in our relationships is because we honestly think it's too ugly to stomach. Most Christians I know have the idea that the truth about them is awful and unattractive. They believe that *they* and *only they* know the real truth, and if anyone were to get even a glimpse of it, they would turn their heads in disgust. I can't even compliment or encourage the average Christian person without them stopping me half-way through to inform me that I'm totally wrong.

> †
> *It is imperative that your perspective of YOU is altered if you ever want true relationship with God.*

They usually recite the usual line, "If you only knew the truth about me." They say this because they sincerely think the truth about them is appalling.

So my question to you is this: *Do you believe that God rejoices in the truth about you?* Think about that for a moment. If you are like most people, you probably believe that God knows the truth about you and He is repulsed by it. You think this way because you are certain that He has kept track of where you have been, and what you have done. Because these things repulse you personally, you can't imagine that God would think any different. When you think about your personal truth, you are immediately confronted with a thousand memories in your mind that are embarrassing and revolting. Most Christians I know don't believe for one moment that God rejoices in the truth about them.

The problem is that most of us associate our personal truth with the host of our personal failures. We have learned to callously define ourselves by the sins we struggle with. When we think about standing in the presence of God, we are terrified because we are sure His eyes are fixed on the very things we try our best to hide. We see these secret things as the ugly truth about us, and we can't imagine God rejoicing in them.

I want to show you something about the Heart of God that I believe will set you free from this horrible mindset. For you to receive what I am about to tell you, you must be willing to let yourself off the hook for what you believe you truly deserve. It is imperative that your perspective of YOU is altered if you ever want true relationship with God. You simply won't give Him your heart if you continue to believe the things about yourself that you do. It is impossible for anyone to have relationship with a God who sees people the way they see themselves. Prepare yourself and hold your breath as you read this next section.

The Truth About You And Your Past

The truth about you has nothing to do with what you have done or where you have been. God rejoices in the truth about you because it is truly something to rejoice about! One of the greatest problems with most people is that they honestly believe that they know the truth about themselves. What they think is the truth is really not truth at all. Most Christians confuse "*the facts of their life*" with "*the truth about themselves.*" This is one of the greatest causes of spiritual death that the Christian world has ever seen. The two are as far apart as the east is from the west. The *facts of our life* have nothing to do with the *truth about us.* God's eyes are fixed on the truth, and He rejoices in it because it's beautiful.

> ✝
> *Most Christians confuse "the facts of their life" with "the truth about themselves."*

God is not bound by time and space. He knows our future as well as our present. When He looks at us, He calls us by what He sees in our future, not by *what we see now*. With God, the future is as solid and real as we see the present. When He looks at us, it's important to know that He is not "hopeful" for what we *COULD become*, but He knows for a fact what we *WILL become*. This is the truth that God rejoices in! This is the name He calls us by and this is the only way He sees us.

Let go of what you believe to be the truth about yourself and open your heart to the things you have been dreaming that you would some day become. These dreams were put in your heart by God, Himself. You must familiarize yourself with them because the truth about you exists deep in the heart of the visions God gives you. Most people reject the vision God has given them because they don't feel they deserve it. This is not only spiritual suicide but it's an outright rejection of truth. God's vision that He has given you is the TRUTH about you. Embrace it, and call yourself by that name because that's the name He calls you.

> *When God looks at you, He calls you by a name that has nothing to do with your present situation or mindset.*

Our God saw the future of a man named Abram, and He gave him the name Abraham. God called a childless man "father of many nations." Then He went on to say, "IT HAS BEEN DONE." It wasn't as if God was telling Abraham that it was possible in the future. He was telling him the truth about his future.

God approached a cowardly man who was hiding in a cave and called him a "mighty warrior." Gideon's reaction was the same as many people today. He began to correct God with a long list of things in his present situation by which he defined himself, but God interrupted him and told him the real truth. He was a "mighty warrior" whether or not it had come to pass yet. It was a fact, and it was a truth that God rejoiced in.

God called Peter by the name of his future. He gave him the name "rock." Peter's present was anything but a rock, but Peter became a rock, that was the truth about Peter.

When God looks at you, He calls you by a name that has nothing to do with your present situation or mindset. Be excited about that and stop calling yourself the lying names of your present. There is a truth about you that is so wonderful and enticing that God cannot contain Himself whenever He looks at you. He sees that and only that. God truly rejoices with the truth about you!

Set Free By The Surprise Of Truth

I received a call from a pastor who was at his spiritual wits' end. This poor man had been secretly struggling with a pornography addiction and he was terrified to approach anyone for help who knew him. Without telling me his name, this precious person began to describe the level of imprisonment that the enemy had put him under. This man was on the verge of totally giving up. He not only felt condemned and ashamed, but he also felt a million miles away from God's Heart. His prayer life had been diminished to nothing more than a faint and parched plea for water once or twice a day. I could tell that every part of this man was in anguish.

He began to tell me how terrified he was of anyone finding out the "truth" about who he really was. This statement caused me to sit up in my chair in dismay and grief on his behalf. I asked him how he felt just after he had given himself over to another bout with pornography. I encouraged him to describe to me what goes on in his heart in the hours following another fall.

He began to describe the levels of anguish and personal disgust that would roll over his spirit in these times. He told me how dirty and shameful he felt inside because of what he had just participated in. Every part of his soul would go into a state of mourning and sadness. The thought of what he had just done was almost enough to make him vomit.

In the midst of this man's honest assessment of these inner feelings I interrupted him with a statement that changed everything. I told him that when God looks at him, He sees his heart, and God is absolutely proud of what He sees. In fact, this man had the very Heart of God and didn't even know it. He despised the very things that God despises and he was sickened by the things that God loathes. The very fact that this precious pastor felt the way he did about the sins he committed was evidence that he had the Heart of God! The truth about this man was NOT in the things with which he was struggling, but in his heart. This is the truth that God sees.

I am not in any way minimizing the destructiveness of pornography. That goes without saying. I am also not attempting to imply that we can all just live in sin because God knows our heart and that's all that matters. This story is a clear example of how internally destructive a life of sin can be. It also represents the destructive power that is ignited when we define ourselves based on that sin rather than truth.

This pastor was gloriously set free that day because the "truth" that was given to him was light years away from what he had believed. The bondage that this man was under was not the pornography; it was the name he began calling himself because of the pornography. When he realized how his Father in Heaven saw him, he began to immediately see himself in that same light and the moment he did, he was set free. It is imperative that you understand that God rejoices in the truth about you! Therein lies the secret to freedom from every sin with which you struggle. It is the truth that sets us free, and your truth is not what you have done, or where you have been. Your truth is found in your heart! It is that in which God rejoices.

Love Always Protects[14]

After my father left me at the age of six, my mother remarried about a year and a half later. Our house went from having three boys and a newborn baby girl, to having six children. My older brother Kevin was two years older than me. My younger brother Brian was about three years younger. I was right in the middle. When my mother remarried, I gained two more siblings, David and Michelle. David was fifty-five days older than Kevin, so they immediately paired off and became best friends. Michelle was three months older than Brian, so they paired off and became best friends. I was now not only in the middle, but dead in the middle.

By the time I was seven, my teachers discovered that I had a severe learning disability. Today it is known as dyslexia. In my day, however, dyslexia had not yet been discovered so I didn't have the privilege of wearing the medical diagnosis of dyslexia around my neck, back then we were just called stupid.

I couldn't read to save my life. By the time I reached high school, I was still at a third grade reading level. In fact, I was at a third grade level in every area in addition to reading. Most of my school years were spent sitting in "special reading," drawing pictures and writing short stories. This is what they have the children do when they don't know what else to do with the children. I think it's the school's last ditch effort to prepare them to maybe join the circus or link up with a traveling carnival, so they can at least say that they helped the "special" kids get a job, too.

I had five brothers and sisters who all did very well in school. I was the only one with the problem. I felt singled out by life. It was humiliating to have my baby sister who was seven years younger than me help me sound out the words on my tenth grade homework assignment. I wondered why this was happening to me, and I asked that question more than a million times.

Mrs. Newman

My third grade teacher had the biggest and perhaps the most negative effect on my life. She was the one who discovered that I had a learning disability coupled with an extreme attention deficit disorder. My secretary will solemnly swear that not much has changed today.

Mrs. Newman was a very harsh speaking woman with a gruff voice and a condescending spirit. I can recall looking into her eyes at the age of eight and seeing clearly that she detested me. Being hated by an adult was torturous and humiliating for an eight-year-old little boy. It drained every ounce of confidence right out of me. She defined who I was in this world. I looked up to her because she was my teacher and I truly wanted to please her, but no matter what I did, she despised me all the more.

The God's Honest Truth

This teacher would regularly stand me up in front of the class and humiliate me. She looked at me as if I was stupid. She got a thrill out of watching me break down and cry in front of everyone in the room. There is really no way to describe the horror of what I went through during that period of my life. I still have nightmares about it to this day. It changed the entire course of my life for the next twenty years.

That year, my parents took me to a psychologist for counseling. After spending one hour with me, the psychologist sternly warned my parents that something must be done immediately because he was certain that I was moments away from committing suicide. As I explained to you earlier, *I was already dead.* The day my father drove out of my life, I lost all hope and reason to go on. Mrs. Newman only compounded the anguish and confirmed that my existence didn't really matter.

Every morning as I set out for school, I felt like I was walking to a concentration camp. As I left my neighborhood and walked through the desert, my legs became weak and my heart sank in my chest. The moment my school came into view, I could feel a lump in my throat and my eyes began to burn with tears. Every morning I felt like a dead man walking his final walk to the gas chamber.

There was this *brown metal bridge* that hung over the busy street in front of my school. Crossing that bridge every morning meant that I was crossing from Heaven to Hell. Every morning I stood at the top of that ugly brown bridge, and I peered to the other side, with a dreadful feeling in my heart. As I walked that final twenty yards into what seemed like a furnace of emotional pain and torment, I would look over the side of that bridge and watch the speeding cars race underneath me. I wondered where they might be going in such a hurry. I wished that I could be in one of those cars instead of standing on the bridge to school.

There was a transformation that took place in my heart as I crossed that bridge. I became someone else completely. I had to in order to survive. When school was out and I was crossing that bridge on my way home, I could feel ME meeting back up with ME the moment I got to the other side. The next morning, however, I departed from myself just before I crossed back again to school.

One day I just sat in the middle of that bridge and never went to school at all. I just sat there and thought. I dreamed that there was something wonderful just beyond that old bridge instead of my elementary school. I squinted my eyes to see the faces of the people driving beneath me. I even considered jumping off that bridge and ending it all. All day, I just sat there and thought. I thought about my father and where he might be. I imagined he was sitting on the bridge beside me holding my hand. I dreamed that he would walk across with me and sit with me in class to protect me and comfort me. When I opened my eyes, he was not there, so I just sat there.

As the years passed by, I often wondered where God was during that time in my life. Why didn't He protect me from all those terrible things? How could He just sit there and allow this woman to hurt me so? Surely God was aware of what was happening. Why didn't He do anything to stop it? Where was this protection of His that I had heard so much about?

The World's View Of Protection

Few people would dispute the fact that love always protects. However, it all comes down to what they believe protection is. As a child, I had my own understanding of what it might be. I wasn't far off from what the rest of the world believes today. I have found that we live in a day and age where the definition of *protection* has been given a new twenty-first century meaning. As a result, many times we end up unintentionally cursing those we intended to protect.

Parents, in their effort to protect their children from sickness, sanitize every inch of their homes with all the newest disinfectants and cleaners. Their children could literally eat off the floor by the time they are finished. This is all done for the purpose of protecting their kids from harmful bacteria. The problem is that we are now finding out that children *need* bacteria to help develop their immune system. Now children are getting sick and almost dying from things as simple as a head cold because their body has never been exposed to bacteria.

It is ironic that sometimes what is thought to bring protection can actually be a curse in disguise.

It is ironic that sometimes what is thought to bring *protection* can actually be a curse in disguise. I am not saying that we all shouldn't keep a clean home; I am just confronting the mind-set that many of us have when it comes to what *protection* really is. We have come to believe that it means that nothing bad will ever happen to us. It is always associated with *physical* pain or discomfort. Because we live in a world where flesh is everything, it is not surprising that we define just about everything as it pertains to the flesh. Protection is no different.

Our world has clearly defined protection as pertaining purely to the flesh. They pride themselves for "using protection" when they have sexual intercourse with someone they barely know. As long as the flesh is protected, then it doesn't matter what they do. What is even more astounding is that if we buy into this tangled philosophy we are considered *wise* by the world's standards.

Once again, this upside-down version of protection ends up being a curse in the end, because there isn't a condom made that can protect the *spirit* and the *heart* of a person who engages in this behavior. When we are fooled into thinking that covering the flesh is more important than covering the heart, we are setting ourselves up for unparalleled emotional disaster.

The fact is, the world has taught us to hate *protection of the heart.* When the heart is protected, the flesh goes hungry. I cannot tell you how many times women have come to me asking me for godly and fatherly protection in their dating life. They honestly want my advice, and they promise to put themselves under my covering and listen to everything I say, because their past choices have proven deadly.

The problem is that the moment the first prowling guy comes on to them, and I take a stand on their behalf, they inevitably storm out of my office angry with me for *protecting their heart* from an obvious wolf. They despise protection of the heart because it doesn't allow immediate gratification for their flesh. Several weeks or months later, they come back with a broken heart and a host of spiritual scrapes and bruises because the man they wanted only wanted one thing.

> *When the heart is protected, the flesh goes hungry.*

Anytime something is defined by the flesh it cares only about the *here and now.* There is no *vision* in the world's view of protection. The world cannot see past tomorrow. If something is causing pain now, then there must not be any protection involved. Even if the pain is necessary for the purpose of protecting something bigger in the future, people will generally reject it. Our world simply does not believe that love always protects.

The God's Honest Truth

Mechanical Protection Mentality

The problem with our modern day definition of *protection* is that it is both shallow and nearsighted. When we see *protection* as only having to do with physical or emotional harm, we drastically depersonalize it. It becomes a mindless and heartless law that is the same for every person in every situation. When we coddle this *cookie cutter view of protection* we are also depersonalizing our God. We are taking something that has a personality and is meant for the

Eventually we begin to expect everything of God to work in a one size fits all manner.

heart and we are standing it alongside things that are heartless in their nature, such as gravity or time. Eventually we begin to expect everything of God to work in a one-size-fits-all manner. It's kind of like a vending machine or a calculator. This mind-set is not conducive to relationship. Its aim is *anti-relationship.*

We have all heard stories where someone was in a car accident and they escaped a head-on collision without a scratch. Our first response is to say that God was *protecting* that person. There is nothing wrong with believing that God played a major role in that situation, however, when we create a once-and-for-all definition of *God's protection* based on an incident such as this, we are gravely mistaken. What about the thousands of loving people who didn't escape without a scratch? What about the people who died in head-on collisions? Was God not protecting them? The moment we define protection in this way we are forced to assume that God's protection was lifted from those who were injured in car accidents as opposed to those who were not.

I believe that these *robotic expectations of protection* have woven themselves into every area of our religious thinking. The moment something bad happens in our lives, we immediately assume that God must have lifted His hand of protection. We frantically examine our lives and check for any reason why He might be angry with us, in an effort to explain why this terrible thing was allowed to happen. Unfortunately, there is always some area of personal failure that we can put our finger on so without missing a beat, we just accept our deserved punishment and go on. Perhaps, if we do better next time God will reconnect His *protection machine* to our lives.

Eventually, His ways become a mystery to us because they don't coincide with what is robotically supposed to happen. God becomes like a soda machine that has a mind of its own. It's not supposed to, but for some mysterious reason it does. This is why so many Christian people behave very much like folks do when the soda doesn't come down the chute. They become enraged and start slamming the machine with their fists in frustration. This isn't supposed to happen. They followed all the rules. They put the exact required amount in the slot. They pushed all the right buttons, yet they didn't get what they expected.

> ✝
>
> *Just about every Christian will agree that God protects, but very few believe in their heart that God ALWAYS protects.*

This is why if you ask most Christian people if they believe that God always protects, their answer is a resounding NO. Just about every Christian will agree that *God protects*, but very few believe in their heart that *God ALWAYS protects.* So we say things like, "If that person doesn't turn from what they are doing, God will lift His hand of protection from them." We have become certain that He does this because under our *mechanical definition of protection*, it truly seems to be going that way.

The best we can do is come up with teachings that seem to make sense of it all. So we describe God's protection as an umbrella

The God's Honest Truth

that if we step out from underneath, we will get rained on. Then we come up with a list of things that we must always be doing in order to stay under His *umbrella of protection*. Before long, an entire theology is developed to support our one-dimensional understanding of *God's protection*. It becomes contingent upon us following a list of laws and guidelines in an effort to earn it.

God's Protection Is Never Used Against You

God will never threaten to lift His protection to teach you a lesson. I am astounded at the number of people who think He does this. Though we have all heard the stories where it seems that God is using His protection as a tool to get His point across to someone, I assure you, that these testimonies are

> *God will never threaten to lift His protection to teach you a lesson.*

being translated by the teller, according to their own perceptions of Him. They are only evidence of the level of misunderstanding of God's heart that people in this generation have.

God protects you because He loves you. Not because you are being good and following the rules. Protection is a sacred thing with love. It is never used to manipulate or control. He would never threaten to take it away for the purpose of *getting your attention*. Just as we would never think of using this against our children, God won't do it with you. There are plenty of loving ways to get someone's attention without using fear.

Loved ones, you must know for sure that God will never, ever lift His hand of protection from you. Your security is sacred to Him. Without it, you are nothing and He knows that. We live in a world where things go wrong. Bad things happen to all people eventually. It's just a fact of life.

Don't ever suspect that God removed His protection in an effort to correct, rebuke or punish you when something bad happens in your life. He never once promised us that nothing bad would ever happen to us. As long as you are here on Earth, you will experience adversity and pain. Everyone does. You *must* know in your heart that when you do, it's not a sign that God has ceased to protect you.

God's Protection Is Totally Free

Thousands of well-meaning Christians daily offer up their prayers to "Father God" for His hand of protection over their family, business and home. They approach Him with fear and intimidation saying, "Father God I've paid my tithe this month so please protect my business. Father God, hold back the hounds of Hell from attacking my family. Father God please put angels around my home to guard it and protect it." What they really mean to call Him in their hearts is, "GOD FATHER." This is precisely the heart of what we believe about Him in this generation.

God has never changed, nor will He ever change, however THINGS have changed.

Modern day Christianity's teaching on the subject of *paying tithes*, is perhaps the greatest and most convincing evidence that as a whole, we don't believe *God always protects*. We see Him as a mafia kingpin who requires us to *pay Him off* for His protection. This picture we have painted of our Father in the twenty-first century is repulsive and heartbreaking.

Once again, this teaching is derived from an Old Testament verse that applied to Old Testament times. None of the New Testament writers talked about paying tithes! You would think that at least once, Paul would have mentioned it in his many letters to the churches if it still applied to this age. Why didn't Jesus sternly warn us to pay our tithes? The reason is because the New Testament age is pro-relationship! If you love, you will find 10% offensive because you will want to give everything. It is only through love that we are lifted out from underneath the law. It is imparative that you understand the New Covenent Age is NOT a time-zone it is a state-of-heart.

NO, I am not suggesting that *God has changed* from the way He was in Old Testament times. God has never changed, nor will He ever change; however, THINGS have changed.

January 13th 1996, at eleven o'clock in the morning, I married my beautiful wife Angie. On January 12th, only one day earlier, there were boundaries and limitations to our relationship that prohibited us from experiencing intimacy on certain levels. Twenty-four hours later, however, those boundaries were removed completely and Angie and I were free to experience intimacy on an entirely new level. It is important to understand that *I had not changed* one little bit within those twenty-four hours, but THINGS changed.

> ✝
> *Until we understand what has changed because of Christ, we will always be bound and gagged by the old unmarried mentality.*

Until we understand what has changed because of Christ, versus before Christ, we will always be bound and gagged by the old *unmarried mentality*. In many ways the Church resembles a couple that has only *dated* for fifty years, but never entered into marriage. Something begins to stink in a relationship that stubbornly rejects consummation. This is what most of our teachings do today. They reject the intimacy that God gave His Son for and embrace an anti-relationship mentality of solitude.

What would you think if I told you that every week when I get my paycheck, I gave my wife 10% for her bank account, and kept 90% for my personal account? You would say I had a troubled marriage. You might also say that my wife and I were struggling with the whole idea of the *oneness* of marriage. The fact is my wife and I share one bank account. Everything I have belongs to her and everything she has belongs to me. This is the heart of the New Testament.

In the Old Testament times, people PAID. In the New Testament times we GIVE. The difference between the two is the revelation of LOVE. I believe that we hold on to the Old Testament mentality because we are struggling with the *oneness* of marriage that God desires to have with us. Understand that you do not have to pay God for His protection. God always protects you and it's free because He is married to you. He is now one with you because of what was accomplished on the cross.

> *In the Old Testament times, people PAID. In the New Testament times we GIVE. The difference between the two is the revelation of LOVE.*

Understand that it is not my intent to discourage you from giving ten percent of your income or more to your church. In fact, if you attend a church, you are obligated by "love" to support that establishment. However, when doing so we must not think that we are either earning God's blessings or purchasing His protection. These things are free because your Father in Heaven also freely gives from a Heart of love.

The Heart Of Protection

Only a few hours after my wife and I had arrived at the hospital, we were holding hands and steadily breathing together.

Her contractions had escalated in a matter of hours and before we knew it, she was ready to begin pushing. As I held her hand and counted to ten with each agonizing contraction, she mustered up what little energy she had left to pass our fourth child into the world. This baby came so quickly that the nursing staff didn't even have time to prep the room for delivery. It seemed that it was all over before it began.

As I was cutting the cord, I noticed that something was wrong with the baby. She wasn't breathing normally. She was gasping with her entire body to get air into her tiny lungs. When I pointed it out to the doctor, he acknowledged that there was indeed a problem. A nurse came and tried to suction out her mouth in an effort to clear the air passages, but it didn't seem to help. They gave her a petite oxygen mask and put her under a heat lamp to warm her, but she continued to struggle.

As I kept one eye on my baby daughter and the other on the doctor, I began to seriously worry for her safety. I was worried because the doctor appeared to show very little concern for what was happening. I suppose he knew I was watching his response and using it as a *worry compass,* but his lack of concern troubled me all the more.

In the next twenty minutes, my daughter was taken from us and put in the hospital nursery to be kept under close supervision. This was particularly hard on my wife, because she had not even had a chance to hold our child. The head nurse came into our room several minutes later and explained that because our baby was born so fast, she was not able to get all the embryonic fluid out of her lungs. The nurse told us that this was very common with children who come out so quickly, but they just wanted to keep an eye on her for the next several hours to make sure she was okay.

For the next several hours, I stood outside the nursery and watched my daughter fight for her life. Watching her body seize up at every breath was almost more than I could take. Every so often, the resident nurse would look up from her desk at my daughter and then go back to what she was doing. This began to eat at me because it didn't appear that this person was giving my daughter the attention she needed. Truthfully, it didn't even seem like she cared.

After about five hours of this absurdity, I boldly forced my way into the nursery and directly confronted the nurse face to face. I was sick and tired of seeing my baby suffer, and I wanted something done about it now! Why couldn't they just extract the fluid from her lungs? Why couldn't they call in a specialist? Why weren't they doing anything but watching? Something needed to be done immediately, and it didn't appear that it was going to happen unless I lit a fire beneath them.

The head nurse was called in to speak with me about my concerns and answer my questions. In my impatience I had only one question: "What can be done NOW to help this baby?"

Her answer was deliberate and premeditated, and I will never forget it as long as I live. She looked me squarely in the eyes and said, "There is a lot we can do NOW to help your daughter, however, we are choosing not to do anything. We are giving this child time to *declare herself* before we step in and help." She explained to me that, "helping her now could actually be hurting her in the long run." She said, "This baby needs to fight for her life so she will become a strong adult in the future."

I appreciated that answer so much that I ran to my room to write it down. When I came back to the nursery I stood over my struggling daughter and bent over her and whispered in her ear, "Breathe baby, breathe. Breathe baby breathe." In the next few hours, baby Eva had won the battle! She was lovingly bundled up and safely returned to her mother's arms.

The Support Beams Of Life

God's protection for His children cannot be defined according to the flesh alone as we have done in this generation. Remember that God is a *heart person*, and we are created in His image. Though the flesh and the heart are interwoven, it is imperative that all things of God are seen and understood through the lens of the heart and not the flesh. The flesh is temporary, but the heart is eternal.

God's protection is a Father's promise to always hold us up in the midst of all circumstances. Love bears up under anything! It is the support beam that will never give way even in the midst of unimaginable pressure. The pressures and pains of life are not evidence of a lack of protection; they are the very things that prove God's protection. Understand that there is no escape from adversity and hardship as long as we live in this world.

> †
> *...it is imperative that all things of God are seen and understood through the lens of the heart and not the flesh.*

Bad things not only happen to good people, but they happen to all people. The good news is, that God will never cease to support and grow our heart regardless of what is thrown at the flesh. Love always thinks this way. It's all about the heart.

My baby daughter's struggle with breathing was due to a *purely physical condition*. Though there was much that could have been done *physically* to help her right away, the nurse was more concerned about her *heart*. It was her future character, her attitude and her inner willpower that was at stake. In this same way, God will never override the heart to save the flesh. Everything

He does is for the benefit of the heart because that's the part of you that lasts forever.

Love Inoculates The Heart

When my oldest daughter, Landin, was getting her first vaccination shots, it was a dark and dreary day in the Hufford home. Watching her go through the pain of that brought my wife and I to tears. I can remember the horror in her eyes when the first needle pierced her skin. I literally laid my body over hers and cried with her through the experience.

She had a look of disillusionment on her face that seemed to be searching for the answer as to why I was the one holding her down. It was as though she thought I was causing this pain deliberately, and she was couldn't understand why. Unfortunately, she was too young for me to explain that I did this because I love her. I did it to protect her from something that could possibly kill her in the future. It had to happen.

The only way to be safe from hardship and suffering is to endure it.

When we get a vaccination shot, we are actually being injected with the very thing we are trying to avoid. With a smallpox vaccination, they are purposefully shooting smallpox into our body. The same is true with the measles, the mumps and even the flu. Ironically, this is what it takes to be inoculated from these deadly diseases in the future.

Many people live bitter lives because of the pain of their past. They constantly rummage through all the terrible things that happened to them when they were growing up. They even become angry with God because He wasn't there to protect them. Their whole life was unfair and painful, and they spend the rest of their days going over it and over it. In the midst of their self-pity, they never stop to ask themselves what it is they have been inoculated from because of these experiences. Rather than embrace who they are today as a result of those vaccinations of the past, they choose to focus on the pain of the shot.

People who grow up in a stressful home where tension is always looming in the air have been inoculated from losing their mind in tense situations later in life. They become uniquely qualified to endure certain social climates because of what they went through in their past. On the other hand, if someone lived in a home of total peace all the time where confrontation never took place and they walked into a room today that was full of stress and tension, they would almost certainly lose their focus.

Every emotional vaccination that we have received in our past is uniquely fit for what our future holds.

Children who grow up in countries that are at war, become inoculated from the fear of death. Army boot camp is really a grueling few months of physical and emotional inoculations from the strain of war. This principle is true in every area of life. Football players are inoculated from being knocked unconscious when they are slammed into the ground, because at practice they were slammed over and over and over again. Anytime you take your shots like these guys do, there is very little that can affect you from that point on. The only way to be safe from hardship and suffering is to endure it.

Your Protection Has To Do With Your Purpose

Every emotional vaccination that we have received in our past is uniquely fit for what our future holds. If I were going to Calcutta, India on a missions trip, I would undergo a series of vaccination shots that specifically pertain to diseases that are common in

Calcutta. What would be the point in getting a mumps vaccination if the mumps were not in Calcutta? Only the things that pertain to that specific area would be shot into my body to prepare me for the journey. In the same way we have to understand that with God, our protection has to do with our purpose.

When God was creating you, He also created a purpose for your life. He knew ahead of time what kind of family you had to grow up in, in order to prepare and shape your heart for your ultimate purpose in life. God did not delight in the abuse you may have endured when growing up, nor did He cause it to happen. He was there with you, crying and holding your hand, just as I was the day my daughter Landin received her shots. It's worth it to Him because He knows that it has everything to do with your future purpose. When you fulfill that purpose you will be at your maximum level of happiness and satisfaction. That's the thing about a purpose. It is custom made for you, and when you reach it and live inside of it, you will find supreme fulfillment because it was specifically fitted to your personality. Fitting into your purpose in life is everything!

The Bridge To My Purpose

Ten years ago, I arrived in Phoenix, Arizona from Hollywood, California for the purpose of attending the Masters Commission program at Phoenix First Assembly. Masters Commission is like an evangelism boot camp that trains people in outreach and youth ministries. I had sold everything I owned and moved to Phoenix to attend this nationwide program in hopes that it would be my entrance into the ministry.

The first day it began, I was driving to the church down a road that I had never been on before in my life. My heart was reeling with anticipation for what the coming weeks and months would hold for me. As I was praying and thinking about everything I had been through in the last thirty years that had lead up to this moment, I casually looked up from the road and THERE IT WAS.

I almost stopped breathing when I saw it because *it wasn't supposed to be there*. Nevertheless, almost twenty miles away from where I grew up as a child there stood the *brown metal bridge* I used to cross to school every day. Evidently it had been picked up from where I used to live and brought to this little street I was driving down.

As I raced beneath the bridge on my way to church, I looked up and there stood a little boy looking over the side at me. Without warning, I began to cry. My mind was flooded with the memories of that terrible bridge and the hours I spent on it as a child. In that moment, the Lord began to speak to me about my purpose in life.

He began to reveal to me that everything I went through as a child was for the purpose of preparing me for my purpose in life. It had to happen! I was called to listen and understand hurting people. I was called to love those who felt abandoned and encourage those with low confidence. And I truly did love them. My heart bled for them. I couldn't help myself; it was just a part of me. Every single grueling experience that I had endured as a child was preparing my heart for a ministry that would bring the maximum amount of joy and contentment in my life.

Looking back on the pain of my past, in the light of what I am doing now, I wouldn't change a single thing. He was protecting me all along. It was worth it, and I would do it all again. Just as King David thanked God for broken bones, I daily find myself praising Him for allowing me to be inoculated for a ministry that has brought absolute fulfillment in my life.

It was He who held me up when my teacher would humiliate *me* in front of the class. It was He who walked me across the bridge to school when I was eight years old and terrified. He was even there the day I sat on that bridge and contemplated jumping off. He was holding me up in the midst of pressure and torment, and He has never failed me yet. Love always protects!

Love Always Trusts[15]

My house is beginning to look more and more like a daycare center. We now have four daughters ranging from five years old to eight weeks. From morning to night the sounds of giggling, whining, crying and laughter can be heard in every room. There is rarely a moment of peace and quiet. Believe it or not, after a hard and stressful day at work, I actually look forward to coming home to the chaos of the screaming quartet. It's where I belong and I wouldn't give it up for the world.

Ever so often, I am reminded of the sheer power and responsibility of my position as their father. It's a million times more than just providing food and shelter. That's about three percent of my job. My real calling springs to life the moment I look into their eyes and I see their unconditional wholehearted trust in me. It's almost more than I can bear.

If they knew the truth about my humanity, they would surely withdraw their confidence in daddy. Nevertheless, they fall asleep in my arms in a public place without even a hint of worry. They leap off the edge of the pool into my arms without reservation. They beg me to play "blast off" where I throw them high into the air and catch them while their mother nervously watches. The sun rises and sets at my command as far as they are concerned. No other man is better looking, stronger or smarter than me. My words determine the course of their lives, my eyes reveal who they are and my kisses bring healing to their "owies."

It is difficult for me to imagine that someday their trust might wither away from me. The thought of that happening makes me ill. If that gaze of "believe" in their eyes were to fade away when they looked at me, I am not sure I would know who I was any more. Within that look, lies the power that drives me to do great exploits on their behalf. It kills every selfish part of me and purifies my heart. I could never imagine their trust withering away.

Beating Up Trust

Very few people in today's world believe in their hearts that love always trusts. While the majority would unanimously agree that it *should* trust, they would tell you that the reality is that it just simply doesn't.

Our understanding of the concept of *trusting* has taken a serious beating in this generation. We define *possessing trust* according to how it pertains to us in the here-and-now. We want to know if we can trust someone to be faithful to us, or to tell us the truth. We question whether or not a person can be trusted to keep our secrets or to not talk badly about us behind our back. If someone proves him or herself worthy of our trust, then we finally *possess trust.*

All people start out with a zero balance of trust in today's thinking. Whatever trust they get from that point on is earned.

Once it is earned, the person suddenly becomes worthy of our trust, or "trustworthy." If they do one thing wrong, however, they are catapulted back to a zero balance and made to start all over again. If they fail in one area, every other area is immediately closed to them as well.

This is a losing game all the time because the person, who requires their trust to be earned, is usually subconsciously looking for a reason to take it back. Though they claim that it can be earned from them, they begin to frantically come up with reasons to take it back the moment they feel like they might have to open themselves up to it. They will purposefully take the slightest mishap and blow it up to

> *Having a lack of trust has become a sign of strength in today's society.*

look like a mountain of betrayal so they can keep themselves comfortably closed off and self-protected. The person earning the trust eventually realizes that the cards are stacked against them and they eventually give up altogether.

Many people simply don't trust anyone anymore. There are two kinds of non-trusting people in the world. The first one is what I call the quiet *non-truster*. Usually this person has made a decision early in life that trusting is of no use to them, and they have given up on humanity as a whole. These people just live in a dark hole of solitude, and have learned to be comfortable.

The second non-truster is much louder. You can usually tell who they are because for some reason they feel like they have to announce it to the world. What they are really meaning to portray is that they are strong. Having a lack of trust has become a sign of strength in today's society. All the heroes in our favorite action movies have renounced trust altogether. It's not only seen as independent and powerful, but a lack of trust is also perceived as wisdom. It comes with the title of "streetwise." The number one rule of thumb on the streets or in the world in general is to not trust anyone, ever. It's the greatest form of self-protection we know. We build walls around our hearts so that no one gets in and no one gets out.

Trust is very much like *protection* in that the true significance of the word has evolved into a shallow and superficial meaning in our minds. As long as *trust* is seen from this selfish upside-down perspective we will never truly taste its beauty and possess its power. We will also ultimately define the Heart of God and our relationship with Him in accordance with what our heart believes about this subject. Evidence of this is seen all throughout our religion's reasoning.

The Christian View Of Trust

When I first became a Christian, I ran a homeless ministry in downtown Los Angeles. On several occasions, I invited homeless people to come and live with me. One woman in her forties lived with us for about eight months. Diane had been drunk since she was eighteen years old and had been living on the streets for twelve years. She made incredible progress during her stay with us, and we became good friends.

One day, however, Diane relapsed. She stole my typewriter and my brother's leather jacket and disappeared. After scouring the inner city, we finally found her and brought her home. I sat with her personally for three days, until she was completely sober again. The moment I left for work on the fourth day, Diane left for the inner city with *my* leather jacket and my brother's bass guitar. We searched and found her again and brought her home. After she was sober again, she left with a pair of expensive boots and one of our cell phones. Believe it or not, we repeated this scenario several more times until we never found her again.

My view of "Christian trust" was different from the world's view of trust; however, it was just as shallow and small-minded. I thought that Christians were to show unconditional trust in all areas pertaining to all *things*. It was the extreme opposite end of the world's view. I soon found out that trust is not about THINGS, but about a position of the heart.

This misguided view of "Christian trust" has proved to be a huge stumbling block for thousands of well-intentioned people. We have become an easy target for the world. I've watched women stay with an abusive or alcoholic boyfriend who is cheating on them simply because he said he would stop. She thinks that trusting him is the Christian thing to do. Con artists have learned to play the "God card" when approaching people in a church parking lot for money. It works every time. Even the homeless have learned that if they hold a sign that says, "God bless," they will get the Christian handout. While not every Christian is this naïve, there are many who honestly believe that they are supposed to be.

...trust is not about THINGS, but about a position of the heart.

After being personally ripped off so many times because of my ill guided concept of trust, I became fearful of a *trusting God.* If God is love and love always trusts than I wasn't sure if I could trust God. He might release Charles Manson from prison or call an ex-child molester to work in the Church nursery. The thought of God being so naïve and trusting frightened me to death.

What Does It Mean To Trust As A Christian?

Trust is not only about specific *things* and *situations* like our world has taught us. Trust is a posture of the heart. Love cannot be achieved without trust because trust IS the doors of the heart.

If we define trust from the perspective of the flesh, we will miss it completely. Trust comes from the heart and has to do with heart things. It is not only possible to have both a practical wisdom along with a Kingdom heart, it is required! Jesus said to be wise as serpents and harmless as doves.

This balance is absolutely necessary. The world has taught us that trust is either all or nothing. There is no middle ground. Either we trust someone completely in every area, or we don't trust him in any area. This is not true of Kingdom trust. It doesn't open and shut the doors of the heart. Kingdom trust clearly defines what issues call for wisdom, and what issues call for trust. The two are as far apart as the east is from the west.

It is possible to deny an ex-child molester a position in the church nursery and keep our heart doors open to him at the same time. It is possible to not allow someone to abuse us and still keep our heart opened to his heart. Just because we may not give a man who has a gambling problem the position of church treasurer, doesn't mean that we have to close our heart to him.

What the world fails to see is that *trust* is not about *topics*. Topics require wisdom and have very little to do with trust. Though I don't hand my five-year-old daughter the keys to my car and tell her to take it for a spin, that doesn't mean that I don't *trust* her. She doesn't know how to drive. Her feet wouldn't reach the gas pedal. She couldn't even see over the dashboard. My decision has nothing to do with *trust* and everything to do with *wisdom*. Trusting my daughter is far deeper than a set of car keys. When we attempt to make driving a car at the age of five a *trust issue*, we are transplanting a *heart word* into a fleshly climate and ultimately **killing it.**

> † *Kingdom trust clearly defines what issues call for wisdom, and what issues call for trust.*

The world has taught us that trust is about *topics* because worldly thinking is predominately selfish. All self-centeredness views heart things from a fleshy perspective, and the result is an upside-down definition of truth. The statement, "I love pizza" is a perfect example of *heart words* being trivialized and altered to a casual and tacky shallowness.

Trusting God

When we get in the habit of playing out the world's interpretation of trust in our earthly relationships, we eventually conduct ourselves the same way in our relationship with God. In the world, if someone doesn't come through for us, we close him off

> ✝
> *God hears our hearts over our mouths.*

altogether. Rather than pinpoint the exact area in which he failed us, and use practical wisdom in that specific area, we assume that he cannot be trusted in *any* area, and we lock him out of our hearts for good.

This attitude becomes the blueprint for our interactions with God as well. If something bad happens in our lives, we assume that God can't be trusted in any area and we close our hearts off from Him completely. If we don't get the *things* we want *here and now*, then we find Him more and more difficult to trust. Rather than sit down and take an honest look at the specific incident in which we feel He failed us, we just write Him off all together.

We do this because our eyes are on the physical things that we want and not on the true desires of our heart. We determine His trustworthiness by whether or not we get the promotion at work, or the car we prayed for. If He provides the extra money to make our bills, then He has earned our trust. If our car breaks down, or we get an extra bill we didn't expect, then God's trustworthiness is in question. The moment something doesn't happen in the *here and now arena*, we shut Him off completely.

One of the things that we have to understand about the Heart of God is that He hears our *hearts* over our *mouths*. We are in the habit of asking Him for things that are totally contrary to what our heart desires. Most people are not even in touch with their own heart, so when God answers the prayers of their *hearts* over the prayers of their *mouths*, they are totally mystified and perplexed. Their entire life is full of answered prayers only they don't know it because they never heard themselves ask for it in the first place. Because they didn't get the THINGS that their mouth asked for here and now, they stop trusting God from their heart.

I know men who have totally closed their hearts off from women. They don't trust them as far as they could throw them. I also know women who feel this exact same way about men.

> ✝
> *Most people are not even in touch with their own heart, so when God answers the prayers of their hearts over the prayers of their mouths, they are totally mystified...*

Their heart is so miserably untrusting and clogged because of the pain of their past that they are actually fearful of the idea of opening up to a man. Ironically, both these men and women who feel this way almost always pray (with their mouths) and ask God to send them a mate. When it doesn't happen, they lose all trust in God because it didn't appear that He answered their prayer. The problem is that God *did* respond to their prayer, but they just don't remember praying it. Remember, God is a *heart* person. He listens and speaks only to the heart. If your mouth is praying, "please, send me a mate" and your heart is praying, "Please keep all members of the opposite sex away from my heart" your answer from God will be in accordance with your *heart's prayer*, not your mouth.

I believe that this is the reason why most people's prayers seem to dissolve into thin air the moment they leave their lips. They are really not prayers at all, because they are so disconnected from the truth of what's really on the person's heart. When we pray for someone to be healed, but we could care less if they are healed or not, we aren't praying at all. We are just exercising our gums. Many married people pray every day that God will break through their individual walls of protection and create a deeper intimacy in their relationship; however, if the truth be known, neither one of them desires closeness with the other in the least. The thought of it makes their heart sick. After years of anguish and loneliness in their marriage, they lose all trust in the power of prayer because they honestly feel that they've tried it. If they were to be totally honest with themselves, they would come to the conclusion that they got exactly what their hearts wanted, nothing!

> *When we pray for someone to be healed, but we could care less if they are healed or not, we aren't praying at all.*

The Bible says to trust in the Lord with all your *heart*, and lean not on your own understanding. It is God who gives us the desires of our hearts, but if we don't know our own hearts, then we won't think He ever gives us anything. This one principle alone can totally change the way you hear and understand Him. We find Him difficult to trust because we have been talking and listening from our HEAD, and we have been expecting Him to give us the desires of our flesh. Once things are turned right side up, relationship can flourish and spring to life.

Here And Now Things

So many misinformed Christians think that *giving God their heart* means *giving God their things*. Because they feel that their heart may be wrapped up in their stuff, they conclude that God must want their stuff. So they begin to play the *things-here-and-now-game* with God because this is how they themselves associate earning trust. They dangle their stuff like a carrot in front of His face, hoping to entice Him into giving His trust to them.

Sadly, they are assuming that He thinks like humans do. Until that opinion of Him is abandoned completely, they will continue working to earn His trust all their lives, never realizing that they had it all along. Remember, Kingdom trust is not to be defined from a fleshly perspective. Any time we reduce the beauty of God's open heart towards us to a few earthly topics, we are redefining Kingdom things and trivializing truth.

When I hear someone proclaim that God is "waiting for them to be trustworthy" before He can give them a new position of authority, my response is a quote from one of my favorite movies, "The Princess Bride."

"You keep saying that word. I don't think that word means what you think it means."

God's trust cannot be summed up by one or two things, He doesn't give us when we ask. Just because He doesn't put us in a leadership position, doesn't mean that God does not trust us. There are thousands of reasons why it just might not be right for us at that particular time. Selfish thinking always forces it to be a trust issue, but that just doesn't make it so.

> ✝
> *Anytime we place the word "trust" in place of "wisdom," terrible things happen to our relationship with Him.*

Perhaps God is teaching us something else at the time, and the extra stress of leadership would be counterproductive to that path. It might even be that we simply are not emotionally ready for the weight that comes with such a position, and He would rather wait until we have less on our plate. Whatever the reason, we can be sure that the issue is not *trust*, but *wisdom*.

Many people pray for God to send them a mate, however, their life is entirely too hectic and busy for a relationship. They haven't even stopped to take a practical look at their daily schedule before asking God for something that couldn't survive three days if He gave it to them. Until they thin out their schedule, they wouldn't make a good mate for anyone. God's wisdom cannot allow Him to toss

It is important to God that we know without a shadow of a doubt that He ALWAYS trusts us.

that person the keys to a relationship that they are incapable of driving at this point in their life. It's not about trust; it's about wisdom. God can do this and keep His heart fully open to that person at the same time because God always trusts!

It is imperative that we understand the difference between God's *trust* and His *wisdom*. Anytime we place the word "trust" in place of "wisdom," terrible things happen to our relationship with Him. The moment we believe that He doesn't trust us, we begin to feel rejected by Him. The feeling of rejection causes a natural human reaction to take place. We shut our hearts down and close ourselves off from intimacy with God.

We all have within us the need to know that we are trusted by our Father. We define ourselves and our worthiness by how open we feel His heart is to us. If we perceive it to be closed, we will spiritually and emotionally implode. The name, "unworthy" will follow us wherever we go. This is devastating to the human heart, because whatever our creator believes about us is what we will ultimately become. His trust is the very thing that holds us together.

It is important to God that we know without a shadow of a doubt that He ALWAYS trusts us. His heart is never closed. This inner knowledge produces trust and openness within us towards Him. Trust that is willing to submit to His wisdom at any cost without feeling like He has closed His heart towards us is essential, but not possible unless we believe this principle.

Do You Believe That God Always Trusts You?

The question really is; do you believe that God's heart is always opened to you regardless of your situation in life? While the answer for you might be an easy YES, I wonder what answer your *heart* would give. I have found that with all the religious jargon in the world today, it is next to impossible to believe that God's Heart is always open to us whatever our situation in life. Our heads believe it, but our hearts can't even conceive it.

Many of us can't fathom God having an open heart, because of the many times we have been black-balled by fellow Christians in the past for something we did or did not do. The moment we step out of line with the rules of our denomination, we find that people who were our best friend the day before, now refuse to have anything to do with us. The slightest slip in one area of our lives becomes public knowledge and reason enough to withhold trust in

When we find ourselves performing for God in order to prove to Him that we are trustworthy, we are telling Him that we believe we have to earn His

every area of life. It's difficult *not* to make assumptions about the Heart of God through the actions of His children.

If you were sitting in your car at a stoplight and looked over to the car next to you to find your pastor smoking a cigarette, while waiting for the light to change, what kind of things would go through your mind? If you are like most people, you would immediately think to yourself that you couldn't ever trust anything he said from the pulpit from that day forward. This is the common reaction that many Christians today have been taught to have. They behave this way because this is how they think God behaves. Remember that we all will ultimately be conformed to the image of who we believe our Father in Heaven is. How can we believe that God never closes His heart doors towards us when the majority of our Christian brothers and sisters do the exact opposite?

> ✝
> ..."backsliding" is built on an inner belief that God closes His heart off to people who make mistakes.

When we feel like we have to wait a day or two after we sin before we can approach God with confidence and boldness, we are declaring in our hearts that we don't believe *God always trusts.* When we find ourselves performing for God in order to prove to Him that we are trustworthy, we are telling Him that we believe we have to *earn His open heart.* When we feel extra bold and secure in His presence because we've been particularly good in the past week or two, we are subtly admitting that we don't believe His heart is *always* opened to us. Anytime we feel closer and more accepted by Him as a result of a rule we followed or a religious principle we practiced, we are guilty of believing God does not always trust.

I believe that the entire infrastructure of the concept of "backsliding" is built on an inner belief that God closes His heart off to people who make mistakes. It is not until a person is willing to repent and "do right" by God that they feel God's heart is open to them again. The entire process of "backsliding" begins with misconceptions about the Heart of God that propels a person further and further from Him.

A person sins, and he immediately feels that God has turned His heart from him. They decide to wait a few days before approaching Him, and in the midst of those few days, they sin again. Now they are forced to wait an additional few days, and almost always they sin once more in that time. Before they know it, they have assumed a life emotionally separate from the Lord for several years. All the while, they are subconsciously scanning their religion to see if God would have them back. They are waiting for a sign to tell them that God's heart is open to them once more. Once they find it, they crawl back to Him in repentance. This entire scenario could have been avoided if the truth about God was never compromised.

Open Heart Surgery

One of the learning channels that my wife and I watch regularly had a special on emergency room traumas. We usually don't allow gory movies into our home, but this was an educational channel, so it kind of made it *legal gore*.

One of the first patients to arrive in the emergency room had been shot in the chest. There were about six doctors around him working feverishly to save his life. At one point he "flat lined" and they brought out the shockers to bring him back to life. When that didn't work, they decided to massage his heart manually. To do this, they brought out a big saw and literally cut right through his sternum. They made doors in his chest so they could get to his heart. Once this poor man was completely opened up, the doctor reached inside of him and massaged his heart until the man had a pulse again. It was the most astounding thing I had ever witnessed.

In the midst of watching this play out in my living room, the Lord spoke to me and said, "This is relationship." He began to show me that this is exactly what God requires in every relationship He has. Total openness! Complete vulnerability! For any relationship to be authentic, the heart doors of both people must always be opened.

Imagine the level of trust that this young man had to have while lying on the operating table. He was wholly opened and naked. Every hidden part of him was exposed for the purpose of saving his life. If he had refused access to his heart, he certainly would have perished. Relationships are exactly the same way. If the heart doors are not opened at all times, you will die. This principle runs throughout every aspect of love. It is a very picture of who God is when He comes to you.

The very last scene of the life of Jesus was every bit as gory as that show I watched that day. He was completely naked, spread eagle and opened up. Jesus Christ was God introducing Himself to the world. It was a perfect picture of how God expresses Himself in the context of relationship. He keeps nothing hidden from His children. Everything has been exposed for you to see, because that is what

> *For any relationship to be authentic, the heart doors of both people must always be opened.*

relationship requires. Don't ever think that God will stop trusting you if you mess up. He is the very author of trust and openness. It is impossible for Him to contradict who He is. Rest in that and rejoice, because your Father in Heaven loves you and *love always trusts*!

Love Always Hopes [16]

It didn't matter on this day if the other kids made fun of me or picked me last for their team. It didn't matter if I couldn't read or write as well as the other children, or if I sat alone in the lunchroom. It didn't even matter if the teacher humiliated me in front of the class and sat me in the corner. Today, it just didn't matter because I was holding something deep inside of my heart that no one could take away. It got me through the day. It made awful things trivial and sad things happy. This day was different from any other day because this was the day my parents showed me the tickets to Disneyland that they had bought the day before. We were going in three months, and nothing else mattered between now and then.

At any moment, when the depression started to set in, I would just remind the depression that I was going to Disneyland in three months, and it would leave me alone for another day. When worry would begin to tangle my mind the night before school, I would remind the worry that I was going to Disneyland in three months and it quieted down and left me. If loneliness whispered lies into my ear, I responded by telling the loneliness I was going to Disneyland in three months, and the loneliness wasn't allowed to come along. Nothing could hurt me for the next three months because I had been given a hope to anchor myself to. As long as the tickets were pinned to the refrigerator, and the date was set on the family calendar, I was bigger than the normal me.

My mind would go there ahead of time, as if to practice and rehearse the things I might do. I would picture myself waiting in line for a ride with popcorn in one hand and a corn dog in the other. At night when everyone else was sleeping, I would lie in bed and close my eyes, and if I tried really hard I could almost hear the sounds and smell the air of the Magical Kingdom. I would get that feeling of contentment in my heart that reminded me of when I used to lie under the Christmas tree and look up at the lights and ornaments dreaming of Christmas Day. There is nothing like that feeling in the air. It overpowers every bad thing in life and there were many nights that it rocked me to sleep in its arms like a caring mother with her child. When I was there, in that state of mind, it didn't matter what else happened, because I had hope to tow me through it.

The Evolution Of Hope

When most people think of "hope," a certain feeling comes to their minds. It's viewed as a dreamy fantasy that isn't certain, but it's great to imagine. In the midst of struggle and turmoil, a *hopeful* person might say, "maybe this or that could happen," or "perhaps it could be so." Irrespective of their situation, they "hold out hope" by being optimistic and positive. They are holding on to a dream and refusing to be affected by their surroundings.

Whether or not that dream ever comes to pass is not the issue; it's just the fact that the dream is there that matters.

Children *hope* they can be a ballerina or a professional baseball player. Women *hope* they don't gain weight when they get older and men *hope* they make a lot of money and get that big promotion at work. Terminally ill patients *hope* that they get better and beat the sickness. Prisoners *hope* that they will be released early, and everyone else *hopes* they won't. Football teams *hope* to win the Super Bowl and people who buy lottery tickets are *hoping* to win.

Though most of these things are possible, they are not probable, however, our view of hope chooses to make them at least appear probable for the moment. It gives us a slice of something we need to get us through the day. If it doesn't happen, that's okay, too; at least we didn't give up *hope*. The evolution of the meaning of hope in our minds

> *The problem with today's definition of hope is that it has been reduced to wishing...*

begins to resemble the very things we are in the habit of putting it into. Hope becomes possible, but not probable.

The problem with today's definition of hope is that it has been reduced to *wishing* for something that might or might not happen. There is no guarantee. It's just a dream of what could possibly take place, but it's not a true picture of what will take place. I suppose there isn't anything wrong with wishing and dreaming, but when it takes the place of hoping, or is seen as the exact same as hoping, we are making a grave mistake.

Children start out with about ninety percent dreams and ten percent truth. As they get older, they begin to experience more and more truth and eventually they replace the dreams and fantasies with facts and reality. Very few adults are as *dreamy* as children, because they have found that most of those dreams they had as a child were not authentic or even possible. For instance, an umbrella cannot make you fly and wooden puppets don't become real boys. After believing in those fantasies and being let-down by them so many times, most people eventually come down from their dreamy mind-set and live in the real world.

When we associate hope with dreams, we are treading on dangerous ground because the inevitable end of that mind-set will be hopelessness. This is, in fact, what has happened to the word *hope* in our generation. We have redefined it to mean *wishing* or *dreaming*. When we say that love always hopes, we immediately get a childish fantastical view of love that is difficult for any thinking person to relate to. Until we define the truth about what hope is, we will never be able to possess it and keep it safe in our hearts.

The Hope We Have In Christ

Every time I read in the Bible about the hope we have in Christ, there was always a check in my spirit. The Apostle Paul would talk about how Jesus Christ had risen from the dead and

> *Until true hope is restored and understood, it will be impossible to know what to do with it and how to use it.*

was now at the right hand of the Father interceding for us, and then out of the blue Paul would say he *hopes* this is true. "Which is it?" I would think to myself, "is it true or not?" It almost had a tone of uncertainty to it when I read it. How can you know something is true and then *hope* it's true in the same breath? Truthfully it sounded to me like Paul wasn't sure whether Christ rose from the dead or not.

If *God is love* and *love always hopes* then that must mean that *God always hopes*. This brings up an entirely different question.

Why would God need to hope for anything? Doesn't He know the beginning from the end? Is it true what some people say about Him, that He chooses not to look at the end so He can experience the ride along the way? Does God block out from His mind what He knows will happen so He can hope it will happen with us? That sounds a bit weird to me.

I couldn't imagine God hoping something will happen when He already knows for sure whether or not it will. Why would hope even need to be there? What would be the point of hope if you knew for sure the end of a thing? If you watched a rerun of a football game and already knew who was going to win, would you find yourself *hoping* that they would win? They're going to win whether you hope or not, so what difference would it make?

The problem with our modern day understanding of the word "hope" is that we have twisted its meaning in the same way we have twisted the words "protect" and "trust." The new revised definition comes out looking like the exact opposite of the real thing. Each time we do this in the English language we set ourselves up for unparalleled destruction. Until true hope is restored and understood, it will be impossible to know what to do with it and how to use it.

The Purpose Of Hope

When God created hope, it had a specific purpose. Hope is very precious and important to every Christian person. Life depends on hope and God made it that way. It is very dear to His heart because of the power it possesses for His children. When a person loses their hope, they basically lose their life. It is everything to a child of God. We can't even have faith without hope. Our entire faith is held together by the hope we have in God. If that hope is taken away or drained, the aftershocks will rock throughout every area of our lives. The very purpose of hope will be lost and we will be left empty and vacant.

The purpose of *hope* is for it to be inserted into truth. This is the most important element of hope that you must understand before we go another inch in this book. Hope must always be inserted into truth. If it is placed in anything else other than truth, it will die!

When hope is placed in truth, it tows us through everything in life. There is nothing a person cannot endure if their hope is placed in truth. It was created for truth. There is a hitch on the back of truth that connects to hope and pulls us through circumstances and situations that we could not otherwise make it through.

The problem is that God also gives us choice. We have a choice where to tie our *hope rope.* There is also a hitch on the back of every lie that fits perfectly with hope, but it tows us to death and destruction. Any time we willingly choose to tie our hope to something other than truth, we will eventually be dragged to our death and lose all hope.

Hope has become dangerously distorted in this generation. We have come to believe that hope is *not for sure* because we have hitched it up to things that are not for sure. Our definition of hope has changed to fit our misuse of it. Because of the fact that we choose to put it in things that *could be* or *might be,* we have experienced constant let-downs. Those let-downs have stamped a false image of the meaning of hope on our hearts. Eventually we begin to lose hope because its new meaning doesn't have something that we need attached to it.

> ## ✝
> *We have come to believe that hope is not for sure because we have hitched it up to things that are not for sure.*

Instead of being irreplaceable and essential it becomes *nice to have* but not indispensable.

When we lose our hope, we lose our faith as well. This is why so many women will tell you that they have lost all faith in men. They lost faith because they put their hope in men who proved that they were not worthy of it. They hitched their *hope rope* to obvious lies and deception because those lies made them feel good for the moment and then allowed themselves to be towed around until they lost everything. All the while, they said to themselves, "I hope he changes." Instead of putting their hope in the truth about that man, they chose to put it in the lies they told themselves about him. Sometimes it works and sometimes it doesn't. This is precisely from where the modern day definition of hope was born. Sometimes it works, sometimes it doesn't.

Hope must always be inserted into truth. If it is placed in anything else other than truth, it will die!

When a person comes to me and tells me that they have lost their faith, my first response is to ask them "What have you put your hope in?" Almost always I find that they had put it in a string of lies that were sure to fail them.

Hope was designed by God to be inserted into truth and nothing else. We *lose hope* when we gamble with it in an effort to get what we want here and now. When we tie it to something that we know in our hearts is a lie, but we wish in our heads that it isn't, we are gambling with our portion of hope that God has given us. The end result is always the same: hopelessness.

Men date women who are sleazy and flirtatious, and then they hope she will settle down when they get married and change her ways. When she starts flirting with his friends and the marriage finally ends, his hopes are dashed to the ground. Women will marry a man who has been divorced three other times with the hope that he won't leave her as well. When it happens, her hope is crushed and killed and she loses faith in men altogether. Some people give up their job because they met a guy whose sister's cousin's boyfriend's mother's aunt has an uncle who says he would hire them in a heartbeat. Before they know it, they are living on the street and without hope.

The most awful thing about all of this is that many of us actually attribute these actions to being "acts of faith." We think it's Christian behavior to place our hope in things regardless of the truth that surrounds them. This is how many Christians see godliness because this is how many people see God. They honestly feel that it's in God's heart for them to insert their hope into anything and everything. The act of *hoping against all odds* feels Christian to them. It has become associated with faith. This is grieving to God because it assumes that He desires His children to build their homes on sinking sand. Hope was never meant for what *could be* or what *might be*, it was meant for what *will be*. When we attach this false definition of hope to our religion, we create a machine of destruction that ultimately topples everything in its path.

> *Hope was never meant for what could be or what might be, it was meant for what will be.*

Before we know it we begin to *hear* God encouraging us to hope for the craziest things all in the name of faith. After trial and error, hope becomes almost impossible to sustain because its altered meaning bites us so many times. The ultimate and unfortunate result is that we don't even hope in God any more. His very existence takes on the look of our definition of hope itself. Maybe He is real and maybe He isn't. Maybe He loves me and maybe He doesn't. He just might come through for me, but then again, He just might not. It's nice to think He will but one can never be sure.

Hope Is For Long Distance

Hope is important because it's designed for the long run of life. It is the prize at the *end* of the race. Faith is what causes you to take each step along the way. When hope is put in truth, its power is unstoppable! There must be a truth at the end of every race that makes the race worth running. If that truth is in question, it then becomes a wish or a dream and there is no power for the runner to keep running when the road gets bumpy and steep. It must be *for sure* if hope is going to receive its power from being placed in it.

When I owned a painting company years ago, I used to pay my workers at the end of each week. Once, however, I was going out of town and decided to pay them at the beginning of the week before the work was done. When I returned home from my vacation, I found that very little was done. They basically sat around all week with no motivation whatsoever to lift a finger. Though I could blame them for not having the integrity to finish the job, I knew immediately that the real fault belonged to me. I took away their hope. Their paycheck at the end of the week was their hope. It was a sure thing that they would get at the end of the race. When I gave it to them at the beginning, they became powerless in their hearts to continue. Needless to say, I never did that again. Tampering with hope is devastating to the long run of life.

> *Hope is important because it's designed for the long run of life.*

This is why God is so grieved when we cause people to question whether or not they will make it to Heaven when they

Heaven is guaranteed to you because you need that guarantee!

die. When we do this we are tampering with the most precious thing God has set before them. We are calling the prize at the end of the race into question and we are covering it with doubt and uncertainty. The ultimate result is that the runner's hope is lost and the power to keep going is depleted. It is impossible to do this to someone and love them at the same time!

As an eight-year-old boy, God knew that I needed hope to get me through the terrible times in my life. He provided Disneyland tickets that I could look up and see every time I came home at night. It was a done deal. I was going to Disneyland in three months. No one could take that from me. I needed that in order to make it through each day. If my parents had begun to threaten to tear up those tickets if I did something wrong, in an effort to manipulate me to be a good little boy, I would have lost my hope.

This is precisely what we are doing to God's children every time we insinuate that they might not be going to Heaven. Understand, loved ones, God will NEVER threaten to tear up the Disneyland tickets if you are bad. He isn't stupid. God knows you need those tickets. The power of you knowing that those tickets are yours, and no one can take them from you, is the same power you need to help you be a good little boy and girl. Heaven is guaranteed to you because you need that guarantee! There is power in you knowing that it's yours at the end of the race. It propels you forward and pulls you past the filth of life.

If you are a Christian and you don't believe that you are *eternally secure* in Christ, you need to know something. *You*

The God's Honest Truth

have no hope. All you have is a wish and a dream. Until you know for sure that you belong to God and you are going to be with Him when you die, you will remain in a state of constant hopelessness. Everything in your life will waver, including your faith. This is precisely why so many Christians come and go from their faith all the time. They don't know for sure that they are okay with God. It all depends on their works and actions rather than what He promised.

God has given us this hope as an anchor for our souls. The moment the anchor is taken away, our souls begin to waver and drift. It is absolutely essential that our hope is protected and preserved. Without it, we will die. Perhaps this is the main problem with most honest Christian people in the world today. Nothing is for sure when it comes to God. They are never sure where they stand

If you are a Christian and you don't believe that you are eternally secure in Christ, you need to know something. You have no hope.

with Him. He just might send them to Hell if they mess up a bunch of times in a row and then die, or worse yet, if they died in the middle of committing a sin. They just can't be absolutely certain where they are going when they die. It all seems to depend on the mood God is in when their time comes. The only hope they have is in themselves. Rather than be towed by the hope that God gives them, they say things like "God wants *ME to tow the line.*" They tow themselves throughout life wishing and dreaming that it will all be okay in the end.

I once heard a terrible story about a gang of cruel racists who captured a black man and tied him to a rope that was hitched to the back of their truck. They dragged this poor man throughout the city until his body literally dissolved into nothing. This is precisely what I see in the Christian world today. People have attached their hope to lies and have been dragged to the point where there is nothing left of themselves. It's an awful way to die.

My grandfather was an icon in his denomination. He wrote hundreds of Christian hymns that are sung in churches across the country, even to this day. He was truly the sweetest man I had ever met. His character was beyond anything I have ever seen in anyone. At one point, when he was ninety-six-years old, he began to lose his mind because of the medication he was on, and he didn't recognize his wife anymore. One evening, when they were about to climb into bed, he informed her that he was a married man and he would not sleep with her. That night, as he slept on the couch, my grandmother cried herself to sleep because she had a husband who was so faithful to her that he wouldn't even cheat on her with her. That's integrity.

In my grandfather's last few years of life, he would sit around the house depressed and hopeless. When my grandmother would ask him what was wrong, he would just respond by saying, "it's hopeless; I can't make it to Heaven." He was at a point in his life where he realized how truly sinful he was on his own. Because he grew up in a denomination that taught him that God would withhold Heaven from people who didn't earn it, he came to the end of his life without any hope at all. The only hope he had was in himself and his ability to *tow the line*. Even a man with monumental integrity such as he had, could not tow himself to Heaven and he knew it.

Misery And Fear In Exchange For Hope

People who don't have hope in God have to use other recourses to motivate them throughout their life. Usually things like pain and fear are used as a replacement. Their only power that tows them through difficult times is the knowledge that if they don't make it through, they will ultimately burn in Hell for eternity.

Imagine having death as your only source for empowerment. Sadly, this is the case with most Christians in the world today: either they tow the line, or else. This is why many people become defensive the moment I attempt to cut their line and give them a new one. They honestly feel that they need that line to get them to Heaven. Cutting it or giving it up is unthinkable. What would be there to motivate them to do right if it wasn't for the fear of the hellish consequences if they didn't?

Why is it that most people know for sure how to get to Hell, but they can never really be certain that they are going to Heaven? When did Hell get so much power over Heaven in our minds? If you don't believe that you are going to Heaven for sure, the only power you have to tow you through life is the power that comes from Hell. Misery and fear of imminent doom is the only thing that will motivate you. Make a decision today that your hope will not be put in anything but the truth of what God has promised and guaranteed you: HEAVEN.

God's Hope In You

The reason why God has hope in you is because God knows the truth about you. Remember, hope is always placed in truth. God's hope for you has to do with a truth that He has seen with His own eyes. When God looks at you today, He sees you in the future and He calls you by that name. It's not as if God

He doesn't hope in you because He is not sure of the ending or outcome. He hopes in you because He is completely certain of it.

is trying to encourage you into what you *could be* or *might be* if you did all the right things in your life. He is telling you that

He has seen your future *for a fact* and He knows for sure what you will become. God's hope in you is placed in the truth of your future.

When I hear people say that God has *given up hope* with them, I am totally mystified and perplexed. Many preachers talk about a time in some people's lives where all hope is lost, and where God takes His hands off of them completely. This is ludicrous because they are assuming that God thinks like we do today. They think that He is in the habit of putting His hope into things that are not definite and secure. They are holding on to the tangled definition of hope that the world twisted it into. Rest assured, this way of thinking has nothing to do with the truth of God's heart. He doesn't *hope* in you because He is not sure of the ending or outcome. He *hopes* in you because He is completely certain of it. This is exactly how He wants you to use your *hope*. That's what it's for. *Love always hopes* because *love rejoices with the truth*. The two go hand in hand. You can't have one without the other.

Hope Speaks Of Worth

It is important that you know that your Father hopes in you because it speaks of your worth. When we think that God has

His hope in you is evidence that you're worth is greater than you could ever imagine.

lost hope in us, we are declaring to ourselves that He no longer sees any value in putting His hope in us. You are worth every ounce of hope that God has for you. His hope in you is evidence that you're worth is greater than you could ever imagine. The evidence of that worth is seen in the fact that He gave His only Son, so that you might have life. You mean everything to Him.

If we insinuate to people that God has lost hope in them, we will have communicated to them that God finds no inner value in their hearts. This is devastating to the human heart. Not only do we need *hope* to survive, but we need to know that God *hopes* in us if we want to survive. The moment we lose sight of this or feel like it is fading away, we will cease to matter in our own eyes. Every child searches their father's eyes to find that *hope* in them. They were not only created to have it in their father but they were created to receive it from him as well.

Love always hopes because when you love someone, you can see things in them that they themselves cannot see. This is essential for love to survive. It needs to see beyond the natural realm in order to last forever. True love causes us to see truth, and when truth is seen, hope is anchored to it.

It Is Never God's Desire That You Lose Hope

Your hope is so precious to God, because it leads you to wonderful things and sustains you in the midst of trials and tribulations. It's your covering and safeguard. Hope is the very thing that keeps your eyes open and your heart beating. It means everything to God because it's your mother in the faith. He will do anything to see that you never lose your hope.

I have heard many people say that God will allow terrible things to happen to people who put their hope in anything but Him. This is an awful thing to say about Him. God cares so much for you and your hope that He will even supply more hope where you have wasted yours. Just like a father handing his child coins to toss into a wishing well, God will continuously supply hope even to those who waste it away. He does this because He knows that His children need hope to survive. It is never His desire to see us hopeless, even if it happens as a result of our bad choices and sinful disposition.

Children need something to look forward to. Nothing grieves the Heart of God more than when a child who has absolutely nothing to look forward to. The eyes of such a child go dark and dim and their countenance becomes tired and grey. Even if it is as trivial as going to Disneyland in three months, God will provide it because it gets that child through life. It's that important to God because it's that important to the child.

When our wasted hope in untrue things comes to an end, and we are empty inside and without hope, God is there, supplying a new dose of it, because without it we will never get better. I have watched in amazement at His faithfulness in supplying hope to a generation who compulsively gambles it away on things that are sure to fail. He cares more about our well-being than He does about Him receiving our attention. In spite of what many people say, God never desires to see His children hit a rock bottom state of hopelessness. He would rather we have hope in the wrong things than no hope at all.

> *God cares so much for you and your hope that He will even supply more hope where you have wasted yours.*

Guarding Your Hope

Because of the fact that hope is so essential to our well-being, it must be guarded and protected with our very lives. There is only one way to ensure that our hope grows and flourishes to its full size. You must commit to truth! It is imperative that you never allow yourself to ingest anything but pure truth. The moment something is added or taken away from it, the consequences are grueling. You must guard what you allow yourself to listen to and believe. Everything must be weighed and measured by the one infallible scale that God has given us.

If anything other than love is used to gauge the authenticity of truth, it will deceive you and the end result will be a total loss of hope. Hope is kept alive by the truth, the whole truth and nothing but the truth. It simply cannot survive without it.

Every one of these aspects of love that we have covered in this book is interdependent on the other. Love is like a delicate ecosystem that depends on everything within it to sustain itself. Even the smallest eliminations can cause the biggest disasters. If we were to take something as small as ants or crickets off of our earth, the far-reaching effects on our planet would be devastating. The truth of God's heart is very much like this. This is why we must never even suggest some of the fearful things that we do about Him. If we imply that God might turn His face from one of His children in a specific circumstance, we are creating a chain reaction of tiny explosions that gets worse and worse down the line of our theology. The far-reaching effects on our religion are devastating.

> ✝
> *If anything other than love is used to gauge the authenticity of truth it will deceive you and the end result will be a total loss of hope.*

Every ingredient of love must be present in order to preserve the truth about God's heart. The moment we are *envious* we become *impatient* and *self-seeking*. If we are *proud* we become *easily angered* and *rude*. If we are *boastful*, we cannot be *kind* and we refuse to *rejoice with the truth*. If we don't *rejoice with the truth*, we will eventually lose our *hope*. Love requires each and every aspect to be in perfect alignment.

When a religion overlooks or disregards one aspect of love, it ultimately ends up redefining the face of God, Himself. Over time, He begins to appear despicable and unattractive to people. It is absolutely imperative that we commit to truth and reject the hype and jargon that has fueled our churches for so long. The only way to do this is to love; anything less that that is nothing at all. God is knowable, but to know Him, you have to love people. All truth comes through our love for people. God is love.

Love Always Perseveres[17]

When the Titanic set sail, it was considered by all to be the "unsinkable ship." It was made of iron and was bigger than any cruise liner around. All the ingredients were present for a boat that would persevere through anything. Great care was taken to see that the best of everything was on board, including crystal chandeliers, expensive china and silver flatware. It was truly a five star experience for its lucky passengers.

After that historical moment, when the Titanic sank to the bottom of the ocean after hitting the iceberg, many people exchanged ideas as to why this happened. For years there was constant speculation as to what went wrong. Some people believed that the ship was cursed because of a comment that was made about how "not even God could sink it." Others wondered how it was that an iceberg could sink a ship that was made of iron. The survivors claimed that the Titanic broke in half just before disappearing under the cold icy waters. Scientists argued with them for decades, claiming that it was impossible for something made of iron to break in half. It wasn't until the location of the sunken ship was discovered several years ago that the real answers began to come to the surface.

The deep diving camera proved that the Titanic was indeed in two pieces at the bottom of the ocean floor. Further studies showed that the iron used on the Titanic *had not been tested.* Because of the fact that they were rushing to complete the project by a certain time, they had decided not to take that one little step of *testing* the quality and durability of the iron. This proved to be a fateful choice. Tests done after the fact have proved conclusively that the iron used to build the Titanic was as brittle as a pane of glass. It was doomed for failure the day it set sail.

The reality of the Titanic is that it really wasn't a boat at all. *It was faking it.* There was no way to tell the difference as it left the harbor with people clapping and music playing because it seemed to have everything. Who would have thought that what looked like a boat, floated like a boat and felt like a boat would soon turn out to be a coffin?

The Test Of Authenticity

We have covered many different aspects of love thus far, and they all have one thing in common. *They can all be faked.* It is possible to fake patience and kindness. Anyone can fake not being envious or boastful or proud. Selflessness can be acted out and anger can be easily hidden. People can pretend not to keep records of wrongs, and it doesn't take much to act as though we don't delight in evil. Protection, trust and even hope can be faked as well. Every single aspect that we have covered so far can be counterfeited to fool the most experienced onlooker.

There is one last thing that is the final step to discovering the authenticity of love. Until it has been added to everything else, love is really not love yet. It may look like it, float like it and even feel like it, but it's only a mirage. Before love leaves the assembly line and is given the label of authenticity, IT MUST BE TESTED!

Though all the ingredients may be present, they do not equal *love* until they have been put through the fire and have proven themselves. This testing is absolutely essential. Love needs testing not only to prove itself, but also to survive, thrive and grow. Without testing, love matters not. It is useless and dormant. It has no purpose or function. It's about as useful as an ice sculpture of a horse. It looks nice, but it won't take you anywhere. Eventually it will all melt away and be forgotten.

Testing is the final proving element for everything in life. Before a professor is called a professor, he must first pass the tests that prove he is a professor. Though he may have all the knowledge inside of him, and he may have taken all the right classes, it amounts to nothing until he passes the test. A soldier is really not a soldier until he has been proved in the heat of battle. He may look like a soldier, dress like a soldier and carry a gun like a soldier, but until he passes the test *under fire*, he is just *a guy playing soldier*. Everything in life is this way. The mark of authenticity is never given until the appropriate tests have been passed.

> *Before love leaves the assembly line and is given the label of authenticity, IT MUST BE TESTED!*

It is not by accident that "love always perseveres" was put at the end of this long list of statements about love. Testing always comes at the end. It's the last thing that must happen once everything else is in its place. There is one way, and only one way, to know for certain whether something is love or not. *It has to make it through the fire.* It must persevere. All of the previous fourteen elements that we have discussed may be present, but if love does not persevere through the fire, IT IS NOT LOVE. This is the one and only element of love that cannot be faked. It will either persevere, or it will melt away.

This one principle about love is probably the most overlooked and downplayed aspect in the world today. We build our relationships the same way we built the Titanic. Testing it before we set sail is the last thing on our minds. Ironically, this is the most important part of all, and it is continuously and routinely disregarded in this generation. We minimize the *need* for perseverance in relationships today because something inside us already knows the truth and doesn't want to admit to it. As long as it makes us feel good here and now it doesn't matter if it perseveres in the future.

> ✝
> *...if love does not persevere through the fire, IT IS NOT LOVE.*

Couples who divorce will nonchalantly make excuses in an effort to cover up the truth of why their love didn't persevere. They'll replace "it failed the test" with something more palatable, like "we just grew apart." We have a whole list of better-sounding justifications that we commonly use to explain away the ugly truth. They range from, "we just went in different directions" to "we just weren't meant to be together." Unbelievably we even attempt to blame God for it failing by saying, "I don't think this was the person God had for me." Rather than admit that it just couldn't take the heat, we prefer to act as if there was some justifiable and pretty-sounding reason why it dissolved in the midst of opposition and adversity. The answer to whether or not it was love can be found in the question; "are you still with that person?" If not, it failed the test and it wasn't love. It may have looked and felt like love, but I assure you, it wasn't love at all. It was proven by the fire and when the fire came, it melted.

The world has also taught us that *true love* should never be tested at all. Testing it would be a lack of faith and it would diminish its beauty. The world gets offended if we even dare test it, because it feels so unbelieving and suspicious.

I get nervous when couples sit in my office only weeks before their wedding date and tell me that they have never been in a fight together. It's as though they are thinking that adversity hasn't come their way because of the authenticity of their love for each other. This is a grave mistake. One of two things is happening in relationships like this.

First of all, a couple who's never experienced adversity is most likely avoiding it at all costs. When it begins to come upon them, they sidestep it and escape it just in time. Something in them fears it because of what it might prove to them in the end. Rather than face it and see what their "love" is made out of, they run. They avoid testing like the plague and pursue peace at any cost, even at the cost of never being personally known and understood.

> *The world has also taught us that true love should never be tested at all.*

Secondly, I personally feel that couples that never fight are probably not talking about things that really matter deeply to either one of them. Therefore there is no reason to feel passionately about anything enough to argue about it. Either way, these relationships are sitting ducks. My advice to anyone in this position is to postpone your wedding date until you have been in a few arguments together. Don't run from the testing; embrace it.

Would you get on a new roller coaster that had never been tested before? Would you fly on an airplane that had never been flown before? Would you take a medication that had not been tested and approved? Why then would anyone consider marrying someone with whom they had never argued with before? I am not endorsing marriages that fight and bicker all the time. This is a clear sign of selfishness, however, those relationships are just as brittle as relationships that never ever argue at all.

Perseverance And Opposition

You must have opposition, discouragement, adversity and suffering in order to have perseverance and endurance. These are the very things that our generation identifies as evidence of the non-existence of love. When these things surface in a relationship, we have been taught that it *must not be love* because they are present. On the contrary, these things are essential for love to exist. The world has taught us that love is supposed to make these things go away, but the truth is that nothing will make these things go away. They are a part of the world we live in. There is no escape from them. The purpose of love is to persevere and hold up in the midst of them. Unless they come upon you, your love cannot be tested and proved. Don't avoid them; embrace them.

> *You must have opposition, discouragement, adversity and suffering in order to have perseverance and endurance.*

When I was in high school, I used to lift weights religiously. I repented of that years ago. I have found that there are two kinds of weightlifters in the world. There are the guys who lift for power and muscle, and there are guys who lift for endurance. The endurance guys are usually lean and wiry. I've always thought they were just making excuses for their skinniness, but I have come to learn the importance of what they were doing. They were putting themselves under a continuous state of opposition in an effort to develop a strength that would carry them in the long run of life. The bulky guys, who lifted for power and muscles, were seeking *a one-time strength* and a nice body. In the end, endurance is a million times better than power. Our world has turned love into a picture of bulky-attractive-power and has downplayed and minimized love's need for endurance.

We come from a religious world of *power-seeking Christians* who teach that true spirituality never experiences opposition, discouragement and adversity. Somehow we are supposed to rise above it all and escape trials and tribulations if we are truly spiritual and right with God. If these things are in our lives, we have learned to see them as evidence that we are doing something spiritually wrong because with God these things don't exist. This is rubbish! When the fire comes, the power seekers have no endurance because they have spent all their time praying away all their trials and tests. They bind all the demons so that nothing will oppose them and they escape adversity at every turn. The problem is, they become weak and frail in their hearts and they don't last in the long run of life. The moment an iceberg comes their way in the form of a member of the opposite sex or a hefty wad of money, they break in half and sink to the bottom of their spiritual oceans, because they avoided the testing at any cost.

The Origin Of Adversity

We have been taught in churches that all suffering and adversity is the result of the fall of Adam and Eve. If they had never fallen, we would never experience adversity of any kind. Our theology believes that it was never in God's plan that these things visit us. It might surprise you to find that this way of thinking is completely wrong.

Adversity is a beautiful thing. It was created by God, Himself. It produces perseverance, and love always perseveres. How could God be love, and love always persevere if adversity wasn't from God? Satan was originally created as adversity. When he fell from Heaven, he became our adversary. Though *that* was definitely not in God's plan, adversity was.

The Bible says that even Jesus learned obedience through suffering. If Jesus was the second Adam and was completely without sin, why would suffering *teach* Him anything? Everything in this world grows and is tested through adversity. Even trees become stronger through drought and storms. They need these things to develop deeper roots and strong branches. Should we assume that if Adam and Eve didn't sin, there would be no wind, either? We hate suffering and adversity so much that we have excommunicated it from our theology. There is nothing in Scripture that suggests that there would have been no adversity if Adam and Eve had not fallen. Everything in the Bible points completely to the contrary. It even goes as far as to tell us to *rejoice* in our sufferings. Why? It's because suffering produces perseverance. Everyone who is godly in Christ Jesus will suffer.

Testing produces something in the tested that lasts a lifetime. We need to be tested, and so does our love. The purpose of a test is not to see whether or not you fail, but it is to strengthen you internally. Perseverance requires testing for it to develop and grow.

> *Adversity is a beautiful thing. It was created by God, Himself.*

The Foundation Of Love

The whole reason why love always perseveres is because of love's foundation. The purpose in testing love is not to see whether it *passes or fails*, but it is to prove whether it *is or isn't*.

Understand that though perseverance is learned in life, it is *immediate* in love. The Bible doesn't say love *learns* to persevere, it simply says that love

The foundation of love is death.

always perseveres. Just as love does not learn to be patient or kind, these things are immediate when love is present.

The foundation of love is what makes it unstoppable and immovable all at the same time. Unless the proper foundation is laid, love will never survive even the slightest breeze. Foundation has everything to do with perseverance.

The strength of a house depends entirely on its foundation. If the house is built on sand, it will fall flat when the first storm hits it. If it is built on a rock, it can withstand most everything.

The reason why the world has taught us that perseverance is of minimal importance in love is because the world has also taught us to either lay *no foundation at all* or to lay *a flimsy and worthless foundation*. Everything in worldly thinking concerning relationships is sinking sand.

The average amount of time a couple knows each other before they have sexual intercourse in this day and age is about two months. Sadly, the same is true among Christians. The problem with this is that *sex* ends up becoming the foundation of the relationship. Remember, whatever is put down *first*, is the foundation. When you build a house, the *first* thing you do is lay the foundation. Everything else is built on that. In relationships, if sexual intercourse takes place at the beginning of the relationship, it suddenly becomes the foundation. Sex was never meant to be the foundation of a relationship. It was designed by God to be the *consummation*. The foundation of relationship is love.

Love's foundation may startle you when you first read it so buckle your seatbelt. The foundation of love is *death*. If you die to yourself you can endure anything in your relationship. The power of endurance and perseverance comes alive when you are in it for someone else rather than self. Perseverance in love is for the sake of the other person, not for your sake. The only way to possess it is if the relationship is not about you. The final test of perseverance is really a test to see if you are in it for you or for others. If you are dead to self, you will withstand anything. If you are alive to self and dead to the other person, the relationship will dissolve and sink.

> *The final test of perseverance is really a test to see if you are in it for you or for others.*

Our marriages today have no endurance because most people are in it for themselves. This is precisely why the first year of marriage is commonly known as the most difficult year of all. It is so hard because each person is being crucified from selfishness. They are learning that life is not about them. They either die, or they divorce. Many marriages that I counsel remind me of the main character in every horror movie I saw as a teenager: *they just won't die.*

In the weightlifting world there is a saying, "No pain, no gain." In the world of relationships there is a similar saying, "No death, no life." Until the foundation of death is laid, love will have no perseverance and it will surely fail the test. It can have every single ingredient to it that we have talked about in the previous chapters, but until a person is dead to him or herself, and alive to the other person, it is NOT love.

The God's Honest Truth

Perseverance And The Purpose Of Your Life

There is nothing that we cannot do if we are doing it for the sake of others. There is nothing we cannot endure when it's for someone we love. When we die to our selfish desires and our constant inclination to protect and serve ourselves, there is absolutely nothing we cannot accomplish.

The greatest stories ever told are when a mother who weighs a hundred and ten pounds picks up the back end of a car to save her baby boy, or when a father runs through fire to save his children. These heroic acts were empowered by the love these people have for someone else. This is the power of love. These demonstrations of love are essential in proving love. So many husbands say to their wives, "I would die for you," but what the wife really needs to hear is, "I've already died for you." The truth of that will definitely be tested and proved many times throughout their relationship. Love is not satisfied with *illustrations* of its power and genuineness. Love requires *demonstrations.*

God's Demonstration Of Love

Jesus gave illustration after illustration of what love was, and then at the end of His life, He gave us the greatest demonstration the world had ever seen. It was the final thing that *had to happen* to prove that what He said and did was authentic. The truth of His death to self had already taken place before the foundation of the world, but the

> *Love is not satisfied with illustrations of its power and genuineness. Love requires demonstrations.*

time came when He had to demonstrate it in the physical realm. He endured the pain of the cross for the sake of others. This is why He was able to take every blow and bear every lashing. He did it for you and me.

The death of Christ was not *just* for the sake of atoning for sin; it had to happen for the purpose of proving His love. Love is not love until it is proven. The only way Jesus could have accomplished His purpose of revealing the Father's Heart to the world is if He publicly died to Himself and rose to live in us. This is the very essence of all relationship! The sacrifice of Christ took place before the world began, because God wanted relationship with us and that is what is required for all relationship. Even if Adam and Eve had never sinned, Christ would have been sacrificed before the world began. The sacrifice took place for the purpose of relationship and it just happened to atone for sin later on. The atonement for sin that later came about because of the sacrifice is evidence of perseverance through death. This is why God will persevere with you for all eternity. He has already died to Himself.

> *The sacrifice of Christ took place before the world began, because God wanted relationship with us and that is what is required*

Living in the heart of the ones you love can only happen if you die to yourself. Until this happens, people will always remain a mystery to you. Men will never understand their wives and women will never understand their husbands until they stop living their lives for themselves and start living for the other person. Death is the foundation of every true relationship in the world. Until you lose your life, you will never find it. This was the message that Jesus preached throughout His entire ministry.

God's patience is never running thin with you, because God is not in it for Himself. God can handle being misunderstood by the Church and being blamed for every bad thing that happens in the world because God is not in the business of protecting Himself. The only way to hurt God is to hurt you. His life is about you. And because of this, His love endures forever.

What Do We Believe?

The world has taught us that love does not always persevere. In fact, we have even adopted the attitude that says, "Nothing lasts forever." Because of the fact that we downplay and diminish the significance of perseverance with love in today's society, we also minimize it when it comes to the Heart of God. This is why it's so easy for people to imply that God might be getting to a boiling point with the world today. It's why so many of us believe that He just might wash His hands and give up on us completely.

The Antichrist Spirit In Religion

The non-perseverance view of God's heart is seen throughout most of our Christian thinking and reasoning in this generation. Some people honestly believe that they have gone from saved to unsaved and back to saved again, some fifty times in their life. They don't believe for a minute that God's love for them perseveres because they haven't embraced the "death" of Christ fully in their hearts.

I have referred to this way of thinking in past chapters as an "Antichrist mentality." Because the foundation of love is *death*, and because *God is love*, it is imperative that we understand and believe in what took place on our behalf as a result of the death of Christ. I want to park here for a moment and explain exactly why I have used such a harsh term as "Antichrist spirit."

Many beautiful things happened between God and us as a result of the death and resurrection of Christ. Unfortunately, most of those things are completely disregarded in today's theology. We have become so enamored with the Old Testament traditions that we have patterned our teachings and doctrines after them and have denied the wonderful age we live in today.

Everything from Bible reading, church attendance and the way we pray have all been affected by Old Testament thinking. Popular teachings on worship, generational curses, fasting, tithing, receiving blessings and even hearing the voice of God have all been poisoned by our denial of Christ's death. They have all become *works* teachings that decline to be adopted by God and prefer to remain slaves and servants.

The purpose of the Old Testament is to point the way to Christ. For some reason, however, the Church continues to run back to the Old Testament principles as if to completely deny the changes that Christ brought about. The only way to do this is to blatantly reject the work of Christ done on our behalf and embrace a manual way of *doing religion*.

Believe it or not, most of what we have been taught in Christianity is a complete rejection of Christ. We have become no different than the Jews who rejected Christ two thousand years ago. Remember, accepting Christ does not mean that we accept the historical person of Christ *only*. It means that we accept everything He did and accomplished through His

> *Believe it or not, most of what we have been taught in Christianity is a complete rejection of Christ.*

death and resurrection. We must be willing to believe, receive and live within that freedom of relationship He purchased for us.

If we deny God's perseverance with us or suggest that it might be running short, we are in the same sentence, rejecting the death of Christ. We have to understand that the foundation of everything God is, begins with death. The moment we take our eyes off of that death, we will begin to see God only through pre-death eyes. That's Old Testament.

The only way to know the truth about God's limitless perseverance with you is to come into the age of grace and leave law-minded-thinking. If you consider that He died for you, it changes everything. God is perseverance! He went through the fire and was found to be without defect. He paid ahead of time for all of your sins, so don't ever worry that His endurance is running thin. The foundation of God's love for you is *death* and love that is dead to self, always perseveres!

Love Never Fails [18]

I had been a Christian for about three months, and I was living in Hollywood, California, working as a chef in a popular restaurant. Several of my coworkers had also come to the Lord, and together we formed a weekly Bible study and prayer meeting. Already at this time, I had been preaching on the streets of Los Angeles and delivering food to the homeless. Because of my involvement in ministry, and because I had won most of these people to the Lord, they all looked up to me and considered me their pastor. It was an honor and a challenge that probably shouldn't have been put on such a young Christian. Nevertheless, I was up for the task and spent most of my free time studying and reading everything I could get my hands on, in an effort to be better prepared to disciple these people.

During this early period of my Christian experience, I was not unlike many Pentecostals that we see on Christian television. *I was a power-seeker.* I had read just about every book on the market that dealt with spiritual warfare. These things fascinated me, so I immersed myself in the thousands of teachings on "casting out demons" and "healing the sick." I purchased tape packs and videos where actual exorcisms were recorded, along with a step-by-step "how to" teaching for every Christian. I truly wanted to be the greatest "demon caster-outer" the Church had ever seen.

There is an entire language that goes along with this side of Christianity that I had learned to speak fluently. I "took authority" and "bound demons" and "pleaded the blood" over just about everything in my path. If I were a demon, I would have been terrified of me, because I knew all the tricks of the trade. I carried anointing oil, a Bible, and a list of especially powerful anti-demon verses just in case. My home had been prayed over (with the seven-fold prayer of faith I had learned in a book), and I had stationed angels at the four corners of my property while marching around it seven times and claiming it in Jesus' name. Every window and door in the house was drenched in anointing oil, and I had even written Bible verses on the ceiling above my bed. In the morning, I would put on my spiritual armor and go out to battle the forces of evil that awaited me at work.

Because of my deep knowledge in spiritual warfare, it became a subject that I often talked about. The language of *that world* began to leak through into my everyday conversations. My closest friends knew me as a fearless authority on that subject, and so it was no surprise when two of them came to me for help.

Scott and Saline, a young married couple, approached me about a young woman that they had staying with them at their apartment. They told me that they were sure she was demon possessed. They asked me if I would be willing to stop by their apartment after work and minister to her. Immediately, my heart began to pound within my chest. It was a combination between fear and excitement. "It all came down to this." I thought to myself. Everything I had studied for so long was all about to be put to the test.

After agreeing to help them out, I retreated back to the kitchen of our restaurant and began feverishly praying a million miles an hour. I had about forty-five minutes until I got off work, so I had to make the best of my time. Just as I was doing faith exercises and searching the cupboards for olive oil, Scott walked in the kitchen and informed me that I would be all alone with this woman because he and his wife were going out of town. Now I went from fear and excitement to just plain fear. I kept it well hidden and just replied, "No problem."

In the next forty minutes, I prayed every spiritual warfare prayer I had ever learned. I was speaking in tongues so fast, that I think even God needed an interpretation. I called prayer chains just in case I needed back-up and I even left work early and drove around their block seven times, claiming it for God. Just before I knocked on the door, I put a little anointing oil on my fingers hoping to shake her hand and surprise the demons. My heart was racing as I waited for her to answer the door.

Slowly, the doorknob began to turn as if a child were behind it, trying to work it open. Then the door quietly opened to just a crack and stopped. I could see her peeking through at me when she said, "Are you the pastor?" I had never been called *pastor* before, but I knew she was expecting me so I said, "Yes, I am." After allowing me to come inside, I could see that she was absolutely terrified. "It must have been the Spirit of God inside of me," I thought to myself. I held out my oil soaked hand like a spiritual bear trap on the end of my wrist, and I tried to get her to shake it. When she shook my hand, to my amazement, nothing happened! No shrieks or screams, no split pea soup or uncontrollable growling. Nothing!

I wondered if she might not be demon possessed, because of her unresponsiveness to my anointing oil hand shake. I asked her what the problem was, and she began to tell me about a demon that lived inside of her who spoke audibly to her all the time. It made things fly across the room and hit her if she didn't obey his commands. She even told me his name. I asked her if I could pray with her and she consented with one stipulation; I wasn't allowed to use the "J-word." Obviously, she was speaking about the name of Jesus.

This was paralyzing! It was like training a soldier in the use of an automatic weapon and then stripping him of it moments before battle. How in the world was I supposed to cast this demon out, without using the name of Jesus? Everything I had learned up to this point hinged on me using that Name. Without it, I was useless.

Over the next hour and a half, I proceeded to launch out into every spiritual warfare tactic that I had learned in the past six months. I pleaded the blood, rebuked the demon, and I called down the blessings, but nothing happened. I was dead in the water. I truly felt like a traveling snake oil salesman who had come to the end of his bag of tricks.

After sitting with her for more than two hours, and quite frankly, feeling embarrassed and a bit faithless, I just relaxed my heart and waited for the answer. While I was waiting for God to speak, I caught a glimpse of this poor terrified little girl sitting in front of me. She had not had a moment of rest in days. This precious girl was so wrapped up in fear that she could barely sit still. All at once, my heart began to bleed for her. I walked across the room and took her in my arms and held her tightly. I loved her from the bottom of my heart. It was as if she were my baby daughter. Everything inside of me melted into her, and I cried with her as we held each other.

This wonderful girl was set free that very moment. Her name was Joy, and she had reclaimed it in my arms. I learned that day that tricks are for kids. Though I was stripped of using the Name of Jesus, I found that if I became Jesus, all the power of the Universe was at my fingertips. It was love that set her free. From that day forward, my entire ministry has been built on that foundational truth. GOD IS LOVE. Nothing can stand up to that, nothing!

The Way To Love

Because the English language has so many different definitions of the word love, it is sometimes difficult to know exactly what the Bible means when it says to *love* people. We use the word *love* to describe our feelings for everything from our favorite foods to our spouse and children. It's difficult to know exactly where on the scale the love of God fits in. Is it somewhere in-between our love for pizza and being *"in love"* with our spouse? How will we know when we have achieved it? How will it feel? Until we get to the answer to this question there will always be a vague assumption as to what the *love* of God is and how we put it into action.

If you have ever been *"in love"* before, you will agree that there is nothing like it in the world. It consumes your entire being. Your whole life is about that person. You literally meditate on them night and day. Everything you do is for them. It's as though you have swallowed that person into your heart and spirit, and you see deeper inside them than anyone else on the planet does. You would gladly die for that person and in a sense you already have. Unless you are with them you feel empty and lost. Your personal fulfillment comes rushing in the moment you see a smile on their face. When you are with them, you can't keep your hands off of them. Every part of you longs to snuggle up close to that person and it's almost as if you are trying to put them on like a glove. There is truly nothing in the world like being in love!

Being *"in love"* is such a huge thing that it consumes every part of our souls. We have come to see it at the ultimate high point of love that is usually experienced only a few times in life if we are lucky. Because of its magnitude and power it must never be taken lightly or handled flippantly.

> *Anything less than "in love" is just a shallow counterfeit.*

Many of us have even developed a fear of it happening to us, because of all that we lost in the past as a result of it. Being completely drained can be terrifying. We have come to believe being *"in love"* once or twice in a lifetime is just about all the body, soul, and spirit can take. After that, there is simply nothing more to give.

The revelation that I want you to get after reading the last seventeen chapters might strike you as being a bit idealistic and even downright impossible. I want you to brace yourself and open your hearts completely. The love of God that we are supposed to have for people is not somewhere *in-between* our love for pizza and being *"in love"* with our spouse.

The Love Of God IS Being "In Love!"

We are supposed to be head over heels *in love* with people. There is no middle ground when it comes to love. It's either all or nothing. Love always means to be "in love." Anything less than "in love" is just a shallow counterfeit. The only way to fulfill the teachings of Jesus is to be *in love*. Everything He said to do in regard to others is the very thing that people who are *in love* do without thinking. It takes being *in love* to accomplish the last fifteen aspects of love described in our original Scripture. You can't just *really like* a person and fulfill what God requires in this verse. There is simply no humanly possible way to do these things unless you are totally and completely *in love* with others.

This revelation might appear a bit disheartening to most people who read this book, because it seems impossible. Most people have never even considered that this is what the Bible means when it says to love one another. They don't consider it simply because it doesn't seem realistic. The order feels entirely too tall for any normal human being to fill. Because most people can't conceive of this being possible, they resign themselves to a belief system that waters down the real truth until it can be comfortably swallowed. Over time, an evolution takes place in our thinking. It redefines the meaning of "in love" and reduces it down into a cold list of works and deeds. We become more concerned as to *what a Christian should DO* than we are about *how a Christian should feel*. This works mentality completely misses the heart of God.

How Is It Possible?

When my wife was pregnant with our second child, I was both excited and concerned. I was concerned because I could not fathom myself loving this child as much as I already loved my first child. Already, I had given every part

> ✝
> *...the capacity for love within the heart of human beings is limitless.*

of my heart to Landin. There was nothing left of me. She was my world. I lived and breathed for her, and every moment of every day was completely surrounded around her. My mind and soul was saturated with her always. How could I possibly love another child this much? There simply wasn't anything left of me to give. I was secretly terrified at the prospect of having another child, because I felt like I would have to take away some of my love for Landin in order to have something to give to Sidney.

When Sidney was born, I didn't know how to act with her. I spent the first few days of her life feeling totally guilty, because my heart had not kicked in like it did with our firstborn. I was afraid to hold her, or spend time with her, because I honestly didn't feel like I could give all of myself to her. What was left to give?

About a week after we brought Sidney home, something happened. One day, when I was holding her, our eyes met and she smiled at me. That little smile pierced straight through my silly fears and landed directly in the center of my heart. Instantly something flooded into my soul and I became warm with love all over again. In a matter of weeks, I found that there were parts of me that I didn't even know existed. I became so in love with Sidney that I could hardly stand it. From that day until the present, Sidney has remained in the center of her daddy's heart.

> *When you allow that love to govern your life, rather than allowing your life to govern that love, you will have discovered the secret to "walking in the Spirit."*

By the time little Emma came along, I wasn't worried in the least. I had already learned the most beautiful lesson of life with Sidney. I learned that the capacity for love within the heart of human beings is limitless. There is no end to how much love one person can possess for others. Now I have four daughters, and I am *in love* with all of them, and it continues to grow and grow each day. I could have a thousand children and be head over heels in love with each and every one of them. There are no limits to how much love one person can give.

The problem is that most people never allow themselves to be *stretched* by love. They will hold themselves back from giving their all, because they don't think it's possible to give more. Until we are willing to cross over the line of small-mindedness into the world of ever increasing love, we will always be bound by our own human perceptions of what is possible and impossible. That, *stepping over*, is precisely what is happening when a person puts their faith in God. It's the willingness to give yourself completely to the love that God puts in your heart for a person. When you allow that love to govern your life, rather than allowing your life to govern that love, you will have discovered the secret to "walking in the Spirit."

Love Never Comes To An End

Remember, if God is love and love comes from God, it is shallow thinking to believe that we could ever run out of love for people. The only thing that blocks the flow of God's love through us is the selfishness *in* us. The reason why our past experiences of "loving people" seemed to deplete us to the point of emotional emptiness is because we were doing it upside-down. We were in it for ourselves. This is the opposite of love. Love is never self-seeking. The moment we believe that the experience of love is receiving it, our

The only thing that blocks the flow of God's love through us is the selfishness in us.

supply will die off. When we care more for others than we do ourselves, we can receive an unlimited supply of love from the author of love Himself.

True love never comes to an end because God never comes to an end. I have had many people tell me that I have a lot of love to give. This really isn't true at all. Within myself, there is very little love. I suppose I have as much as anyone else. I have enough to love my wife and kids and possibly one or two friends, but that's about it. When it comes to people in general, there really isn't any love left inside of me to give out. This is why I need God to constantly replenish my supply. The moment I open my heart to a new person, He is there, flowing a tidal wave of fresh love through me and into that person. As long as my heart is opened, there are no limits to how many people I can be *in love* with and how deeply I can love them.

The problem is that we have to *want* to do this. I have found that most Christians are not moved by this message because it flat out tells them that if they want to know God, they have to be *in love* with people. Most people just aren't interested in doing that. It's not appealing to them, because they don't see any immediate personal benefit attached to it. This is why so many of us become so saturated with the practices of our religion. It's a way to bypass and avoid love by preoccupying ourselves with the pretty colored rules and regulations. If we focus on being caught up on our tithe, making sure we attend Church and pray regularly, we are somehow able to keep our minds busy enough to overlook the very foundation of our religion: love.

> *...the reason why Christianity has become the fastest declining religion in America is because we don't love people.*

I am convinced that the reason why Christianity has become the fastest declining religion in America is because we don't love people. We spend more time trying to convince people that we love them by performing the symptoms of love than we do actually loving them. Feeding the hungry and clothing the poor does not mean that we love them. We can even lead people to Jesus Christ

The God's Honest Truth

without loving them. We have learned to "act out the symptoms of love" without actually possessing it. The problem is that this apathetic religious behavior eventually exposes itself because it always fails.

We have become experts in avoiding love. We have ministries called: "deliverance ministries" where we attempt to deliver a person from their emotional problems by casting out a demon or saying a formulated prayer. These ministries are born out of a loveless heart. Rather than spend the time listening and loving the person, we hope to find a religious solution that allows us to bypass caring for the one in need. Most deliverance ministries are just plain pussy-footing around love, because they don't want to go there. It's a thousand times easier to declare someone to be demon possessed than it is to hold him or her in our arms and share their burden. If they don't get delivered right away, we find some spiritual way to blame them. We accuse them of holding back un-confessed sin or just plain having a lack of faith. All this is done in an effort to let ourselves off the hook of having to love them.

Love Is Never Without Effect

The literal Greek meaning of "love never fails" is "love is never without effect." There will always be an effect when love is directed towards something. It is never ineffective.

I believe that we have lost sight of this amazing truth, because we have lost sight of love. We have exchanged *love* for *acts of love* that are meant to look and feel like love but they come from emptiness. Because we have done this for so long, we have calculated the power of love by assessing the effects that these heartless and religious *acts of love* have on people. Many times they have no effect at all.

The world is basically unaffected by the love of the Church, because the Church has been taught to hate the world. The most we do is *tell* the world about the love of Christ. Unfortunately, they never get to see a demonstration unless they become a Christian. Then, and only then will they get a taste of it. The taste that they do get is usually not the real thing either because for the most part, the Church only preaches about the love of God without actually having it itself.

The world is unaffected by the giving people of the Church because most Christian givers *only* give to the church and stiff the world. Just ask the waitresses at the restaurants next to your church.

We have subscribed to a mixed up theology that says to abandon the world and seclude ourselves in the body of Christ.

This is essentially what the gift of prophecy is. It's a gift of sight that is available to everyone who loves.

This mentality is an anti-love mind set that believes that God loves us more than He does them. Remember loved ones, God sent His only Son to die for the sins of the WORLD! God is not still a little angry with the world. He loves the world with all His Heart, and so should you. Remember, the only difference between *you* and *them* is *Him*.

Love Never Fails Because It Sees All

There was a time in my ministry where I would pray and wait for the Holy Spirit to give me revelation into a person's heart in order for me to counsel them. Occasionally, I might get a Scooby snack here and there, but more often than not, I came up empty. It wasn't until I became in love with the person in my office that I could see everything inside their heart perfectly.

Because I love my children, there is nothing that they can hide from me. I know their every emotion and motive. When we have company over, I can tell immediately if they are showing off, embarrassed, or shy. My friends may not see it, but I see *all* because I love them so much. The same is true with my wife. I can see right through her all the time. I have always believed that husbands who don't understand their wives are husbands who love themselves more than they do their wives. The quickest way to understanding a woman's heart is to *not want anything from her.* This is the foundation of love. When you have arrived at selflessness, you will see all.

This is essentially what the gift of prophecy is. It's a gift of sight that is available to everyone who loves. When we refer to how God sees everything and knows everything, it's important to understand that His ability to do this comes straight from His love for His children. It is small-mindedness to think that God is all knowing just because He is everywhere at once. His all-knowing character is completely dependant upon His all-loving attitude. Think about this for a moment. Just because you are in the presence of another person, doesn't mean that you know everything about them. It's not until you are in love with that person that this kind of vision is revealed to you. The same is true with your Father in Heaven. The very fact that He knows and sees everything in you is evidence of His continuous and never-failing love for you.

> *We can either have faith to access the power of God or we can have love and become the power of God.*

The Power Of God

Too many of us spend our time trying to build our faith in an effort to access the power of God. We memorize Scriptures, repeat the name of Jesus and claim promises in an effort to get a hold of God's power. Some people follow big-name evangelists around the country in hopes of getting prayed for so that the power of God would rest on them. There are books, tape series, and conferences that are specifically designed to show people how to access the throne of God's power. I've even watched pastors spend hours and hours in their prayer closet begging God to give it to them. The power of God has truly become the most desired commodity in Christianity.

> ✝
> *God is not interested in what works; He is only interested in what counts.*

Ironically, in a generation of Christian power-seekers, we seem to be at our most powerless state in the history of our religion. Perhaps this is because to be a "power seeker" one must first be self-seeking. God never told us to seek His power, He told us to seek Him. God is not power; God is love.

We can either have faith to access the power of God or we can have *love* and *become* the power of God. Faith is important, but faith without love is useless. If you have love, nothing can stop you. Love is unstoppable! It topples over everything in its way. You can bind the demons, tear down the spiritual strongholds and even rebuke the Jezebel spirit, but if you don't love, you are wasting your time. You can link yourself to a prayer chain, speak in tongues and fast yourself to skin and bones, but if you don't love people, you are just spinning your spiritual wheels and going nowhere. No amount of spiritual armor, anointing oil and seed faith offerings will ever take the place of love. All of these things are wonderful, but remember this; if you love, you will have fulfilled every single one of them! Love IS the power of God. It is the fulfillment of every word in Scripture.

Remember loved ones, we were never called to access the power of God, we are called to become the power of God. Anyone can access His power through the many avenues that I stated above. All of them work! God is not interested in what works; He is only interested in what counts. We may find spiritual formulas that work for us, but they don't count for anything. Just because it works, doesn't mean it counts. Just because someone gets healed because we used the Name of Jesus and a bottle of anointing oil when we prayed for them, doesn't mean that we are any closer to the heart of God than we were the day before. The only thing that counts is faith expressing itself through *love*.

It might surprise you to know that a person who *isn't* a Christian but *loves* people has more of God's power than a person who *is* a Christian and *doesn't love* people. All of God's power resides in your love for other people!

Receiving Love

I have said over and over that the experience of love is not when you receive it, but when you give it. This is absolutely true; however, there is one side note that must be stated. If you can't *receive* love from other people, you will eventually run dry. The only way to receive anything from God is to receive it through His people.

Many people have a false view of spirituality. They believe that they shouldn't need to receive anything from anyone if they are close enough to God. After all, the Bible says that God will meet all our needs. While this is true, you must ask yourself, "How will He meet your needs?" Understand that everything God does in our lives is done through someone else. If we can't receive from people, we can't receive from God.

Love requires both a giver and a receiver for it to exist. Until both wires are engaged, love cannot be detonated. Bypassing people and going straight to God is not an option. The only way to get to God is through His people. You can't have one without the other. Receiving love is every bit as important as giving it.

> *...it is the love of God that will bring everything that He started in your life to completion.*

The difference is found in what we actively seek. Do we seek to *give* love or to *receive* it? A heart that truly seeks to *give* it will always receive it, but the heart that seeks to *receive* it, rarely gives it. One way to know if your love if authentic is to ask yourself if you can receive it back from others. Refusing to receive love from other people is a sign that we are emotionally turned off from people.

God's Love For You Never Fails

Most people I know claim to have left the Lord once or twice before they finally came back for good. What they don't know is that they never left the Lord, because He never left them. The reason why they "came back" is because Jesus never stopped living inside of them. Their repentance is evidence that Christ's love never fails. Living a life of sin is not fun when Jesus lives inside of you. Eventually that consistent never leaving love of Christ will soften anyone's heart. His love for you is never without effect.

God's love for you never fails to be turned "on." His love is not like a spotlight that shines in some places and not in others. His love is not a strobe light that flickers on and off over and over. God's love for you is like a soft white light that sheds illumination everywhere. It doesn't click on when you are good and dim when you are bad. It isn't especially bright when you are following the rules or involved in ministry. His love is always shining the same for you no matter what you do or where you are in your life. It's the one thing you can count on never changing.

God's love for you will never run out because God IS love. He sees everything and knows everything about you because His eyes are filled with love for you. Everywhere you go, He is there. Every time you speak, He hears you and every single day of your life, He will live inside of you because His love never fails.

To fail is to try, and not succeed, or to start something and not finish or complete it. Understand that it is the love of God that will bring everything that He started in your life to completion. His love for you never fails. He has counted the cost of building you, and He will complete what He has started with the power of His love. To even think or wonder whether or not God will bring you to the place He promised, is to believe that love fails. You are secure in Him because He is not only the Author of love but He is the meaning of love.

When the Bible says that you are supposed to live *in God* and He would live *in you,* it is referring directly to love! There is no other way to live inside someone. God is telling you that He not only loves you but He is *"in love"* with you. He is head over heels in love with you! Imagine that.

God's Honest Truth

God is patient because He understands everything in your heart. He knows why you do what you do and He is never surprised or taken off guard. God is kind and He desires to touch you in your heart. The heart is always His aim and He never misses.

God does not envy. He never desires to take for Himself what others have but He longs to give away all that He has and

He is never tempted to take things back because He didn't get the attention. God does not boast or brag about the highest truth about Him, but He willingly lowers Himself beneath you in order to lift you up. God is not proud of the opinion that He doesn't need anyone. He desires relationship with you and He continuously makes Himself vulnerable for the purpose of making that possible. God is not rude. He never leaves things unfinished or unspoken. He does not give the silent treatment or play hide and seek, but He makes everything about Himself known and keeps nothing hidden.

God is not self-seeking. He is gratified and fulfilled when you are glorified. His eyes are always seeking the best for you, and He is never worried about what He gets in return. God is not easily angered or provoked to any mood other than love. He is not high maintenance and He never wants you to walk in fear of offending or hurting Him. God keeps no record of wrongs because He refuses to call you by the name of your past. He doesn't hold things over you or against you. He continuously and eternally wipes your record clean so that He can clearly focus on your heart.

God does not delight in evil and He is not tempted by luring lies and fantasies. He does not desire romance because His heart desires the real you. He cannot be enticed with ideas that would benefit His Kingdom at the expense of you. God rejoices in the truth about you because it is so wonderful and meaningful to Him. God always protects you from caving in, in the midst of unbearable pressure and anguish. He provides a strength that holds you up through the storms of life and carries you to your very purpose, which is to be His child.

God always trusts you with His Heart doors open to you at all times; no exceptions! God always hopes in you because He knows that He knows the end of your story. God always perseveres and proves Himself to be what He claims to be. He stands through the storm and walks through the fire only to demonstrate the authenticity of His love for you. God never fails, because He is driven by His very essence: love. It's the part of Him that sees everything inside of you and knows every inner emotion, thought and feeling. His love for you soaks through every outward thing that stands in its way and saturates your spirit, soul and body forever.

The God's Honest Truth[19]

From the time I was a little boy attending our family church in Phoenix, Arizona, I've listened to people talk about how to know the heart of God. I have heard no less than a thousand different teachings on this incredible subject. Some say that to know the Bible is to know God. Others teach that knowing Him only comes through hours of dedicated prayer time. Theologians look for Him in the original Greek and Hebrew text of the Scriptures, and pastors tell us to show up and take notes through every sermon. I've heard that I could find Him through passionate worship, generous giving and tireless works. It's been said that if we follow the laws of God we will know His heart. Others preach that we must be witnessing and leading people to God in order to know Him. Knowing His heart has been the quest of every well-meaning Christian person from the time Jesus walked the earth until the present date.

The moment we find someone who seems to know Him personally, we study that person and watch everything they do in an effort to duplicate their life. We read their books and listen to their teachings. We book counseling sessions with them and ask them to pray for us. We do our best to follow everything they do and say in hopes that someday, something might click within our spirits and we could have with God what they have. We do this because we honestly want to know His heart and we will stop at nothing until we do.

Not only do we wish to *know His heart*, but we also want to *hear His voice*. We want to know when He speaks to us, and understand exactly what He is saying. Most every Christian I know seeks to hear the voice of God in their every day life. These desires to know and hear Him are built within every one of our hearts. They spring from our sincere and inalterable need for true relationship with our Creator. Something inside every person on Earth desires to have intimacy with their Father in Heaven.

What is grievous about this generation is not their *lack of desire* to know the heart of God, but it's their lack of knowing the heart of God in spite of their desire to do so. It crushes my spirit, when I see the sincerity in the eyes of precious people as they run through the *spiritual obstacle courses* of their religion in an effort to get close to Him and end up just as lost and lonely as they were before. When I watch people try

> *Unless we are given untainted truth, we will continue in this aimless pattern of seeking God where He is not.*

their best to piece together all the different teachings, and follow all the doctrinal laws, and perform all the spiritual requirements in order to know His heart, but still come up empty, my heart breaks a thousand times over. What is worse is that every year a

The God's Honest Truth

whole new handful of teachings come out that adds to the confusion and contradiction of our religion. Unless we are given untainted truth, we will continue in this aimless pattern of seeking God where He is not.

How can we seek Him if we don't know what He looks like? If we don't know who He is, how will we know if we have found Him? If I told you to pick a friend of mine up at the airport, but gave you no description of what he looked like, how would you ever find him? This is exactly the predicament we are in when it comes to seeking God. He has been given a million different descriptions that all contradict each other and the end result is that there are countless well-meaning Christians walking aimlessly through the airport of life, looking for a God they've never seen. Ultimately, they end up standing in the middle of the confusion holding up a sign like a limo driver hoping that God somehow finds them.

Stranger God

To know the heart of anyone, you must know the contents of their heart. Until you know everything that resides within a person's heart, you really don't know that person. We have gone on a long journey together, and by now you might be feeling like you know me pretty well, after reading the last eighteen chapters. Perhaps you have made a few decisions about how I might react to certain situations, or what I might say in specific circumstances. You might even be accurate on some accounts, because you have learned pieces of me by simply reading this book. Though you may feel a certain closeness to me at this point, I assure you that you don't know me from Adam.

> *To know the heart of anyone, you must know the contents of their heart.*

If you had not seen my picture on the back of this book, what would you imagine that I looked like? Would you recognize the sound of my voice simply because you read my book? Just because a person reads a book of mine doesn't mean that they have any knowledge of me, personally. There are famous authors all over the world whom people feel like they know, but I assure you, if they went to their houses and knocked on their doors, they would call the police and have them dragged off to jail. There are famous actors that we all feel like we know personally but the fact is, we don't know them at all. This is precisely why stalkers do what they do. They are convinced that they have something *real* with that famous person, and they can't understand for the life of them why the person doesn't know them.

> *Christianity has become a religion of stalkers. We read about God in the Bible, we analyze His works and we memorize stories about Him, and then we think we know Him.*

I think Christianity has become a religion of stalkers. We read about God in the Bible, we analyze His works and we memorize stories about Him, and then we think we know Him. We witness to people about a Jesus that we read about in a book, but we ourselves have no idea who He is. Though God would never have us arrested and send us off to jail, He waits for us to know His heart before real relationship is established.

Relationship is not real until both people know each other's hearts. Many people feel a closeness to God because they can openly pour their hearts out to Him and hold nothing back. They know in their minds that He loves them and sees everything within them. He hears their prayers and answers them. They might even hear His voice and develop a dialogue with Him. Though this is truly beautiful, it still does not constitute relationship. Just because someone pours out their heart to a stranger on a flight to New York, doesn't mean that they know the stranger. I have hundreds of people a year come into my office and talk to me about their deepest problems and struggles. They open themselves up completely to me, but at the end of an hour session, they still don't know *my* heart. I am not upset with them for that, because that's why I'm there for them, but the fact is, they don't know me. We speak back and forth, we work on their life and they reveal all of themselves to me, but until they know the contents of *my* heart, I am just their counselor.

I think this is how God feels with most people. He is their personal shrink. He knows everything there is to know about us, but we don't know Him in return. God has no problem being our counselor; in fact, He even calls Himself that, but until we know what resides *within* His heart nothing will change. There are not a thousand ways to accomplish this. There is *only* one!

To Know Me Is To Love Me

If I were to empty the contents of my heart out before you, you would find five separate things. I will list them in no particular order: Angie (my wife), Landin, Sidney, Emma and Eva. These five people make up the total sum of what resides in my heart. If you take them away, there is simply nothing left. They are all that is within me and there is nothing else that matters besides them.

I can talk to you until we are both blue in the face, but until you know these people, you will never know my heart. They are me, and I am them. If you give one of them a cup of cold water you are giving me a cup of cold water. If you buy a present for one of them, you do it for me. If you don't do it for them, you don't do it for me. If you steal from one of them, you are stealing from me. If you are friends with them, you are friends with me. There is simply no other way to know my heart unless you know their hearts. There is no way to touch my heart without going through them. The quickest and only way to my heart is found within the hearts of my wife and children.

If you love Landin, but you don't really care for Sidney, *you don't really care for me*. If you don't like my wife, but you love my children; *you don't like me*. You can't love some of them and not others. It's either all or nothing. If you don't like me, you don't like them. If you don't like *one* of them, you don't like *all* of me. If you don't make an effort to know them personally, you can never know me personally. Everything about me is found in them and everything about them is found in me. My entire heart is filled with them and *only* them. You can read every book I write and listen to every sermon I preach. You can counsel with me for countless hours and we can even have dinner together, but the fact remains, until you know and love my family, you will never know and love me.

I have people who serve me in my ministry night and day. They have made their entire lives about helping me and supporting the cause I stand for. I love them and appreciate them with all my heart. Some of them slave through two jobs and still find the time to work for me. They stand up for me, when others backstab me. They give their money to me, and they donate all their time. These people are very dear to my heart. I sometimes cry when I sit around and think about all that these people have selflessly done for me. They are precious and loved by me more than they will ever know. They serve me, work for me, give to me and support me, but because they don't know my wife and children, they don't know my heart. I am not suggesting that they wouldn't, if they had the opportunity, but I'm just stating the fact that they don't know them, and because of that, they don't know me.

I also have people in my life that won't lift a finger for me. They never do anything in my name. They don't give me money, they don't partner with me in my ministry, and they haven't read any of my books or listened to a single sermon of mine in over a year. However, they know my wife and children, personally. Their entire lives are centered around knowing and loving my family. Because of this, these people know and love my heart.

I know pastors who spend six hours a day reading and studying their Bibles. I am all for that! The pages look like a battle zone. Everything is underlined, highlighted and starred. There are notes scribbled in all the margins and key words are circled on every line. They have memorized over two thousand different Scriptures and can recall them in an instant, but they are basically indifferent to people. These men think that they know the heart of God, but what they don't know is that they are being grossly deceived.

I also know people who read their Bible about five minutes a week. They secretly kick themselves for not doing it more, but they just find it hard to understand. The whole subject makes them feel uncomfortable, because of all that has been preached about it, so they shrink away from it and do their best to give it a glance every now and then. In their personal lives, however, they are wholeheartedly in love with people. Every part of them wants to spend time with others, listening and loving on them. Because of this and this alone, these people know God intimately.

Telling someone what is on your heart is easy. Even God will tell you what is on His heart. Intimacy is when you know what is IN His heart.

I know people who spend five hours a day in their prayer closet. They pray two hours in the morning, one hour at noon, and another two hours before bed. Their eyes are glazed over, because they spend so much time crying before the Lord. When it comes to people, however, they are just apathetic and disinterested. They secretly wish that they could hide themselves away in a cave up in the mountains and just be alone with God forever. Though these people may have the spiritual appearance of knowing the Heart of God, they are as far away from knowing Him as the east is from the west.

I also know people who pray a total of three minutes a day. They are afraid to approach God because their religion has made them completely aware of their shortcomings and failures. They constantly wonder if He is angry with them, and if they are going to end up in Hell for the things they have done. However, *they love people* with all their hearts. Their life is about getting to know others deeply and loving them. These people have an intimacy with God that is irreplaceable! They know Him intensely and wholly because they love and know His children.

> *The total sum of God's heart is people.*

Telling someone what is *on* your heart is easy. Even God will tell you what is *on* His heart. Intimacy is when you know what is *IN* His heart. All of the religious practices that I have mentioned in this book are all valid things because they pertain to what is *ON* God's heart. We must never think that practicing them will give us access to the inside of His heart. There is only one way to know the inside of God's heart, and that is to know and love His children. The total sum of God's heart is people.

There is no question in my mind that in the end there will be millions who thought they knew Him, but didn't, and trillions who were convinced that they didn't know Him, but really did. This last chapter is meant to be a spiritual report card of sorts.

It all comes down to this. Do you love people or not? You can follow every religious rule and ritual, but if you don't love people, you don't love God. You can practice all the sacraments, but if you don't know the hearts of people, you will never know the heart of God. There is no other way. Make no mistake about it.

It's Time To Show You God

Several weeks ago, I came home early from work because I was feeling a bit under the weather. As I was lying on the couch, my daughter Sidney was sitting on our reclining chair next to me, watching a "Barney" video. I was already feeling sick, so I tried my best to block out the amazingly irritating sound of Barney's voice, because it was more than I could handle.

Just as I was about to relocate myself to another part of the house in an effort to preserve my sanity, my eyes fell on my precious daughter Sidney. She was completely entranced by this purple dinosaur. Her eyes were wide with wonder, and her face was shining with imagination. She did not know I was watching her, in fact, she didn't even know I was in the room at that point, so I took full advantage of this opportunity. I found myself gazing at her in loving awe.

In a matter of seconds, tears began to run down my cheek. My entire world was sitting on a reclining chair watching Barney. She is the most precious person I have ever known. I would not only die for this little girl, but I have already died for her long ago. There is nothing left of me. She is everything. I admired every curve and crevice in her face. I studied her big brown eyes and cute little pudgy nose. Even her fingers brought me to tears. They are so small and perfect. Her precious little lips that look like her mother's lips are my favorite feature.

Before long, I lost track of where I was and I reached out and grabbed her and held her close to me. I told her I loved her over and over again, and kissed her a thousand times.

Inside of me, there is a flame of love for that little girl that I can feel burning in my chest. It burns for all of my children. It started with my wife long before they were born. For the last nine years, that flame has grown to an internal forest fire. Sometimes it literally takes my breath away when one of them walks into the room and smiles at me. My entire life is guided by that flame inside my heart.

As we come to the close of this book, I want to leave you with something that I believe will be the most powerful revelation you will have ever heard in your life. This final truth is the granddaddy of all revelations that this book has to offer. If you get what I am about to tell you, I believe that you will be able to hear the voice of God with absolute clarity from here on out. You will know the deepest parts of His heart, and I can guarantee you that in the next three months, you will receive revelations about Him that will stun your spirit. Never again will you wonder whether or not God is speaking to your heart. Never again will you need someone else tell you how He is, or how He thinks. You will finally be able to take your "*what would Jesus do*" bracelet off because you will become the Jesus in your heart, mind and soul. This final revelation is the very destination that this entire book has been heading. That burning flame that you feel inside your heart when you truly love someone is more than just a feeling.

That Flame Is God!

You don't need to look for Him anywhere else. He is not somewhere up in the sky or far off on a mountaintop. He isn't traveling with an evangelist waiting for you to show up, so He can touch your heart. He isn't conjured up at a camp meeting worship service or a Wednesday night prayer meeting. He lives inside of you! God is love.

I have watched thousands of people over the years desperately search for the "fire of God" in prayer meetings, conferences, and worship services. They scream at the top of their voices and fall on the ground waiting for it to hit them. They weep and wail and cry out to Him to send it to them. Many people will move their entire families across the country chasing it, because someone told them it was here or there. It's been prayed for, prophesied about, and preached from every pulpit in America and all the while, it existed in the hearts of people who love. The fire of God IS love!

> *All of the answers in the universe are found in that flame of love inside your heart.*

If you can grasp this one truth, it will change your life forever. All of the answers in the universe are found in that flame of love inside your heart. If you analyze that flame, you will find all wisdom and grace; you will possess supernatural understanding and untainted spiritual insight.

Consulting The Flame

I have watched parents cry out to God for wisdom in rearing their children. They have lost sight of what to do next. They beg God to lead them to a Scripture or a Christian book that will give them the answers they seek. God's response goes something like this:

"Consult the flame."

If you look to that flame of love you have for that child in your heart and consult it, you will know how to act and react.

Discipline will become precise and godly every time. The flame reveals the inner parts of your child's heart to you. It shows you exactly what to do in every situation. The problem is that most of us get angry and frustrated and we intentionally look away from the flame, or we even blow it out for a moment. We forget that we love our child. The moment we do this, we become instantly deaf, dumb and blind. Then we need a Bible verse or a book to bail us out. If you keep your eyes on the flame, all the answers will come.

I will never forget the day when my daughter Landin was running around the hotel we were staying in the night before we went to Disneyland. She was so excited she could hardly contain herself. Without even thinking, she ran by her sister Sidney and slapped her on the back as hard as she could. Sidney immediately broke out in a level 8 cry. I grabbed Landin, and I looked into her eyes with complete disbelief as to what I just witnessed.

> *The flame reveals the inner parts of your child's heart to you. It shows you exactly what to do in every situation.*

As I fired off the words, "what are you thinking" my eyes portrayed a father who had no idea who this child was or where she came from. I saw my precious little daughter drink that look into her little spirit and her heart broke right before me. *Immediately the flame burned me.* It showed me the level of inner pain I had just caused my daughter by giving her a look that suggested I didn't know or understand her. Right away, I took her in my arms and said, "Daddy knows that you didn't mean to hit Sidney. You were just excited, weren't you? Daddy understands, but you can't hit her even when you are excited."

The flame not only convicted me, but it gave me the exact words to make it right. It showed me a clear picture of what I

The God's Honest Truth

had done and it gave me instant blueprints on how to rebuild what I destroyed. All of the answers to parenthood are found in the flame because God is the flame. God is love.

Husbands and wives pray for wisdom from God to help them in their marriage. They struggle to the point of divorce because nothing comes. Their hearts become cold and dead. They counsel with a pastor in an effort to hear God's voice in the matter because they can't hear Him on their own. God's response is to:

"Consult the flame."

Look at that husband or wife that you used to love so much and remember how it felt. Search your heart for that flame that used to burn so hot that it made you sick. Find it and consult it! Understanding is found in that flame. Grace lives there. Marriage counseling is for people who blew the flame out and refuse to relight it. At the very best, it will just help you to get along better in the context of a flameless marriage. If you

It is not the Bible that makes the flame come to life; it's the flame that makes the Bible come to life!

embrace the flame of love inside your heart, there is nothing your marriage cannot overcome. There is nothing that is beyond understanding or to difficult to embrace. If you keep your eyes on the flame your relationship will spring to life and never die.

Christians tell me every day of the week that when they read the Bible, it has become mundane and boring. They've tried switching translations in an effort to mix the words up a bit, but eventually they find themselves right back where they started. God's response to this is to:

"Consult the flame."

All Scripture must be seen under the light of the flame of love. The moment it is read without the lens of love before it, it will die in your hands. It is not the Bible that makes the flame come to life; it's the flame that makes the Bible come to life! Scripture becomes difficult and impossible to translate *only* when a person waivers in their heart as to whether or not God is love. The moment we lose sight of

The purpose in reading our Bible is to allow our heads to come into alignment with the flame of love that burns within our hearts.

this beautiful truth we are faced with scary verses that seem to prove He is the opposite of love. The Bible must be seen through the flame or its beauty and life will become invisible.

The Bible was never meant to be a "hand book for living." This saying comes from a law-minded mentality. *The Bible is a revelation of God's heart.* It's *a revelation of love.* Unless it is seen *through love,* it will sadly become nothing more than a manual of do's and don'ts. Understand that the entire Bible hangs on the flame we are talking about. The flame is the Word living inside of you! The purpose in reading our Bible is to allow our heads to come into alignment with the flame of love that burns within our hearts. The entire Bible already exists within the flame. If you have to run to your Bible for an answer, it's because you either don't have the flame or you refuse to consult it.

All of Christianity must be seen through the flame of love. Our entire religion is based on it. Every aspect of God's character is revealed in that flame as well. His desires, His tone and His countenance can be known only in the flame. You can study theology, memorize the entire Bible, and even serve others until you are blue in the face, but if you do not love people, you do not love God. Our entire Christian walk is lived out through our love for others. Without this, everything else amounts to a pile of dung. Possessing the power of God means absolutely nothing! Though we may cast out demons, heal the sick and perform wondrous miracles in His name, if we have not love in our hearts, we don't know Him, nor have we ever known Him.

After listening to one of my sermons, a delightful young woman approached me and said, "I can tell that you spend a lot of time in prayer to get these revelations about God's heart." She was right, but not in the way she was expecting. I did spend a lot of time with God, but it wasn't in the traditional sense. I hadn't locked myself in a prayer closet for multiple hours crying out to Him for a revelation of His character. I spent hours driving around town in my pickup truck contemplating the love I have for my wife and kids. I analyzed it and studied it until it began to speak to me. I fanned it and grew it until it consumed all of me, and there was nothing left. I learned to consult it and strip it of all its beauty and wisdom. Eventually, it began to speak the truth of God's Heart to me, and the things that it said were more stunning and beautiful than anything I had ever heard in any sermon in my life. I found that all true revelation comes from the flame. Never again did I search the Scriptures for hours waiting for a sermon to pop out at me. Every sermon I write today was found in the flame of love that I possess for the people in my Church.

All Scripture must be seen under the light of the flame of love. The moment it is read without the lens of love before it, it will die in your hands.

That flame gives me boldness to speak the truth regardless of the consequences to me. It kindles a desire within me to set people free and bring them to liberty at any cost. No opposition will come against me that is stronger than my love for these people. The love of God inside of me brings me through the most awful and vindictive persecution. My family and I have

> *...all true revelation comes from the flame.*

undergone unimaginable persecution from the most unlikely sources, because of this message. I have been blackballed from entire ministries and rejected by friends and collegues. Lies have been told about me, and my words are endlessly misquoted and taken out of context, all in an effort to destroy my credibility and suffocate the simple truth of love that I preach. I have found that people either love religion, or they love people. If their heart is attached to the former, they will almost always hate me, and everything I stand for. None of this matters to me, because the flame carries me through it all. It counsels and calms me in the midst of dirty looks and condescending snickers I get in church hallways. It calms me because I know love and no one can tell me that it is something that it is not. I have seen it and touched it. It speaks to me and I reply. I know that I know that I know that this is the truth about God's heart.

The Lost Boy's Generation

If you don't have love in your heart, you become like the "lost boys" in the movie "Peter Pan." They had never seen or known a "mother" in all their lives. They asked Wendy, "What's a mother? Tell us about a mother." This is exactly where I see most of the Church today. They need someone to tell them about God. They ask over and over for another story about Him so they can visualize the One they never knew. Then they put all the stories together and try to paint a picture of Him. Over time, the stories become embellished and twisted. They take on a new form and eventually become a contradicting series of *spiritual urban legends.* Finally the end result is a picture of God that bears no resemblance to the flame of love. It goes virtually unnoticed, because very few people have that flame themselves. The moment someone ignites that flame within their heart and consults it, they find that their religion has been utterly destroyed while they were gone. They can either ignore it and continue on with their religious traditions, or reject the lies and stand for the truth. The question is, what will you do?

The Flame Comes From God

If you are worrying because you don't feel like you have this love, please don't fret. God is not asking you to conjure it up on your own. He is that flame. All you have to do is be willing to receive Him. Accepting Jesus Christ into your heart is more than just believing in the traditional Jesus Christ and asking Him to live within you. It's opening yourself up to loving others! When your heart is open and willing to burn with love for people, God will live inside you.

Accepting Jesus Christ into your heart is more than just believing in the traditional Jesus Christ and asking Him to live within you. It's opening yourself up to loving others!

It's as simple as that. He will reveal everything about Himself to you through the love for others that you have opened to receive from Him. All truth and revelation is yours when you are ready.

The thing about love is that it casts a spell on the lover that makes the object of love appear to them as truth. Whatever it is that we love suddenly becomes truth to us. If we love religion and tradition, those things will appear to be truthful. If we love hype and flamboyance, they will take on the form of truth in our eyes. Love sends a powerful delusion, so that the lover will believe the lie and so be condemned.

Pure truth can only be discovered when love is pointed the right way. It all comes down to what it is that we love. Authentic truth is found only in the love of people! When you have that, you will have opened the doors to every truth in the universe. Then, and only then, will you know "The God's Honest Truth!"

The God's Honest Truth *(Teaching Series)*
Intimacy exists just beyond the boundaries of religion. Relationship requires you to let go and venture out. Prepare your heart for one of the most radical teatching series this generation has ever seen concerning the Heart of God. Every part of your Christian life is about to be changed forever. Experience the power of TRUTH as we journey deeper than ever into the Heart of God.

Experience this amazing 16 week series in
DVD, and CD Audio formats

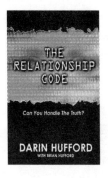

The Relationship Code
The Relationship Code is the first marriage teaching written for both single people and married couples. For the single person, it is a goal to obtain, a guide to personal growth, and a road map to godly character. For married couples, it is the spark of life that will set their relationship on fire.

This incredible teaching is also accompanied
by a Teaching Series, and Study Guide

Available For Purchase Today!
www.darinhufford.com

Additional Audio Titles
(Available in tape or CD format)

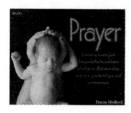

Prayer Series
This series will literally transform your mindset on prayer forever. This sixteen sermon series re-defines prayer in a way that is simple, exciting and real. You'll be surprised to find what you've been missing.

Fear Series
Do you avoid some of what life has to offer due to fear? Do you sometimes feel overwhelmed and overcome by worry and fear? These sixteen teachings define what fear is, where it originates from and how to remove it from your life.

Grace Series
Grace is everything when it comes to your walk. This twelve week series expounds on facets of God's grace that are fresh and unique. Learn the TRUTH about what Grace is and who it's for. This series will cause an explosion in your life that will produce righteousness and joy forever.

Available For Purchase Today!
www.darinhufford.com

Additional Audio Titles
(Available in tape or CD format)

Believe Series
This twelve week teaching series re-establishes what it means to "Believe" in God. The power of "Believe" can carry you through any of life's obstacles. Discover a power that has been lost in years of tradition and religiosity. Discover the power of God and man together!

Confidence Series
Confidence is the very fuel that everyone's internal engine runs off of. Without it, you won't even begin to capture what life has for you. This twelve week series helps you rediscover your confidence, keep it and maintain it. This is a must for anyone in business or ministry!

Life Application Series
Putting the "truth" to work in your every day life. Finding the balance between the spiritual and physical. This is a collection of Pastor Darin's sixteen favorite teachings.

Available For Purchase Today!
www.darinhufford.com

Additional Audio Titles
(Available in tape or CD format)

Devil Series
Most Christians believe that their Devil is as big as their God. Find out how religion has intensified the power of the Devil in our every day lives. Deflating your Devil is one of the first steps to understanding who you are in Christ. This series is both challenging and thought provoking.

Sin Series
We are in great need of a revelation of sin in our generation. This six week series in full of some of the most fresh and stunning revelations on the subject. You will be encouraged and blessed when you listen to this life changing study.

Giving Series
Discover the authentic truth about giving that has been lost for generations. Find out how this beautiful expression can bring both fulfillment and joy to your life. Learn what misconceptions have tainted this subject and how you can alter them to find the heart of truth when it comes to giving.

Available For Purchase Today!
www.darinhufford.com